A BIBLIOGRAPHY
for the
GOSPEL of MARK
1954-1980

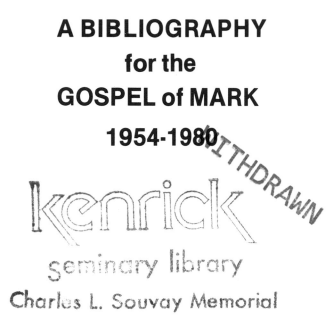

HUGH M. HUMPHREY

Studies in the Bible and Early Christianity
Volume 1

The Edwin Mellen Press
New York and Toronto

Library of Congress Cataloging in Publication Data

Humphrey, Hugh.
    A bibliography for the Gospel of Mark, 1954-1980.

    (Studies in the Bible and early Christianity ;
v. 1)
    Based on entries for "Mark" in the Elenchus
bibliographicus Biblicus, 1954 to 1977-1978; New
Testament abstracts, 1956-1980; and Ephemerides
theologicae Lovanienses, 1978-1980.
    Includes index.
    1. Bible. N.T. Mark--Bibliography. I. Title.
II. Series.
Z7772.M1H85 [BS2585.2]   016.226'3   81-18717
ISBN 0-88946-916-4 (hard)   AACR2
ISBN 0-88946-917-2 (soft)

Studies in the Bible and Early Christianity
    ISBN 0-88946-913-X

Printed in the United States of America

TABLE OF CONTENTS

INTRODUCTION

This Bibliography for the Gospel of Mark provides an index to the journal articles, essays in collected works, and books published since 1954 and through 1980 (a few titles for the early part of 1981 are incidentally included). Works by scholars, for scholars, and in scholarly journals--the results of more than a quarter-century of study of the Markan gospel--comprise the biggest part of the Bibliography; but included also are materials written to interpret that scholarship for a wider audience.

The items listed were based upon the annual reports for "Mark" in the <u>Elenchus Bibliographicus Biblicus</u> (Rome: Biblical Institute Press) from 1954 (vol. 35) to 1977-1978 (vol. 58s). From 1956 to 1980, those annual reports have been cross-checked and expanded by means of the entries for Mark's Gospel in <u>New Testament Abstracts</u> (Cambridge, MA: Weston School of Theology). The "Elenchus Bibliographicus" listings of the <u>Ephemerides Theologicae Lovanienses</u> were also used for recent materials (1978 to 1980).

Whoever uses this Bibliography should find a number of its features helpful:

1) <u>A classification system</u> sorts out the titles in the Bibliography according to their major emphases. Titles are cited under the most appropriate heading. A glance at the Table of Contents will indicate not only the ample extent of the headings and sub-headings but also where those materials may be found in the Bibliography.

2) <u>A cross-referencing system</u> brings the attention of the researcher to titles whose primary emphasis caused them to be listed in one place but whose secondary emphasis also needs to be noted under a different heading. Each item in the Bibliography was assigned a number in the far-left column; and there is often a notation under a particular heading to consult the items referred to by those numbers and cited completely elsewhere.

3) <u>Chronological sequence</u> determines the order of the materials listed under a classification. In the second column (from the left) on each page the date of publication is given and the titles are listed beginning with the most recent and moving back to the least recent. (If two or more titles appear the same year under the same classification, they are then cited by author in alphabetical sequence.) It is a purpose of this Bibliography to bring the researcher's attention to the most current materials on his topic and this chronological indexing accomplishes that.

It should be noted that an <u>article</u> is listed according to the date of its original appearance; subsequent translation (from a foreign language into English) or re-publication (e.g. in a collection of essays) is noted in brackets immediately following the original entry. A <u>book</u>, however, is listed according to the date of its latest edition; if an English translation of a foreign language title has appeared, the book is cited according to the date of the English translation; if a further edition of the foreign language title has appeared after the English translation has been made, it too is cited.

4) Complete publishing information is provided. The full names of authors or editors of books are given as they appear on the title pages of their works and, in the case of authors, those names have been capitalized to make the identification of the full-length treatment of a topic easier. Abbreviations of the series in which some titles appear have been avoided because the references occur so infrequently.

5) Indication of an abstract for a journal article is given in parentheses at the end of the citation. The letter "N" inside the parentheses refers to New Testament Abstracts and the numbers which follow indicate the volume of that journal and the corresponding reference number for the abstract. Thus (N 17-936) refers to volume 17, abstract number 936.

6) Reference to book review listings is given in parentheses at the end of a citation. The letter "E" inside the parentheses refers to the Elenchus Bibliographicus Biblicus and the numbers which follow indicate the volume and corresponding reference number under which the book is first noted. Thus (E 45-1084) refers to volume 45, number 1084. In that volume or in subsequent volumes may be found listings of book reviews for that title.

7) Abbreviated titles for journals have been employed for the most frequently cited journals. The abbreviations are those in common usage and the complete Table of Abbreviations may be found just before the Bibliography. All other journal titles are cited in full and a complete list of the 231 journals used in this Bibliography is given after the Table of Contents.

This Bibliography has sought to achieve usefulness and completeness. Whether one consults it to pursue a theme or to learn what has been written about a particular text in Mark's Gospel, he can have confidence in the accuracy of the citations, their general accessibility and the genre of scholarship reflected in the listing given.

Two other bibliographies for Mark's Gospel exist which can supplement this one for materials prior to 1954. In 1973, Günter Wagner published An Exegetical Bibliography on the Gospel of Mark (Bibliographical Aids 2; Rüschlikon-Zürich: Baptist Theological Seminary) which included some materials back to 1931 and extended its listings up to 1972. It features references to the particular pages within books where a Markan text was treated and it indexes all references from Mark 1:1 - 16:20. That approach is also a weakness of the work, since the indexing is not extended beyond the chapter and verse indications. The other major bibliographical souce is the entries for "Mark" in the two volumes of Bibliographie Biblique 1930 - 1975 (edited by Paul-Émile Langevin, S.J.; Québec: Les Presses de l'Université Laval, vol. I, 1972 [cf. pp. 293-308];

vol. II, 1978 [cf. pp. 654-691]). Volume I surveys 70 Catholic periodicals in French, English, German, Italian, Spanish and Portuguese from 1930 to 1970; volume II extends that coverage up to 1975 and includes 50 other journals and materials by non-Roman Catholic scholars as well. Its classification system, besides the chapter and verse indications, includes 17 general headings for Mark's Gospel, yet the work is somewhat cumbersome to use because of its two-volume format and the necessity of consulting a separate table for the details of editor and publisher in items like essays published as part of a collection.

Neither of these two bibliographies, of course, have items up to 1980, nor do they present as extensive a coverage of the periodical literature as is represented by New Testament Abstracts or Elenchus Bibliographicus Biblicus and reflected in this Bibliography, nor do they index their materials as fully as does this Bibliography.

These introductory comments cannot close without acknowledgement of the help I have received at various stages of the Bibliography's development. Nora Edmonds, Kevin Flood, Donna Lasota, William Schaub and Kathleen Winters Corcoran compiled and checked many of the items. The personnel of the Nyselius Library at Fairfield University were very helpful in checking many items and in according me a place to work on the final manuscript. My colleague John Thiel generously and carefully proofread the manuscript, reminding me often of my human finitude. Support and encouragement have come from many, but mention should be made especially of Paul Achtemeier, whose enthusiasm prompted completion of the Bibliography, and of Dean Steven Weber at Fairfield University who made institutional resources available. Throughout the whole project my wife Ellen has provided the understanding or the tolerance (as the occasion demanded) to keep it moving along. To all these I express my grateful appreciation.

It is my intention to continue to expand this Bibliography periodically to include materials prior to 1954 and subsequent to 1980. A Bibliography on the Gospel of Matthew is now in progress and will be presented in a similar format.

Hugh M. Humphrey

Fairfield University
Fairfield, Connecticut
July 23, 1981

Abr-Nahrain (Leiden)
African Ecclesiastical Review
(Eldoret, Kenya)
American Ecclesiastical Review
(New York)
Anglican Theological Review
(Evanston, IL)
Annual of the Swedish Theological
Institute (Jerusalem)
Antonianum (Rome)
Archiv für Liturgiewissenschaft
(Regensburg)
Assenblées du Seigneur (Paris)
Augustinianum (Rome)
Australian Biblical Review (Mel-
bourne)
Bibbia e Oriente (Genoa)
Bibel und Kirche (Stuttgart)
Bibel und Leben (Düsseldorf)
Bibel und Liturgie (Klosterneu-
berg)
Biblebhashyam (Kottayam, Kerala,
India)
Bible et Terre Sainte (Paris)
Bible et Vie Chrétienne (Mared-
sous)
Bible Today (Collegeville, MN)
Bible Translator (Brussels)
Biblica (Rome)
Biblical Research (Chicago)
Biblical Theology (Belfast)
Biblical Theology Bulletin (Al-
bany, NY)
Bibliotheca Sacra (Dallas, TX)
Biblische Notizen (Bamberg)
Biblische Zeitschrift (Paderborn)
Bijdragen (Amsterdam/Heverlee)
Bulletin de Littérature Ecclési-
astique (Toulouse)
Bulletin du Centre Protestant
d'Études (Geneva)
Bulletin of the John Rylands Uni-
versity Library of Manchester
(Manchester)
Burgense (Burgos)
Cahiers du Cercle Ernest Renan
(Paris)
Catholica (Copenhagen)
Catholic Biblical Quarterly
(Washington, D.C.)

Christian Century (Chicago)
Christianisme Social (Paris)
Christianity Today (Carol Stream, IL)
Christus (Paris)
Church Quarterly (London)
Church Quarterly Review (London)
Civiltà Cattolica (Rome)
Claretianum (Rome)
Clergy Review (London)
Collationes Brugenses et Gandavenses
(Bruges)
Collectanea Theologica (Warsaw)
Colloquium (Auckland/Sydney)
Communio (Seville)
Communio Viatorum (Prague)
Compostellanum (Santiago de Compos-
tela)
Concordia Journal (St. Louis, MO)
Concordia Theological Monthly (St.
Louis, MO)
Crux (Vancouver, BC)
Cultura Bíblica (Madrid)
Currents in Theology and Mission
(St. Louis, MO)
Dansk Teologisk Tidsskrift (Copen-
hagen)
Deltion Biblikon Meleton (Athens)
Dimension (Philadelphia)
Divus Thomas (Piacenza)
Doctrine and Life (Dublin)
Downside Review (Bath)
Dunwoodie Review (New York)
Ecclesiastica Xavieriana (Bogota)
Ecumenical Review (Geneva)
Église et Theologie (Ottawa)
Encounter (Indianapolis, IN)
Ephemerides Carmeliticae (Rome)
Ephemerides Theologicae Lovanienses
(Louvain-Leuven)
Esprit et Vie (Langres)
Estudio Agustiniano (Valladolid)
Estudios Bíblicos (Madrid)
Estudios Eclesiásticos (Madrid)
Estudios Franciscanos (Barcelona)
Études (Paris)
Études Franciscaines (Blois)
Études Théologiques et Religieuses
(Montpellier)
Euntes Docete (Rome)
Evangelical Quarterly (Buxton,

Derbyshire)
Evangelische Theologie (Munich)
Expository Times (Banstead, Surrey)
Foi et Vie (Paris)
Freiburger Zeitschrift für Philo-
sophie und Theologie (Fribourg)
Geist und Leben (Munich)
Gereformeerd Theologisch Tijd-
schrift (Amsterdam)
Gordon Review (Wenham, MA)
Gregorianum (Rome)
Harvard Theological Review (Cam-
bridge, MA)
Hebrew Union College Annual (Cin-
cinnati, OH)
Heythrop Journal (London)
Hibbert Journal (London)
Hokhmah (Lausanne)
Horizons (Villanova, PA)
Humanitas (Brescia)
Immanuel (Jerusalem)
Indian Journal of Theology
(Calcutta)
Indian Theological Studies
(Bangalore)
International Catholic Review Com-
munio (Spokane, WA)
Interpretation (Richmond, VA)
Irish Biblical Studies (Belfast)
Jeevadhara (Kottayam, Kerala,
India)
Jewish Quarterly Review (Phila-
delphia)
Journal for the Study of the New
Testament (Sheffield, UK)
Journal of Bible and Religion
(Brattleboro, VT)
Journal of Biblical Literature
(Chico, CA)
Journal of Ecumenical Studies
(Philadelphia)
Journal of Religion (Chicago)
Journal of Religious Thought
(Washington, DC)
Journal of Semitic Studies (Man-
chester)
Journal of the American Academy
of Religion (Chico, CA)
Journal of the Evangelical Theo-
logical Society (Wheaton, IL)

Journal of Theological Studies (Ox-
ford)
Journal of Theology for Southern
Africa (Rondebosch, S. Africa)
Journal of the Royal Asiatic Society
(London)
Kairos (Salzburg)
Katholische Gedanke (Bonn)
Kerygma und Dogma (Göttingen)
Kirchenblatt für die Reformierte
Schweiz (Basel)
Lateranum (Rome)
Linguistica Biblica (Bonn)
London Quarterly and Holborn Review
(London)
Louvain Studies (Louvain)
Lumen Vitae (Brussels)
Lumière et Vie (Lyons)
Lutheran Quarterly (St. Paul, MIN)
Lutheran World (Geneva)
Marianum (Rome)
Melita Theologica (Rabat, Malta)
Miscellanea Franciscana (Rome)
Modern Churchman (Leominster, Here-
fordshire)
Münchener Theologische Zeitschrift
(Munich)
Naturaleza y Gracia (Salamanca)
Nederlands Theologisch Tijdschrift
(The Hague)
Neue Zeitschrift für Systematische
Theologie und Religionsphilosophie
(Berlin)
New Blackfriars (Oxford)
New Literary History (Charlottes-
ville, VA)
New Testament Studies (Cambridge)
Nexus (Boston, MA)
Norsk Teologisk Tidsskrift (Oslo)
Nouveaux Cahiers (Paris)
Nouvelle Revue Théologique (Tournai)
Nova et Vetera (Geneva)
Novum Testamentum (Leiden)
Orientalia (Rome)
Palestine Exploration Quarterly
(London)
Palestra del Clero (Rovigo)
Perspectiva Teológica (São Leopoldo)
Perspective (Pittsburgh, PA)
Perspectives in Religious Studies
(Macon, GA)

Protestantesimo (Rome)
Rassegna di Teologia (Rome)
Recherches de Science Religieuse (Paris)
Religion in Life (Nashville, TN)
Religious Education (New York)
Religious Studies (London)
Religious Studies Review (Waterloo, Ont.)
Restoration Quarterly (Abilene, TX)
Review and Expositor (Louisville, KY)
Revista Bíblica (Buenos Aires)
Revista de Cultura Bíblica (São Paulo)
Revista Teológica Limense (Lima, Peru)
Revue Bénedictine (Maredsous)
Revue Biblique (Jerusalem)
Revue de l'Histoire des Religions (Paris)
Revue de Qumran (Paris)
Revue de l'Université d'Ottawa (Ottawa)
Revue de Théologie et de Philosophie (Lausanne)
Revue des Études Grecques (Paris)
Revue des Sciences Philosophiques et Théologiques (Paris)
Revue d'Histoire et de Philosophie Religieuses (Strasbourg)
Revue du Clergé Africain (Mayidi, Zaïre)
Revue Internationale des Droits de l'Antiquité (Brussels)
Revue Théologique de Louvain (Louvain)
Revue Thomiste (Toulouse)
Ricerche Bibliche e Religiose (Milan)
Rivista Biblica (Brescia)
Rivista di Storia e Letteratura Religiosa (Turin)
Rivista di Teologia Morale (Bologna)
Roczniki Teologicano-Kanoniczne (Lublin)
Saint Mark's Review (Canberra)
Salesianum (Rome)
Salmanticensis (Salamanca)

Science et Esprit (Montreal)
Sciences Ecclésiastiques (Montreal)
Scottish Journal of Theology (Edinburgh)
Scripture (London)
Scripture Bulletin (London)
Scuola Cattolica (Milan)
Selecciones de Teología (Barcelona)
Semeia (Chico, CA)
Servitium (Bologna)
Southwestern Journal of Theology (Fort Worth, TX)
Springfielder (Springfield, Il)
Studia Biblica et Theologica (Pasadena, CA)
Studia Papyrologica (Rome/Barcelona)
Studia Theologica (Oslo)
Studia Theologica Varsaviensia (Warsaw)
Studii Biblici Franciscani Liber Annuus (Jerusalem)
Studii Clasice (Bucarest)
Svensk Exegetisk Årsbok (Uppsala)
Teología y Vida (Santiago)
Themelios (Leicester)
Theokratia (Leiden)
Theologia Viatorum (Berlin)
T(heological) S(tudents) F(ellowship) Bulletin (London)
Theological Studies (Washington, DC)
Theologie der Gegenwart (Bergen-Enkheim)
Theologie und Glaube (Paderborn)
Theologie und Philosophie (Frankfurt)
Theologisch-Praktische Quartalschrift (Linz)
Theologische Literaturzeitung (Leipzig)
Theologische Quartalschrift (Tübingen)
Theologische Zeitschrift (Basel)
Theology (London)
Theology Digest (St. Louis, MO)
Theology Today (Princeton, NJ)
Tijdschrift voor Theologie (Nijmegen)
Trier Theologische Zeitschrift (Trier)
Trivium (Lampeter, Wales)
Tyndale Bulletin (Cambridge)
Una Sancta (Niederaltaich)

Union Seminary Quarterly Review
  (New York)
Verbum Domini (Rome)
Vetera Christianorum (Bari)
Vie Spirituelle (Paris)
Vigiliae Christianae (Amsterdam)
Worship (Collegeville, MN)
Wort und Dienst (Bielefeld)
Zeitschrift des Deutschen Paläs-
  tina-Vereins (Wiesbaden)

Zeitschrift für die Neutestament-
  liche Wissenschaft und die Kunde
  des Älteren Kirche (Berlin)
Zeitschrift für Katholische Theo-
  logie (Innsbruck)
Zeitschrift für Religions- und
  Geistesgeschichte (Erlangen)
Zeitschrift für Theologie und
  Kirche (Tübingen)

TABLE OF ABBREVIATIONS

AbrN	Abr-Nahrain	CollTheol	Collectanea Theologica
AfricEcclRev	African Ecclesiastical Review	CommViat	Communio Viatorum
AER	American Ecclesiastical Review	CQ	Church Quarterly
		CQR	Church Quarterly Review
Anton	Antonianum	CTM	Concordia Theological Monthly
AsSeign	Assemblées du Seigneur	CurTM	Currents in Theology and Mission
ASTI	Annual of the Swedish Theological Institute	DeltBibMel	Deltion Biblikon Meleton
ATR	Anglican Theological Review	DivThom	Divus Thomas
		DocLife	Doctrine and Life
AusBR	Australian Biblical Review	DownRev	Downside Review
		DTT	Dansk Teologisk Tidsskrift
BeO	Bibbia e Oriente		
Bib	Biblica	DunRev	Dunwoodie Review
BibLeb	Bibel und Leben	EcumRev	Ecumenical Review
BibTheol	Biblical Theology	EphCarm	Ephemerides Carmeliticae
BJRL	Bulletin of the John Rylands University Library of Manchester	EspVie	Esprit et Vie
		EstBíb	Estudios Bíblicos
		EstEcl	Estudios Eclesiásticos
BK	Bibel und Kirche	ETL	Ephemerides Theologicae Lovanienses
BLE	Bulletin de Littérature Ecclésiastique	ÉTR	Études Théologiques et Religieuses
BLit	Bibel und Liturgie	ÉtudFranc	Études Franciscaines
		EvQ	Evangelical Quarterly
BR	Biblical Research	EvT	Evangelische Theologie
BSac	Bibliotheca Sacra	ExpTim	Expository Times
BT	Bible Translator	FreibZeit-PhilTheol	Freiburger Zeitschrift für Philosophie und Theologie
BTB	Biblical Theology Bulletin		
BTS	Bible et Terre Sainte	GeistLeb	Geist und Leben
		GerefTheol-Tijd	Gereformeerd Theologisch Tijdschrift
BVC	Bible et Vie Chrétienne	Greg	Gregorianum
BZ	Biblische Zeitschrift	HeyJ	Heythrop Journal
		HibJ	Hibbert Journal
CahCercErnRen	Cahiers du Cercle Ernest Renan	HTR	Harvard Theological Review
CB	Cultura Bíblica	HUCA	Hebrew Union College Annual
CBQ	Catholic Biblical Quarterly	IndTheolStud	Indian Theological Studies
ChristCent	Christian Century		
ChristToday	Christianity Today	Int	Interpretation
CivCatt	Civiltà Cattolica	IntCathRev/Communio	International Catholic Review Communio
ClerRev	Clergy Review		
CollBrugGand	Collationes Brugenses et Gandavenses	IrBibStud	Irish Biblical Studies

JAAR	Journal of the American Academy of Religion	NovT	Novum Testamentum
		NovVet	Nova et Vetera
JBL	Journal of Biblical Literature	NRT	Nouvelle Revue Théologique
JBR	Journal of Bible and Religion	NTS	New Testament Studies
		Or	Orientalia
JES	Journal of Ecumenical Studies	PalCler	Palestra del Clero
		PerspRelStud	Perspectives in Religious Studies
JournEvang-TheolSoc	Journal of the Evangelical Theological Society	PEQ	Palestine Exploration Quarterly
JournTheol-SAfr	Journal of Theology for Southern Africa	RassTeol	Rassegna di Teologia
		RB	Revue Biblique
		RBén	Revue Bénedictine
JQR	Jewish Quarterly Review	RCB	Revista de Cultura Bíblica
JR	Journal of Religion	RelLife	Religion in Life
JRAS	Journal of the Royal Asiatic Society	RelS	Religious Studies
		RelSRev	Religious Studies Review
JRT	Journal of Religious Thought	RestorQuart	Restoration Quarterly
		RevExp	Review and Expositor
JSNT	Journal for the Study of the New Testament	RevistB	Revista Bíblica
		RevQ	Revue de Qumran
		RevThom	Revue Thomiste
JSS	Journal of Semitic Studies	RHPR	Revue d'Histoire et de Philosophie Religieuses
JTS	Journal of Theological Studies	RHR	Revue de l'Histoire des Religions
KathGed	Katholische Gedanke		
KD	Kerygma und Dogma	RicBibRel	Ricerche Bibliche e Religiose
KirchRef-Schweiz	Kirchenblatt für die Reformierte Schweiz	RivB	Rivista Biblica
		RivistStor-LettRel	Rivista di Storia e Letteratura Religiosa
LingBib	Linguistica Biblica		
LondQuartHol-Rev	London Quarterly and Holborn Review	RoczTeolKan	Roczniki Teologiczno-Kanoniczne
LouvStud	Louvain Studies	RSPT	Revue des Sciences Philosophiques et Théologiques
LQ	Lutheran Quarterly		
LumVie	Lumiere et Vie		
LumVit	Lumen Vitae	RSR	Recherches de Science Religieuse
LW	Lutheran World		
MelTheol	Melita Theologica	RTL	Revue Théologique de Louvain
ModChurch	Modern Churchman		
MTZ	Münchener Theologische Zeitschrift	RTP	Revue de Théologie et de Philosophie
NedTTS	Nederlands Theologisch Tijdschrift	RUO	Revue de l'Université d'Ottawa
NewBlackfr	New Blackfriars	SBFLA	Studii Biblici Franciscani Liber Annuus
NorTT	Norsk Teologisk Tidsskrift	ScEs	Science et Esprit

SciEccl	Sciences Ecclesiastiques	TQ	Theologische Quartalschrift
Scr	Scripture	TS	Theological Studies
ScrB	Scripture Bulletin	TSFBull	TSF Bulletin
ScuolCatt	Scuola Cattolica	TToday	Theology Today
SEÅ	Svensk Exegetisk Arsbok	TTZ	Trier Theologische Zeitschrift
SelecTeol	Selecciones de Teología	TynBull	Tyndale Bulletin
SJT	Scottish Journal of Theology	TZ	Theologische Zeitschrift
SPap	Studia Papyrologica	US	Una Sancta
		USQR	Union Seminary Quarterly Review
ST	Studia Theologica	VC	Vigiliae Christianae
StudTheolVars	Studia Theologica Varsaviensia	VD	Verbum Domini
		VetChrist	Vetera Christianorum
SWJournTheol	Southwestern Journal of Theology	VSpir	Vie Spirituelle
		ZDPV	Zeitschrift des Deutschen Palästina Vereins
TBT	Bible Today		
TD	Theology Digest		
TeolVida	Teología y Vida	ZKT	Zeitschrift für Katholische Theologie
TheolGlaub	Theologie und Glaube	ZNW	Zeitschrift für die Neutestamentliche Wissenschaft und die Kunde des Älteren Kirche
TijdTheol	Tijdschrift voor Theologie		
TLZ	Theologische Literaturzeitung		
TP	Theologie und Philosophie	ZRGG	Zeitschrift für Religions und Geistesgeschichte
TPQ	Theologisch-praktische Quartalschrift	ZTK	Zeitschrift für Theologie und Kirche

I. COMMENTARIES

Scholarly Studies

1 1979 Joachim GNILKA. Das Evangelium nach Markus. 2. Teilband:
Mk 8,27-16,20. Evangelisch-Katholischer Kommentar zum
Neuen Testament 2/2. Zürich/Einsiedeln/Cologne: Benzi-
ger, and Neukirchen-Vluyn: Neukirchener Verlag. 364 pp.

2 Frans NEIRYNCK. L'Évangile de Marc. À propos du commen-
taire de R. Pesch. Analecta Lovaniensia Biblica et Orientalia, Ser. V, Fasc. 42. Leuven: Editions Peeters.
v - 74 pp.
⌜Contains reviews of R. Pesch's commentary originally
published in ETL 53 (1977) and 55 (1979) with a note
devoted to J. Gnilka's Das Evangelium nach Markus 1.⌝

3 Walter SCHMITHALS. Das Evangelium nach Markus. 2 vols.
Ökumenischer Taschenbuchkommentar zum Neuen Testament
2/1 and 2/2. Gütersloh: G. Mohn; Würzburg: Echter Verlag. 760 pp.

4 1978 Joachim GNILKA. Das Evangelium nach Markus. 1. Teilband:
Mk 1,1-8,26. Evangelisch-Katholischer Kommentar zum
Neuen Testament 2/1. Zürich/Einsiedeln/Cologne: Benzi-
ger, and Neukirchen-Vluyn: Neukirchener Verlag. 316 pp.

5 1977 Walter GRUNDMANN. Das Evangelium nach Markus.7 (rev. ed.)
Theologischer Handkommentar zum Neuen Testament 2. Ber-
lin: Evangelische Verlagsanstalt. xvi-460 pp.
(E 58s-4812)

6 O. H. LANGKAMMER, O.F.M. Ewangelia według św. Marka.
Wstep--przekład z oryginału--komentarz. Pismo Swiete
Nowego Testamentu 3/2. Poznan--Warsaw: Pallottinum.
415 pp.

7 Rudolf PESCH. Das Markusevangelium. II. Teil: Kommentar
zu Kap. 8,27-16,20. Theologischer Kommentar zum Neuen
Testament 2/2. Freiburg/Basel/Vienna: Herder. xvi-
576 pp.   (E 58s-4844)

8 1976 Rudolf PESCH. Das Markusevangelium. I. Teil: Einleitung
und Kommentar zu Kap. 1,1-8,26. Theologischer Kommentar
zum Neuen Testament 2/1. Freiburg/Basel/Vienna: Herder.
xxiv-424 pp.   (E 57-3774)

9 1975 William HENDRIKSEN. New Testament Commentary: Exposition
of the Gospel According to Mark. Grand Rapids: Baker
Book House. viii-700 pp.   (E 57-3748)

10 1974 Jean RADERMAKERS. La bonne nouvelle selon saint Marc. 1.
Texte. 2. Lecture continue. Brussels: Institut d'É-

tudes Théologiques.   79 pp.; 449 pp.   (E 56-2975)

11   1967   Ernst LOHMEYER. <u>Das Evangelium des Markus</u>. Übersetzt und
erklärt.[17] Kritisch-exegetischer Kommentar über das
Neue Testament 1,2. Göttingen: Vandenhoeck & Ruprecht.
368 pp.   (E 45-1073)

12   <u>Das Evangelium des Markus</u>. Ergänzungs-
heft von Gerhard Sass.[3] Kritisch-exegetischer Kommentar
über das Neue Testament 1,2. Göttingen: Vandenhoeck &
Ruprecht. 44 pp.   (E 46-1401)

13   1966   Marie-Joseph LAGRANGE. <u>Évangile selon Saint Marc</u>.[4]
Études Bibliques. Paris: Cabalda. 680 pp. (E 48-2428)

14   V. TAYLOR. <u>The Gospel according to St. Mark. The Greek
Text with Introduction, Notes and Indexes</u>.[2] London/New
York: Macmillan/St. Martin's Press. 700 pp.(E 48-2452)

15   F. M. URICCHIO and G. M. STANO. <u>Vangelo secondo S. Marco</u>.
La Sacra Bibbia. Turin/Rome: Marietti. xix-730 pp.
                                             (E 47-2472)

16   1963   C. E. B. CRANFIELD. <u>The Gospel according to St. Mark: An
Introduction and Commentary</u>.[2] Cambridge Greek Testament
Commentary. Cambridge/New York: Cambridge University
Press. xv-494 pp.   (E 45-1064)

17   1960   Philip CARRINGTON. <u>According to Mark. A Running Commentary on the Oldest Gospel</u>. Cambridge/New York: Cambridge University Press. xii-384 pp.   (E 42-1193)

18   Sherman E. JOHNSON. <u>A Commentary on the Gospel According
to St. Mark</u>. Black's Harper's New Testament Commentary.
London/New York: A. and C. Black/Harper's. xii-283 pp./
vii-279 pp.   (E 42-1200)

Works for the General Reader

19   1980   J. LANDIER, F. PÉCRIAUX, and D. PIZIVIN. <u>Avec Marc. Pour
accompagner une lecture de l'Évangile de Marc</u>. Paris:
Ouvrières. 207 pp.

20   1979   Wilfrid HARRINGTON, O.P. <u>Mark</u>. New Testament Message 4.
Wilmington, DE: Glazier. xvi-253 pp.

21   Rudolf PESCH. <u>Das Evangelium der Urgemeinde. Wiederher-
gestellt und erläutert</u>. Herderbücherei, 748. Freiburg/
Basel/Vienna: Herder. 222 pp.

22 1978 Paul J. ACHTEMEIER. <u>Invitation to Mark: A Commentary on</u>
<u>the Gospel of Mark with Complete Text from the Jerusalem</u>
<u>Bible</u>. Image Books. Garden City, NY: Doubleday.
236 pp.

23 1976 Hugh ANDERSON. <u>The Gospel of Mark</u>. New Century Bible.
London: Oliphants. xviii-366 pp.   (E 58s-4786)

24   J. B. PHILLIPS. <u>Peter's Portrait of Jesus</u>. <u>A Commentary</u>
<u>on the Gospel of Mark and the Letters of Peter</u>. London/
Glasgow/Cleveland: Collins & World. 185 pp.(E 57-3775)

25   R. C. STEDMAN. <u>The Servant Who Rules</u>. <u>The Servant Who</u>
<u>Serves</u>. 2 vols. Waco, TX: Word Books. 223 pp.; 231
pp.   (E 58s-4857)

26   Lionel A. WHISTON. <u>Power of a New Life: Relational Stud-</u>
<u>ies in Mark</u>. ₍4:35-9:49₎ Waco, TX: Word Books. 117 pp.
(E 58s-4904)

27   <u>Through Suffering to Victory: Rela-</u>
<u>tional Studies in Mark</u>. ₍10;1-16:8₎ Waco, TX: Word
Books. 137 pp.   (E 58s-4931)

28 1975 Paul J. ACHTEMEIER. <u>Mark</u>. Proclamation Commentaries 1.
Philadelphia: Fortress. 122 pp.   (E 56-2929)

29   William BARCLAY. <u>The Gospel of Mark</u>. <u>Revised Edition</u>.
<u>Translated with an Introduction and Interpretation</u>.
The Daily Study Bible Series. Revised Edition. Philadelphia: Westminster Press. x-373 pp.   (E 57-3728)

30   R. CROTTY. <u>Good News in Mark</u>. Mark <u>in Today's English</u>
Version. Cleveland: Collins & World/Fount Books.
190 pp.

31   C. E. W. DORRIS. <u>A Commentary on the Gospel according to</u>
<u>Mark</u>.[2] New Testament Commentaries 2. Nashville: Gospel
Advocate Co. 408 pp.   (E 58s-4801)

32   Manford George GUTZKE. <u>Plain Talk on Mark</u>. Grand Rapids:
Zondervan Publishing House. 192 pp.   (E 57-3747)

33   B. MAGGIONI. <u>Il racconto di Marco</u>. Come leggere il Vangelo. Assisi: Cittadella Editrice. 219 pp.(E 56-2966)

34   Eduard SCHWEIZER. <u>Das Evangelium nach Markus</u>. Übersetzt
und erklärt.[14] Das Neue Testament Deutsch 1. Göttin-
gen: Vandenhoeck & Ruprecht. 223 pp.   (E 55-2886)

35 1974 David E. HIEBERT. <u>Mark: A Portrait of the Servant</u>. A

Commentary. Chicago: Moody Press. 437 pp. (E 57-3749)

36   William L. LANE. The Gospel according to Mark: The Eng-
      lish Text with Introduction, Exposition and Notes. New
      International Commentary on the New Testament 2. Grand
      Rapids: Eerdmans. 652 pp.   (E 55-2870)

37   Fritz RIENECKER. Das Evangelium des Markus, erklärt.[5]
      Wuppertaler Studienbibel. Wuppertal: R. Brockhaus. 288
      pp.   (E. 57-3780)

38 1973 K. S. L. CLARK. The Gospel according to St. Mark, with
      Notes and Commentary. London: Darton. 162 pp.
                                                   (E 56-2492)

39 1971 Robert A. COLE. The Gospel according to St. Mark.[2] Tyn-
      dale Bible Commentary New Testament 2. London: Tyndale.
      264 pp.   (E 53-2651)

40   Erich KLOSTERMANN. Das Markusevangelium.[5] Handbuch zum
      Neuen Testament 3. Tübingen: J. C. B. Mohr. 180 pp.
                                                   (E 53-2677)

41   Rudolf SCHNACKENBURG. The Gospel according to St. Mark.
      2 vols. Translated by Werner Kruppa. New Testament for
      Spiritual Reading 3. London/New York: Sheed & Ward/Her-
      der & Herder. 152 pp. 169 pp.   (E 53-2710)

42 1970 Bertil E. GÄRTNER. Markus evangelium. Tolkning av Nya
      Testamentet II. Stockholm: Verbum. 412 pp.(E 49-2604)

43   Herschel H. HOBBS. An Exposition of the Gospel of Mark.
      Grand Rapids: Baker Book House. 261 pp.   (E 52-2561)
      [Reprinted as vol. 2 of An Exposition of the Four
      Gospels (Nashville: Broadman, 1977)]

44   Eduard SCHWEIZER. The Good News According to Mark.
      Translated by Donald H. Madvig. London/Richmond: SPCK/
      John Knox Press. 395 pp.   (E 52-2595)

45   C. E. G. Swift, "Mark," New Bible Commentary Revised[3] (ed.
      by Donald Guthrie et al.; London: IVP), pp. 851-886.

46   E. WARMERS (ed.). Markus-Evangelium. Schriftauslegung
      für Predigt, Bibelarbeit, Unterricht 7. Stuttgart:
      Klotz. 300 pp.   (E 52-2607)

47   Wolf-Dieter ZIMMERMANN. Markus über Jesus. Das Evangel-
      ium für unsere Tage interpretiert. Gütersloh: G. Mohn.
      183 pp.   (E 52-2611)

48 1969   Henry E. Turlington, "Mark," <u>The Broadman Bible Commen-</u>
           <u>tary, Vol. 8: General Articles, Matthew-Mark</u> (ed. by
           C. J. Allen et al.; Nashville, Tenn.: Broadman), pp.
           254-402.

49   Josef SCHMID. <u>The Gospel according to Mark: A Version and</u>
          <u>Commentary</u>. Translated by Kevin Condon. The Regensburg
          New Testament. Staten Island, NY: Alba House. 310 pp.

50   Henry Wansbrough, O.S.B., "St. Mark," <u>New Catholic Commen-</u>
          <u>tary on Holy Scripture</u> (London/New York: Nelson), pp.
          954-985.

51 1968   H. A. GUY. <u>The Gospel of Mark</u>. London/New York: Mac-
           millan/St. Martin's Press. viii-191 pp.   (E 50-2576)

52   Ernst HAENCHEN. <u>Der Weg Jesu: Eine Erklärung des Markus-</u>
          <u>Evangeliums und der kanonischen Parallelen</u>.^{2} De Gruyter
          Lehrbuch. Berlin: de Gruyter. 594 pp.   (E 50-2578)

53   Edward J. Mally, S.J., "The Gospel According to Mark," <u>The</u>
          <u>Jerome Biblical Commentary II</u> (ed. by Raymond E. Brown,
          S.S., Joseph A. Fitzmyer, S.J., and Roland E. Murphy, O.
          Carm.; Englewood Cliffs, NJ: Prentice-Hall), pp. 21-61.

54 1967   Ingo HERMANN. <u>Das Markusevangelium. Zweiter Teil (8,27-</u>
           <u>16,20)</u>. Die Welt der Bibel, Kleinkommentare zur Heilig-
           en Schrift, KK 5/2. Düsseldorf: Patmos-Verlag. 124
           pp.   (E 49-2613)

55   Dorothy M. SLUSSER and Gerald H. SLUSSER. <u>The Jesus of</u>
          <u>Mark's Gospel</u>. Philadelphia: Westminster Press. 157
          pp.   (E 49-2651)

56 1965   Rudolf GROB. <u>Einführung in das Markus Evangelium</u>. Zürich/
           Stuttgart: Zwingli-Verlag. 357 pp.   (E 47-2431)

57   Ingo HERMANN. <u>Das Markusevangelium. Erster Teil (1,1-</u>
          <u>8,26)</u>. Die Welt der Bibel, Kleinkommentare zur Heiligen
          Schrift, KK 5/1. Düsseldorf: Patmos-Verlag. 117 pp.
                                                     (E 47-2434)

58   C. F. D. MOULE. <u>The Gospel according to Mark</u>. Cambridge
          Bible Commentary on the New English Bible. Cambridge:
          Cambridge University Press. x-134 pp.   (E 57-3768)

59   Henri TROADEC. <u>Évangile selon S. Marc</u>. Commentaires sur
          les Évangiles. Paris: Mame. 254 pp.   (E 47-2470)

60 1963   D. E. NINEHAM. <u>The Gospel of St. Mark</u>. Pelican Commen-

tary. Harmondsworth: Penguin Books. 480 pp.(E 45-1076)
ᵣReprinted with minor revisions as <u>Saint Mark</u> (Philadelphia: Westminster Press, 1978), 477 pp.)ᵧ

61 1962 J. W. BEARDSLEE. <u>Mark, A Translation with Notes</u>. New
Brunswick, NJ: The Theological Seminary. 100 pp.

62   Paul S. MINEAR. <u>The Gospel according to Mark</u>. The Lay-
man's Bible Commentary 17. Richmond: John Knox Press.
136 pp.

63 1961 K. HENNIG. <u>Das Markus-Evangelium</u>.³ Stuttgarter Bibel-
hefte. Stuttgart: Quell Verlag. 104 pp.

64   J. HUBY, S. J. and P. BENOIT, O. P. L'Évangile selon
<u>Saint Marc. Traduction, introduction et notes</u>. 3rd.
rev. ed. La Sainte Bible traduite en français sous la
direction de l'École Biblique de Jérusalem. Paris: Cerf.
94 pp.

65 1959 Curtis BEACH. <u>The Gospel of Mark. Its Making and Mean-
ing</u>. New York: Harper. 124 pp.   (E 40-2045)

66 1957 Ralph EARLE. <u>The Gospel according to Mark</u>. The Evangelical Commentary on the Bible. Grand Rapids: Zondervan
Publishing House. 192 pp.   (E 38-1606)

67   J. Huby, S.J., "The Gospel according to Saint Mark," <u>The
Word of Salvation I</u> (translated by John J. Heenan, S.J.;
Milwaukee: Bruce), pp. 503-923.

68   C. Leslie MITTON. <u>The Gospel according to St. Mark</u>. Epworth Preacher's Commentaries. London: Epworth Press.
142 pp.   (E 39-1668)

69 1956 Harold ST. JOHN. <u>An Analysis of the Gospel of Mark: The
Son of God as Mark Portrayed Him</u>. London: Pickering and
Inglis. 173 pp.

70   K. Staab, "Das Evangelium nach Markus," <u>Das Evangelium
nach Markus und Lukas</u> (Echterbibel: Das Neue Testament
5; Würzberg: Echter-Verlag), pp. 5-98.

Study Guides

71 1979 W. M. SWARTLEY. <u>Mark: The Way for all Nations</u>. Scott-
dale, PA/Kitchener, Ont.: Herald Press. 244 pp.

72 1978 A. Elwood SANNER. <u>Mark</u>. Beacon Bible Expositions 2.
Kansas City, MO: Beacon Hill Press. 256 pp.

73 1977 T. J. SMITH. <u>Good News about Jesus as told by Mark</u>. At-
lanta/Winona, MN: John Knox/St. Mary's College Press.
95 pp.

74 1976 M. GALIZZI. <u>Un uomo che sa scegliere: Vangelo second Mar-
co I. Voi l'avete ucciso: Vangelo secondo Marco II</u>.
Commento al Novo Testamento. Leumann (Torino): Elle Di
Ci. 168 pp.; 160 pp.   (E 58s-4805)

75 1973 Thomas J. SMITH. <u>The Mighty Message of Mark</u>. Winona, MN:
St. Mary's College Press. 267 pp.   (E 56-2988)

76 1972 I. L. JENSEN. <u>Mark: A Self-Study Guide</u>. Chicago: Moody.
112 pp.   (E 54-3156)

77 1971 Sean Freyne, "Mark," <u>Mark and Matthew</u> (by Sean Freyne and
Henry Wansbrough; Scripture Discussion Commentary 7;
London: Sheed and Ward / Chicago: ACTA Foundation, pp.
1-136.

78 1969 John HARGREAVES. <u>A Guide to St. Mark's Gospel. Revised
Edition</u>. Theological Educational Fund Study Guide 2.
London: Society for Promoting Christian Knowledge. 336
pp.   (E 52-2556)

79 1967 I. H. MARSHALL. <u>St. Mark</u>. Scripture Union Bible Study
Books. Grand Rapids, MI: Eerdmans Publishing Co. 64 pp.

80 1966 W. HAMILTON. <u>The Modern Reader's Guide to the Gospels:
Mark</u>. The Modern Reader's Guide to the Gospels. London:
Darton, Longman & Todd. 78 pp.   (E 48-2421)

81 1963 A. JONES. <u>The Gospel according to St. Mark. A Text and
Commentary for Students</u>. New York: Sheed and Ward. 255
pp.

82 1962 Ernest Trice THOMPSON. <u>The Gospel according to Mark and
its Meaning for Today</u>. (rev. ed.) Richmond: John Knox
Press. 255 pp.   (E 36-1490)

83 1961 Ralph EARLE. <u>The Gospel of Mark</u>. Proclaiming the New
Testament. Grand Rapids: Baker Book House. 119 pp.

84 1960 Gerard S. SLOYAN. <u>The Gospel of Saint Mark. Introduction
and Commentary</u>. New Testament Reading Guide. Collegeville, MN: Liturgical Press. 127 pp.

85 1956 C. C. MARTINDALE. <u>The Gospel according to Saint Mark</u>.
Stonyhurst Scripture Manuals. Westminster, MD: Newman
Press. xxxii-177 pp.   (E 38-1619)

86   1955   Eduard LOHSE. Mark's Witness to Jesus Christ. Tr. from
            the German by Stephen Neill. New York: Association
            Press. 93 pp.   (E 37-1254)

                        II. COMPOSITION

General Summaries

See also 1439.

87   1980   W. S. Vorster, "Mark: Collector, Redactor, Author, Narra-
            tor?" JournTheolSAfric 31:46-61.   (N 25-91)

88   1979   D. Senior, "The Gospel of Mark," TBT 103:2096-2104.
                                                        (N 24-107)

89   1976   N. Perrin, "Mark," The Interpreter's Dictionary of the
            Bible Supplementary Volume (Nashville: Abingdon), pp.
            571-573.

90   "The Interpretation of the Gospel of Mark," Int
            30:115-124.   (N 20-788)

91   1975   W. W. Isenberg, "A Short Catechism of the Gospel of Mark,"
            CurTM 2:316-325.   (N 20-450)

92   1972   Ludger SCHENKE. Glory and the Way of the Cross. The Gos-
            pel of Mark. Tr. (from German: 1969) by Robin Scroggs.
            Herald Biblical Booklets. Chicago: Franciscan Herald
            Press. 71 pp.   (E 55-2881)

93   1970   C. Angelini, "Portrait de saint Marc," ÉtudFranc 20:217-
            220.   (N 15-511)

94   A. Denaux, "Kleine inleiding op het Marcusevangelie,"
            CollBrugGand 16:309-341.   (N 15-512)

95   J. W. Michaux, "L'évangile selon Marc," BVC 93:37-41.
                                                        (N 15-154)

96   1967   C. P. Ceroke, "The Gospel according to St. Mark," New
            Catholic Encyclopedia 9 (New York/London: McGraw-Hill),
            pp. 233-240.

97   1963   S. Sandmel, "Prolegomena to a Commentary on Mark," JBL 31:
            294-300.   (N 8-590)
              Republished in Sandmel, Two Living Traditions: Essays
              on Religion and the Bible (Detroit, MI: Wayne State

University, 1972), pp. 147-157, and in <u>New Testament
Issues</u> (ed. by R. Batey; London: SCM, 1970), pp. 45-
56.]

98   1962   W. J. HARRINGTON, O. P.   <u>The Gospel According to St. Mark</u>.
            <u>The Gospel According to St. Luke</u>.   Doctrine and Life
            Series.   Dublin: Dominican Publications.   57 pp.

99   D. M. Stanley, "Mark and Modern Apologetics," <u>TBT</u> 1:58-
            64.   (N 7-515)

100 1958   G. S. Sloyan, "The Gospel according to St. Mark," <u>Worship</u>.
            32:547-557.   (N 3-359)
               [Republished in <u>Contemporary New Testament Studies</u>
               (ed. by Sister M. Rosalie Ryan, C.S.J.: Collegeville,
               MN: Liturgical Press, 1965), pp. 154-161.]

101 1957   D. E. Nineham, "St. Mark's Gospel," <u>Theology</u> 60:267-272.

Author

102 1978   P. Parker, "The Authorship of the Second Gospel," <u>Persp-
            RelStud</u> 5:4-9.   (N 23-111)

103 1967   K. Niederwimmer, "Johannes Markus und die Frage nach dem
            Verfasser des zweiten Evangeliums," <u>ZNW</u> 58:172-188.
                                                             (N 12-885)

"Gospel" Genre

104 1979   J. F. O'Grady, "The Origins of the Gospels: Mark," <u>BTB</u> 9:
            154-164.

105 1978   Benoît STANDAERT, O.S.B.   <u>L'évangile selon Marc.   Composi-
            tion et genre littéraire</u>.   Zevenkerken/Brugge: Sint-An-
            driesabdij.   vi-678 pp.   (E 58s-4856)

106 1977   Gilbert G. BILEZIKIAN.   <u>The Liberated Gospel: A Comparison
            of the Gospel of Mark and Greek Tragedy</u>.   Baker Biblical
            Monograph.   Grand Rapids: Baker Book House.   159 pp.

107 1976   G. Dautzenberg, "Zur Stellung des Markusevangeliums in der
            Geschichte der urchristlichen Theologie," <u>Kairos</u> 18:
            282-291.   (N 21-735)
               [Translated and digested as "Mark and Early Christian
               Theology," in <u>TD</u> 26 (1978):28-29.]

108 1973   R. Schnackenburg, "'Das Evangelium' im Verständnis des
            ältesten Evangelisten," in <u>Orientierung an Jesus: Zur
            Theologie der Synoptiker: Für Josef Schmid</u> (ed. by Paul

Hoffmann in collaboration with Norbert Brox and Wilhelm
Pesch; Freiburg/Basel/Vienna: Herder), pp. 309-324.

109   1972   G. Strecker, "Literarkirtische Überlegungen zum <u>euaggelion</u>-
Begriff im Markusevangelium," in <u>Neues Testament und Ge-
schichte: Historisches Geschehen und Deutung im Neuen
Testament: Oscar Cullmann zum 70. Geburtstag</u> (ed. by
Heinrich Baltensweiler and Bo Reicke; Zürich: Theolo-
gischer Verlag/Tübingen: Mohn, 1972), pp. 91-104.

110   1970   J. M. Robinson, "On the <u>Gattung</u> of Mark (and John)," <u>Per</u>
<u>spective</u> 11:99-129.   (N 15-157)

111   1969   K. Kertelge, "Die Epiphanie Jesu im Evangelium ₁Markus₁,"
in <u>Gestalt und Anspruch des Neuen Testaments</u> (ed. by
Josef Schreiner; Würzburg: Echter Verlag), pp. 153-172.
₁Republished in <u>Das Markus-Evangelium</u> (ed. by R. Pesch;
Wege der Forschung 411; Darmstadt: Wissenschaftliche
Buchgesellschaft, 1979), pp. 259-282.

112   1967   R. J. Dillon, "Mark and the New Meaning of 'Gospel'," <u>Dun-</u>
<u>Rev</u> 7:131-161.

113   1957   G. Schille, "Bemerkungen zur Formgeschichte des Evangeliums. Rahmen und Aufbau des Markus-Evangeliums," <u>NTS</u> 4:
1-24.   (N 2-537)

Literary Style/Characteristics

See also 348, 492-495.

114   1979   R. C. Tannehill, "The Gospel of Mark as Narrative Christology," <u>Semeia</u> 16:57-95.   (N 24-803)

115   1978   E. E. Lemcio, "External Evidence for the Structure and
Function of Mark iv. 1-20, vii. 14-23 and viii. 14-21,"
<u>JTS</u> 29:323-338.   (N 23-461)

116   N. R. Petersen, "'Point of View' in Mark's Narrative,"
<u>Semeia</u> 12:97-121.   (N 23-454)

117   E. J. PRYKE. <u>Redactional Style in the Markan Gospel. A</u>
<u>Study of Syntax and Vocabulary as guides to Redaction in</u>
<u>Mark</u>. Society for New Testament Studies Monograph Ser-
ies 33. Cambridge/New York: Cambridge University Press.
x-196 pp.

118   1977   F. C. Synge, "A Matter of Tenses--Fingerprints of an An-
notator in Mark," <u>ExpTim</u> 88:168-171.   (N 21-742)

119   1975   D. J. Clark, "Criteria for Identifying Chiasm," <u>LingBib</u>
              35:63-72.   (N 20-457)

120   1974   J. M. Robinson, "The Literary Composition of Mark," in
              <u>L'évangile selon Marc: Tradition et rédaction</u> (ed. by M.
              Sabbe; Bibliotheca ephemeridum theologicarum lovaniens-
              ium, 34; Gembloux: Duculot/ Louvain: Leuven University),
              pp. 11-19.

121   1972   F. Neirynck, "Duplicate Expressions in the Gospel of Mark,"
              <u>ETL</u> 48:150-209.   (N 17-133)
              ₍Republished in Neirynck, <u>Duality in Mark: Contribu-
              tions to the Study of the Markan Redaction</u> (Biblio-
              theca ephemeridum theologicarum lovaniensium, 31;
              Louvain: Leuven University, 1972), pp. 13-72.₎

122   1971   F. Neirynck, "Mark in Greek," <u>ETL</u> 47:144-198. (N 16-167)
              ₍Republished in Neirynck, <u>Duality in Mark: Contribu-
              tions to the Study of the Markan Redaction</u> (Biblio-
              theca ephemeridum theologicarum lovaniensium, 31;
              Louvain: Leuven University, 1972), pp. 139-191.₎

123   F. Neirynck, "Duality in Mark," <u>ETL</u> 47:394-463. (N 16-869)
              ₍Republished in Neirynck, <u>Duality in Mark: Contribu-
              tions to the Study of the Markan Redaction</u> (Biblio-
              theca ephemeridum theologicarum lovaniensium, 31;
              Louvain: Leuven University, 1972), pp. 75-136.₎

124   1964   R. C. Nevius, "The Use of Proper Names in St. Mark," in
              <u>Studia Evangelica II: Papers Presented to the Second In-
              ternational Congress on New Testament Studies held at
              Christ Church, Oxford, 1961</u> (ed. by F. L. Cross; Texte
              und Untersuchungen zur Geschichte der altchristlichen
              Literatur 87; Berlin: Akademie-Verlag), pp. 225-228.

125   1963   A. W. Mosley, "Jesus' Audiences in the Gospels of St. Mark
              and St. Luke," <u>NTS</u> 10:139-149.   (N 8-959)

126   1961   Robert G. BRATCHER and Eugene A. NIDA. <u>A Translator's
              Handbook on the Gospel of Mark</u>. Help for Translators 2.
              Leiden: E. J. Brill, for the United Bible Societies.
              xviii-534 pp.   (E 42-1189)

127   John Charles DOUDNA. <u>The Greek of the Gospel of Mark</u>.
              JBL Monograph Series 12. Philadelphia: Society of Bibli-
              cal Literature and Exegesis. 139 pp.   (E 43-1351)

128   1959   G. G. Bilezikian, "The Gospel of Mark and Greek Tragedy,"
              <u>Gordon Review</u> 5:79-86.   (N 4-659)

129   1956   G. D. Kilpatrick, "Some notes on Marcan Usage," BT 7:51-
             56.

130   1954   Harold A. GUY. The Origin of the Gospel of Mark. London/
             New York: Hodder and Stoughton/Harper Brothers. 176 pp.
                                                         (E 36-1479)

Word Studies

131   1980   C. Bonnet, "Le désert. Sa signification dans l'Évangile
             de Marc," Hokhma 13:20-34.   (N 24-798)

132   1978   P. Ellingworth, "How Soon is 'Immediately' in Mark?" BT
             29:414-419.   (N 23-447)

133   G. Rinaldi, "Nota: Nounechōs," BeO 20:26.

134   1973   V. K. Robbins, "Dynameis and Sēmeia in Mark," BR 18:5-20.
                                                     (N 18-866)

135   1972   G. Blocher, "Menschenmeinung oder Gotteswort," KirchRef-
             Schweiz 128:130-134, 146-149.   (N 17-131)

136   1968   E. J. Pryke, "IDE and IDOU," NTS 14:418-424. (N 13-187)

137   1967   G. D. Kilpatrick, "idou and ide in the Gospels," JTS 18:
             425-426.   (N 12-561)

138   1966   J. J. O'Rourke, "A Note Concerning the Use of eis and en
             in Mark," JBL 85:349-351.   (N 11-720)

139   1964   Richard C. NEVIUS. The Divine Names in St. Mark. Studies
             and Documents 25. Salt Lake City: University of Utah
             Press. 74 pp.   (E 47-2450)

140   1963   J. Mehlmann, "Da Origem e do Significado do Nome 'Salomé'
             (Mc 15, 40; 16,1)," RCB 7:93-107.   (N 9-941)

141   1956   C. C. Cowling, "Mark's Use of hôra," AusBR 5:155-160.

Old Testament Allusions

See also 170, 284, 674, 677, 680, 692, 720, 749, 768, 784, 1005, 1048,
       1049, 1051, 1061, 1065, 1073, 1105, 1108, 1109, 1298, 1299,
       1304, 1318.

142   1975   H. C. Kee, "The Function of Scriptural Quotations and Al-
             lusions in Mark 11 - 16," in Jesus und Paulus: Fest-
             schrift für Werner Georg Kümmel zum 70. Geburtstag (ed.
             by E. Earle Ellis and Erich Grässer; Göttingen: Vanden-

hoeck & Ruprecht), pp. 165-188.

143 1972 H. Anderson, "The Old Testament in Mark's Gospel," in <u>The Use of the Old Testament in the New and Other Essays: Studies in Honor of William Franklin Stinespring</u> (ed. by James M. Efird; Durham, NC: Duke University), pp. 280-306.

144   Klaus BERGER. <u>Die Gesetzeauslegung Jesu. Ihr historischer Hintergrund im Judentum und im Alten Testament. Teil I: Markus und Parallelen</u>. Wissenschaftliche Monographien zum Alten und Neuen Testament 40. Neukirchen-Vluyn: Neukirchener. xi-631 pp.

145 1971 H. C. Kee, "Scripture Quotations and Allusions in Mark 11 - 16," in <u>Society of Biblical Literature 1971 Seminar Papers II</u> (Atlanta, GA: Society of Biblical Literature), pp. 475-502.

146 1968 A. Gaboury, "Deux fils uniques: Isaac et Jésus. Connexions vétérotestamentaires de Mc 1,11 (et parallèlles)," in <u>Studia Evangelica 4,1: Papers Presented to the Third International Congress on New Testament Studies held at Christ Church, Oxford, 1965: Part I. The Scriptures</u> (ed. by F. L. Cross; Berlin: Akademie Verlag), pp. 198-204.

147 1965 Alfred SUHL. <u>Die Funktion der alttestamentlichen Zitate und Anspielungen im Markusevangelium</u>. Gütersloh: Gerd Mohn. 198 pp.   (E 47-2469)

148 1961 S. Schulz, "Markus und das Alte Testament," <u>ZTK</u> 58:184-197.   (N 6-786)

149 1956 I. Buse, "The Markan Account of the Baptism of Jesus and Isaiah LXIII," <u>JTS</u> 7:74-75.   (N 1-43)

Pre-Gospel Sources

See also 203, 845, 1443.

150 1979 W. H. Kelber, "Mark and Oral Tradition," <u>Semeia</u> 16:7-56. [Also published in German as "Markus und die mündliche Tradition," <u>LingBib</u> 45:5-58. (N 24-106)]

151   F. Testa, "I 'Discorsi di Missione' di Gesù," <u>SBFLA</u> 29:7-41.   (N 25-75)

152   T. J. Weeden, "Metaphysical Implications of Kelber's Approach to Orality and Textuality. A Response to Werner

Kelber's 'Mark and the Oral Tradition'," in Society of
Biblical Literature 1979 Seminar Papers 2 (ed. by Paul
J. Achtemeier; Missoula, Mont.: Scholars Press), pp.
153-166.

153   1978   P. B. Lewis, "Indications of a Liturgical Source in the
             Gospel of Mark," Encounter 39:385-394.   (N 23-839)

154   1975   Etienne TROCMÉ. The Formation of the Gospel according to
             Mark. Tr. (from French: 1963) by Pamela Gaughan. Lon-
             don/Philadelphia: SPCK/Westminster. viii-293 pp.
                                                         (E 57-3795)

155   1974   E. Best, "Mark's Preservation of the Tradition," in L'é-
             vangile selon Marc: Tradition et rédaction (ed. by M.
             Sabbe; Bibliotheca ephemeridum theologicarum lovaniens-
             ium 34; Gembloux/Louvain: Duculot/Leuven University),
             pp. 21-34.
                [Republished as "Markus als Bewahrer der Überliefer-
                ung," (tr. by Dieter Lührmann) in Das Markus-Evangel-
                ium (ed. by R. Pesch; Wege der Forschung 411; Darm-
                stadt: Wissenschaftliche Buchgesellschaft, 1979), pp.
                390-410.

156   W. Hendriks, "Zur Kollektionsgeschichte des Markusevan-
             geliums," in L'évangile selon Marc: Tradition et rédac-
             tion (ed. by M. Sabbe; Bibliotheca ephemeridum theologi-
             carum lovaniensium 34; Gembloux/Louvain: Duculot/Leuven
             University), pp. 35-57.

157   J. Konings, "The Pre-Markan Sequence in Jn., VI: A Criti-
             cal Re-examination," in L'évangile selon Marc: Tradition
             et rédaction (ed. by M. Sabbe; Bibliotheca ephemeridum
             theologicarum lovaniensium 34; Gembloux/Louvain: Ducu-
             lot/Leuven University), pp. 147-177.

158   P. Vassiliadis, "Behind Mark: Towards a Written Source,"
             NTS 20:155-160.   (N 18-868)

159   1971   Heinz-Wolfgang KUHN. Ältere Sammlungen im Markusevangel-
             ium. Studien zur Umwelt des Neuen Testaments 8. Göttin-
             gen: Vandenhoeck & Ruprecht. 270 pp.   (E 53-2679)

160   1968   F. Neirynck, "Une nouvelle théorie synoptique (À propos de
             Mc. I, 2-6 et par.). Notes critiques," ETL 44:141-153.
                                                         (N 13-188)

161   1961   M. Karnętzki, "Die galiläische Redaktion im Markusevangel-
             ium," ZNW 52:238-272.   (N 6-784)

162   1955   D. E. Nineham, "The Order of Events in St. Mark's Gospel:

an examination of Dr. Dodd's Hypothesis," in <u>Studies</u>
<u>in the Gospels: Essays in Memory of R. H. Lightfoot</u> (ed.
by D. E. Nineham; Oxford: B. Blackwell), pp. 223-239.

Pre-Gospel Sources: Aretalogies

See also 110.

163 1979 G. Theissen, "Die aretalogische Evangelienkomposition des
Markus," in <u>Das Markus-Evangelium</u> (ed. by R. Pesch; Wege
der Forschung 411; Darmstadt: Wissenschaftliche Buchgesellschaft), pp. 377-389.
  [Originally published in Theissen, <u>Urchristliche Wun-</u>
  <u>dergeschichten. Ein Beitrag zur formgeschichtlichen</u>
  <u>Erforschung der synoptischen Evangelien.</u> (Gütersloh:
  Gütersloher Verlagshaus Gerd Mohn, 1974), pp. 211-
  221.]

164 1975 H. C. KEE. <u>Aretalogies, Hellenistic "Lives," and the</u>
<u>Sources of Mark. Protocol of the Twelfth Colloquy: 8</u>
<u>December 1974.</u> Protocol Series 12. Berkeley, CA: Cen-
ter for Hermeneutical Studies in Hellenistic and Modern
Culture. iv-50 pp.   (E 58s-4818)

165 1973 Morton SMITH. <u>The Aretalogy Used by Mark. Protocol of</u>
<u>the Sixth Colloquy.</u> Berkeley, CA: Center for Hermeneu-
tical Studies in Hellenistic and Modern Culture. 54
pp.   (E 57-3788)

Pre-Gospel Sources: Miracle Collections

See also 1545.

166 1976 A. B. Kolenkow, "Healing Controversy as a Tie Between Miracle and Passion Material for a Proto-Gospel," <u>JBL</u> 95:623-
638.   (N 21-396)

167 1972 P. J. Achtemeier, "The Origin and Function of the Pre-
Marcan Miracle Catenae," <u>JBL</u> 91:198-221.   (N 17-142)

168   J.-M. van Cangh, "Les sources de l'Évangile: les collec-
tions pré-marciennes de miracles," <u>RTL</u> 3:76-85.
                                           (N 17-137)

169 1970 P. J. Achtemeier, "Toward the Isolation of Pre-Markan Miracle Catenae," JBL 89:265-291.   (N 15-523)

Pre-Gospel Sources: Passion Narrative

See also 1179, 1183, 1184, 1188, 1192, 1342.

170   1979   J. Oswald, "Die Beziehungen zwischen Psalm 22 und dem vor-
             markinischen Passionsbericht," ZKT 101:53-66.(N 24-118)

171   1975   R. Pesch, "Die Passion des Menschensohnes: Eine Studie zu
             den Menschensohnworten der vormarkinischen Passionsge-
             schichte," in Jesus und der Menschensohn: Für Anton
             Vögtle (ed. by Rudolf Pesch and Rudolf Schnackenburg,
             with Odilo Kaiser; Freiburg/Basel/Vienna: Herder), pp.
             166-195.

171a 1974   Ludger SCHENKE. Der gekreuzigte Christus. Versuch einer
             literarkritischen und traditionsgeschichtlichen Bestimm-
             ung der vormarkinischen Passionsgeschichte. Stuttgarter
             Bibelstudien 69. Stuttgart: Katholisches Bibelwerk.
             150 pp.

Pre-Gospel Sources: Sayings Collection

172   1979   W. Schenk, "Der Einfluss der Logienquelle auf das Markus-
             evangelium," ZNW 70:141-165.   (N 25-90)

173   1978   D. Peabody, "A Pre-Markan Prophetic Sayings Tradition and
             the Synoptic Problem," JBL 97:391-409.

174   1976   E. Best, "An Early Sayings Collection," NovT 18:1-16.
                                                       (N 20-786)

175   1974   M. Devisch, "La relation entre l'évangile de Marc et le
             document Q," in L'évangile selon Marc: Tradition et
             rédaction (ed. by M. Sabbe; Bibliotheca ephemeridum the-
             ologicarum lovaniensium 34; Gembloux/Louvain: Duculot/
             Leuven University), pp. 59-91.

176   1966   J. Lambrecht, "Die Logia-Quellen von Markus 13," Bib 47:
             321-360.   (N 11-1052)

177   1961   J. P. Brown, "Mark as Witness to an Edited Form of Q,"
             JBL 80:29-44.   (N 6-135)

Relationship to Judaism

178   1979   H. Baarlink, "Zur Frage nach dem Antijudaismus im Markus-
             evangelium," ZNW 70:166-193.   (N 25-83)

179   1978   Michael J. COOK. Mark's Treatment of the Jewish Leaders.

Supplements to Novum Testamentum 51. Leiden: E. J. Brill. xi-104 pp.

180 1973 E. J. Vardaman, "The Gospel of Mark and 'The Scrolls'," ChristToday 17:1284-1287.

181 1971 T. L. Budesheim, "Jesus and the Disciples in Conflict with Judaism," ZNW 62:190-209. (N 16-868)

182 H.-W. Kuhn, "Zum Problem des Verhältnisses der markinischen Redaktion zur israelitisch-jüdischen Tradition," in Tradition und Glaube: Das frühe Christentum in seiner Umwelt: Festgabe für Karl Georg Kuhn zum 65. Geburtstag (ed. by Gert Jeremias, Heinz-Wolfgang Kuhn, and Hartmut Stegemann; Göttingen: Vandenhoeck & Ruprecht), pp. 299-309.

183 1969 O. Michel, "Zur Methodik der Forschung," in Studies on the Jewish Background of the New Testament (ed. by O. Michel, S. Safrai, R. le Déaut, et al.; Assen: Van Gorcum), pp. 1-11.

184 1966 J. C. Weber, "Jesus' Opponents in the Gospel of Mark," JBR 34:214-222. (N 11-239)

185 1959 T. A. Burkill, "Anti-Semitism in St. Mark's Gospel," NovT 3:34-53. (N 4-393)

Relationship to Other New Testament Writings: Mark and Acts

186 1970 P. Parker, "Mark, Acts and Galilean Christianity," NTS 16: 295-304. (N 15-156)

187 1958 A. E. Haefner, "The Bridge between Mark and Acts," JBL 77: 67-71. (N 3-79)

Relationship to Other New Testament Writings: Mark and John

See also 157, 313, 384, 750.

188 1978 R. T. Fortna, "Jesus and Peter at the High Priest's House: A Test Case for the Question of the Relation Between Mark's and John's Gospels," NTS 24:371-383. (N 22-782)

189 E. F. Glusman, "Criteria for a Study of the Outlines of Mark and John," in Society of Biblical Literature 1978 Seminar Papers II (ed. by Paul J. Achtemeier; Missoula, Mont.: Scholars Press), pp. 239-250.

190   L. R. Kittlaus, "John and Mark: A Methodological Evalua-
           tion of Norman Perrin's Suggestion," in Society of Bib-
           lical Literature 1978 Seminar Papers II (ed. by Paul J.
           Achtemeier; Missoula, Mont.: Scholars Press), pp. 269-
           280.

191   A. H. Maynard, "Common Elements in the Outlines of Mark
           and John," in Society of Biblical Literature 1978 Semi-
           nar Papers II (ed. by Paul J. Achtemeier; Missoula,
           Mont.: Scholars Press), pp.251-260.

192   M. Smith, "Mark 6:32 - 15:47 and John 6:1 - 19:42," in
           Society of Biblical Literature 1978 Seminar Papers II
           (ed. by Paul J. Achtemeier; Missoula, Mont.: Scholars
           Press), pp. 281-288.

193   1967 E. Trocmé, "Pour un Jésus public: les évangélistes Marc et
           Jean aux prises avec l'intimisme de la tradition," in
           Oikonomia: Heilsgeschichte als Thema der Theologie. O.
           Cullmann zum 65. Geburtstag gewidmet (ed. by Felix
           Christ; Hamburg-Bergstedt: Reich), pp. 42-50.

194   1956 E. K. Lee, "St. Mark and the Fourth Gospel," NTS 3:50-58.

Relationship to Other New Testament Writings: Mark and Paul

195   1977 K. Romaniuk, "Le Problème des Paulinismes dans l'Évangile
           de Marc," NTS 23:266-274.   (N 21-740)

196   1975 K. Romaniuk, "Zagadnienie paulinizmów w Ewangelii św.
           Marka," CollTheol 45:19-29.   (N 20-790)

197   1969s A. W. Argyle, "M and the Pauline Epistles," ExpTim 81:340-
           342.

198   1968 A. A. K. Graham, "Mark and Hebrews," in Studia Evangelica
           4,1: Papers Presented to the Third International Congress
           on New Testament Studies held at Christ Church, Oxford,
           1965: Part I. The Scriptures (ed. by F. L. Cross; Berlin:
           Akademie Verlag), pp. 411-416.

199   1955 J. C. Fenton, "Paul and Mark," in Studies in the Gospels:
           Essays in Memory of R. H. Lightfoot (ed. by D. E. Nine-
           ham; Oxford: B. Blackwell), pp. 89-112.

Relationship to Other New Testament Writings: Synoptic Problem

See also 173, 311, 608, 1028.

200 1980 Rudolf LAUFEN. <u>Die Doppelüberlieferungen der Logienquelle</u>
           <u>und des Markusevangeliums</u>. Bonner biblische Beiträge
           54. Bonn: Hanstein. 614 pp.

201   Hans-Herbert STOLDT. <u>History and Criticism of the Markan</u>
           <u>Hypothesis</u>. Tr. by Donald L. Niewyk. Macon, GA: Mercer
           University Press.
           [Originally published as <u>Geschichte und Kritik der</u>
           <u>Markushypothese</u>. Göttingen: Vandenhoeck & Ruprecht,
           1977. 241 pp. (E 58s-4860)]

202 1979 H. Binder, "Von Markus zu den Grossevangelien," <u>TZ</u> 35:283-
           289.

203   P. Parker, "A Second Look at the Gospel before Mark," in
           <u>Society of Biblical Literature 1979 Seminar Papers I</u>
           (ed. by Paul J. Achtemeier; Missoula, Mont.: Scholars
           Press), pp. 147-168.

204 1978 J. J. Griesbach, "Commentatio qua Marci Evangelium totum e
           Matthaei et Lucae commentariis decerptum esse monstra-
           tur," in <u>J. J. Griesbach: Synoptic and text-critical</u>
           <u>studies 1776-1976</u> (ed. by Bernard Orchard and Thomas R.
           W. Longstaff; Society for New Testament Studies Mono-
           graph Series 34; Cambridge/New York: Cambridge Univer-
           sity), pp. 68-135.

205   John M. RIST. <u>On the independence of Matthew and Mark</u>.
           Society for New Testament Studies Monograph Series 32.
           Cambridge/London/New York/Melbourne: Cambridge University
           Press. vii-132 pp.

206   H.-H. Stoldt, "Geschichte und Kritik der Markus-hypothese,"
           in <u>Society of Biblical Literature 1978 Seminar Papers II</u>
           (ed. by Paul J. Achtemeier; Missoula, Mont.: Scholars
           Press), pp. 145-158.

207 1977 Thomas R. W. LONGSTAFF. <u>Evidence of Conflation in Mark?</u>
           <u>A Study in the Synoptic Problem</u>. Society of Biblical
           Literature Dissertation Series 28. Missoula, Mont.:
           Scholars Press. x-245 pp.   (E 58s-4831)

208 1974 M.-É. Boismard, "Influences matthéennes sur l'ultime ré-
           daction de l'évangile de Marc," in <u>L'évangile selon Marc:</u>
           <u>Tradition et rédaction</u> (ed. by M. Sabbe; Bibliotheca e-
           phemeridum theologicarum lovaniensium 34; Gembloux/Lou-
           vain: Duculot/Leuven University), pp. 93-101.

209   D. L. Dungan, "Reactionary Trends in the Gospel Producing
           Activity of the Early Church: Marcion, Tatian, Mark," in

L'évangile selon Marc: Tradition et rédaction (ed. by M. Sabbe; Bibliotheca ephemeridum theologicarum lovaniensium 34; Gembloux/Louvain: Duculot/Leuven University), pp. 179-202.

210   F. Neirynck, "Urmarcus redivivus? Examen critique de l'hypothèse des insertions matthéennes dans Marc," in L'évangile selon Marc: Tradition et rédaction (ed. by M. Sabbe; Bibliotheca ephemeridum theologicarum lovaniensium 34; Gembloux/Louvain: Duculot/Leuven University), pp. 103-145.

211   1972   E. P. Sanders, "The Overlaps of Mark and Q and the Synoptic Problem," NTS 19:453-465.

212   1971   H. P. Hamann, "Sic et Non: Are We So Sure of Matthean Dependence on Mark?" CTM 41:462-469.

213   1970   D. L. Dungan, "Mark--The Abridgement of Matthew and Luke," Perspective 11:51-97.   (N 15-153)

214   J. A. Fitzmyer, "The Priority of Mark and the 'Q' Source in Luke," Perspective 11:131-170.

215   1969   Robert Lisle LINDSEY. A Hebrew Translation of the Gospel of Mark. Greek-Hebrew Diglot with English Introduction. Jerusalem: Dugith. 159 pp. ₍Cf. the Introduction.₎

216   1966   J. Jeremias, "Zum Problem des Urmarkus," in Jeremias, Abba: Studien zur neutestamentlichen Theologie und Zeitgeschichte (Göttingen: Vandenhoeck & Ruprecht), pp. 87-90. ₍Originally published in ZNW 35 (1936):280-282.₎

217   1965   R. T. Simpson, "The Major Agreements of Matthew and Luke against Mark," NTS 12:273-284.

218   1959   J. H. Ludlum, "Are We Sure of Mark's Priority?" ChristToday 3:no.24, pp. 11-14; no. 25, pp. 9-10.

219   1954s   L. Vaganay, "Existe-t-il chez Marc quelques traces du Sermon sur la Montagne?" NTS 1:193-200.

Purpose/Sitz-im-Leben/Date

See also 21, 87, 89, 154, 181, 290, 352, 356, 367 - 371, 1449, 1538, 1549.

220   1980   G. E. Ladd, "A redactional study of Mark," ExpTim 92:10-13.

221   A. C. Outler, "The Gospel According to St. Mark," <u>Perkins</u> <u>Journal</u> 33:3-9.   (N 25-87)

222   B. M. F. van Iersel, "The Gospel according to St. Mark-- written for a persecuted community?" <u>NedTTs</u> 34:15-36.
                     (N 24-804)

223   1979   E. Best, "Mark: Some Problems," <u>IrBibStud</u> 1:77-98.
                     (N 24-103)

224   J. F. O'Grady, "The Origins of the Gospels: Mark," <u>BTB</u> 9: 154-164.   (N 24-433)

225   1978   P. J. Achtemeier, "Mark as Interpreter of the Jesus Tradi- tions," <u>Int</u> 32:339-352.   (N 23-108)

226   J. D. Crossan, "A Form for Absence: The Markan Creation of Gospel," <u>Semeia</u> 12:41-55.   (N 23-445)

227   1977   F. de la Calle, "La experiencia cristiana de Jesús, según el evangelio de Marcos," in <u>Jesucristo en la historia y</u> <u>en la fe</u> (Semana Internacional de Teología, Madrid, 1977; ed. by A. Vargas-Machuca; Madrid/Salamanca: Funda- ción Juan March/Ediciones Sigueme), pp. 125-132.

228   K. Tagawa, "'Galilée et Jérusalem': l'attention portée par l'évangéliste Marc à l'histoire de son temps," <u>RHPR</u> 57: 439-470.   (N 22-771)

229   1976   W. Bracht, "Jüngerschaft und Nachfolge: Zur Gemeindesitua- tion im Markusevangelium," in <u>Kirche im Werden: Studien</u> <u>zum Thema Amt und Gemeinde im Neuen Testament</u> (ed. by Josef Hainz in collaboration with the Collegium Biblicum München; Munich/Paderborn/Vienna: Verlag Ferdinand Schön- igh), pp. 143-165.

230   M. Karnetzki, "Die Gegenwart des Freudenboten. Zur letz- ten Redaktion des Markus-Evangeliums," <u>NTS</u> 23:101-108.
                     (N 21-388)

231   1975   M. S. Enslin, "A New Apocalyptic," <u>RelLife</u> 44:105-110.
                     (N 20-97)

232   G. Mangatt, "The Christological Kerygma of the Gospel of Mark," <u>Biblebhashyam</u> 1:19-36.   (N 20-99)

233   1973   Ralph P. MARTIN. <u>Mark: Evangelist and Theologian</u>. Exeter/ Grand Rapids: Paternoster Press/Zondervan Publishing House (1973). 250 pp./240 pp.   (E 54-3172)

234   T. J. Weeden, "The Conflict Between Mark and His Opponents

Over Kingdom Theology," in <u>Society of Biblical Litera-</u>
<u>ture 1973 Seminar Papers II</u> (ed. by George MacRae; Cam-
bridge, Mass.: Society of Biblical Literature), pp. 203-
241.

235   1972   T. A. Burkill, "The Formation of St. Mark's Gospel," in
Burkill, <u>New Light on the Earliest Gospel: Seven Markan</u>
<u>Studies</u> (Ithaca, NY: Cornell University), pp. 180-264.

236   J.-M. van Cangh, "La Galilée dans l'évangile de Marc: un
lieu théologique?" <u>RB</u> 79:59-75.   (N 17-136)

237   1971   B. Mariani, "Il Vangelo di Marco posteriore alla distruzione di Gerusalemme del 70?" in <u>La distruzione di Geru-</u>
<u>salemme del 70 nei suoi riflessi storico-letterari. Atti</u>
<u>del V Convegno biblico francescano, Roma 22-27 settembre</u>
<u>1969</u> (Assisi: Studio teologico Porziuncola), pp. 167-
180.

238   Theodore J. WEEDEN. <u>Mark--Traditions in Conflict</u>. Philadelphia: Fortress. x-182 pp.   (E 53-2727)

239   1970   R. A. Edwards, "A New Approach to the Gospel of Mark," <u>LQ</u>
22:330-335.   (N 15-514)

240   H. C. Snape, "Christian Origins in Rome with Special Reference to Mark's Gospel," <u>ModChurch</u> 13:230-244.
                                     (N 15-159)

241   1969   J. D. McCaughey, "Three 'Persecution Documents' of the New
Testament," <u>AusBR</u> 17:27-40.   (N 14-497)

242   R. P. Martin, "A Gospel in Search of a Life-Setting," <u>Exp-</u>
<u>Tim</u> 80:361-364.   (N 14-496)

243   Willi MARXSEN. <u>Mark the Evangelist: Studies on the Redac-</u>
<u>tion History of the Gospel</u>. Tr. by James Boyce, Donald
Juel, Wm. Poehlmann with Roy A. Harrisville. Nashville:
Abingdon. 222 pp.
    [Translated from <u>Der Evangelist Markus. Studien zur</u>
    <u>Redaktionsgeschichte des Evangeliums</u>.² Forschungen
    zur Religion und Literatur des Alten und Neuen Testa-
    ments 49. Göttingen: Vandenhoeck & Ruprecht, 1959.
    (1rst ed.: 1956)]

244   Karl-Georg REPLOH. <u>Markus--Lehrer der Gemeinde. Eine re-</u>
<u>daktionsgeschichtliche Studie zu den Jüngerperikopen des</u>
<u>Markus-Evangeliums</u>. Stuttgarter Biblische Monographien
9. Stuttgart: Katholische Bibelwerk. 240 pp.
                                     (E 52-2584)

245 1968 Charles MASSON. L'Évangile de Marc et l'Église de Rome.
            Bibliothèque Théologique. Neuchâtel/Paris: Delachaux &
            Niestlé. 128 pp.   (E 50-2601)

246   T. J. Weeden, "The Heresy That Necessitated Mark's Gos-
            pel," ZNW 59:145-158.   (N 13-876)
            [Republished as "Die Häresie, die Markus zur Abfassung
            seines Evangeliums veranlasst hat," (tr. by Hermann-
            Josef Dirksen) in Das Markus-Evangelium (ed. by R.
            Pesch; Wege der Forschung 411; Darmstadt: Wissen-
            schaftliche Buchgesellschaft, 1979), pp. 238-258.]

247 1966 Béda RIGAUX. The Testimony of St. Mark. Tr. by Malachy
            Carroll. Herald Scriptural Library. Chicago: Francis-
            can Herald Press. xvi-138 pp.   (E 47-2453)
            [Originally published as Témoignage de l'évangile de
            Marc. Bruges: Desclée de Brouwer, 1965. 194 pp.]

248   F. Uricchio, "Presenza della Chiesa primitiva nel Vangelo
            di S. Marco," Miscellanea Franciscana 66:29-87.

249 1965 John BOWMAN. The Gospel of Mark: The New Christian Jewish
            Passover Haggadah. Studia Post-Biblica 8. Leiden: E.
            J. Brill. 392 pp.   (E 47-2419)

250 1964 S. G. F. Brandon, "The Apologetical Factor in the Markan
            Gospel," in Studia Evangelica II: Papers Presented to
            the Second International Congress on New Testament Stud-
            ies held at Christ Church, Oxford, 1961 (Texte und Un-
            tersuchungen zur Geschichte der altchristlichen Litera-
            tur 87; ed. by F. L. Cross; Berlin: Akademie-Verlag)
            pp. 34-46.

251   D. F. Bregine, "The Marcan Apologetic," TBT 1:918-922.
                                                           (N 9-553)

252   S. Schulz, "Die Bedeutung des Markus für die Theologiege-
            schichte des Urchristentums," in Studia Evangelica II:
            Papers Presented to the Second International Congress on
            New Testament Studies held at Christ Church, Oxford,
            1961 (Texte und Untersuchungen zur Geschichte der alt-
            christlichen Literatur 87; ed. by F. L. Cross; Berlin:
            Akademie-Verlag), pp. 135-145.
            [Republished in Das Markus-Evangelium (ed. by R.
            Pesch; Wege der Forschung 411; Darmstadt: Wissen-
            schaftliche Buchgesellschaft, 1979), pp. 151-162.]

253   A. J. Stacpoole, "A Note on the Dating of St. Mark's Gos-
            pel," Scr 16:106-110.   (N 9-554)

254 1963 M. Karnetzki, "Die letzte Redaktion des Markusevangeli-

ums," in <u>Zwischenstation: Festschrift für Karl Kupisch
zum 60. Geburtstag</u> (ed. by Ernst Wolf, with Helmut Goll-
witzer and Joachim Hoppe; Munich: Chr. Kaiser Verlag),
pp. 161-174.

255   1960s   S. G. F. Brandon, "The Date of the Marcan Gospel," <u>NTS</u> 7:
               126-141.

256   1957s   N. A. Dahl, "Markusevangeliets sikte," <u>SEÅ</u> 22-23:32-46.
                                                         (N 3-590)
               [Republished as "The Purpose of Mark's Gospel," in
               Dahl, <u>Jesus in the Memory of the Early Church</u> (Minn-
               eapolis: Augsburg Publishing House, 1976), pp. 52-
               65.]

257   1956   W. D. Davies, "Reflections on Archbishop Carrington's 'The
               Primitive Christian Calendar'," in <u>The Background of the
               New Testament and its Eschatology. In Honour of Charles
               Harold Dodd</u> (ed. by W. D. Davies and D. Daube; Cam-
               bridge: University Press), pp. 124-152.

258   1952   Philip CARRINGTON. <u>The Primitive Christian Calendar: A
               Study in the Making of the Markan Gospel</u>. Cambridge:
               University Press.   (E 33-1371)

The Social World of Mark

See also 240, 241.

259   1978   J. A. Wilde, "The Social World of Mark's Gospel. A Word
               about Method," in <u>Society of Biblical Literature 1978
               Seminar Papers</u> (ed. by Paul J. Achtemeier; Missoula, MT:
               Scholars Press), pp. 47-70.

260   1977   Howard C. KEE. <u>Community of the New Age: Studies in
               Mark's Gospel</u>. Philadelphia/London: Westminster/SCM.
               xiii-225 pp.   (E 58s-4817)

261   G. Theissen, "'Wir haben alles verlassen' (MC. X 28).
               Nachfolge und soziale Entwurzelung in der jüdisch-paläs-
               tinischen Gesellschaft des I. Jahrhunderts n. Ch.," <u>NovT</u>
               19:161-196.   (N 22-409)

The Structure/Plan of the Gospel

See also 492, 828, 829, 834-838, 1016.

262   1981   V. K. Robbins, "Summons and Outline in Mark: the Three

Step Progression," <u>NovT</u> 23:97-114.

263   1979   J. Delorme, "L'intégration des petites unités littéraires dans l'Évangile de Marc du point de vue de la sémiotique structurale," <u>NTS</u> 25:469-491.   (N 24-432)

264   Werner H. KELBER. <u>Mark's Story of Jesus</u>. Philadelphia: Fortress Press. 96 pp.

265   E. S. Malbon, "Mythic Structure and Meaning in Mark: Elements of a Lévi-Straussian Analysis," <u>Semeia</u> 16:97-132.
                                                                (N 24-802)

266   A. Stock, "Literary Criticism and Mark's Mystery Play," <u>TBT</u> 100:1909-1915.   (N 23-841)

267   1977   F. Belo, "Lecture matérialiste de l'évangile de Marc et de la grande séquence des pains," <u>Cahiers Biblique</u> 17 of <u>Foi et Vie</u> 77:19-33.   (N 23-836)

268   D. J. Hawkin, "The Symbolism and Structure of the Marcan Redaction," <u>EvQ</u> 49:98-110.   (N 21-737)

269   F. G. Lang, "Kompositionsanalyse des Markusevangeliums," <u>ZTK</u> 74:1-24.   (N 21-739)

270   1976   C. Castro Tello, "Estructura literaria y teológica del Evangelo de S. Marcos," <u>Revista Teológica Limense</u> 10: 31-47.

271   1975   P. F. Ellis, "Patterns and Structures of Mark's Gospel," in <u>Biblical Studies in Contemporary Thought</u> (ed. by Miriam Ward, R.S.M.; Burlington, VT: Trinity College Biblical Institute / Somerville, MA: Greeno, Hadden), pp. 88-103.

272   W. J. Harrington, "The Gospel of Mark: A Tract for our Times," <u>DocLife</u> 25:482-499.   (N 20-98)

273   Francisco de LA CALLE. <u>Situación al servicio del Kerigma</u>. (Cuadro geográfico del <u>Evangelio de Marcos</u>). Colección de Estudios del Instituto Superior de Pastoral 9. Salamanca/Madrid: Instituto Superior de Pastoral de la Universidad Pontificia de Salamanca. 248 pp. (E 57-3755)

274   T. Moser, "Mark's Gospel: A Drama?" <u>TBT</u> 80:528-533.
                                                                (N 20-453)

275   D. E. Nineham, "The Order of Events in St. Mark's Gospel. An Examination of Dr. Dodd's Hypothesis," in <u>Studies in</u>

the Gospels (ed. by D. E. Nineham; Oxford: Blackwell), pp. 223-240.

276   L. Ramaroson, "Le plan du second Évangile," ScEs 27:219-233. (N 20-101)

277   F. Rousseau, "La structure de Marc 13," Bib 56:157-172. (N 20-462)

278   L. Soubigou, "O Plano do Evangelho segundo São Marcos," RCB 12:84-96. (N 20-454)

279   1974   J. Radermakers, "L'évangile de Marc: Structure et théologie," in L'évangile selon Marc: Tradition et rédaction (ed. by M. Sabbe; Bibliotheca ephemeridum theologicarum lovaniensium 34; Gembloux/Louvain: Duculot/Leuven University), pp. 221-239.

280   1973   R. Trevijano, "El plan del Evangelio de San Marcos," Burgense 14:9-40. (N 18-485)

281   1972s   H.Simonsen, "Messiashemmeligheden og Markusevangeliets struktur," SEÅ 37-38:107-124. (N 18-867)

282   1972   R. Butterworth, "The Composition of Mark 1 - 12," HeyJ 13:5-26. (N 16-871)

283   1971   D. Blatherwick, "The Markan Silhouette?" NTS 17:184-192. (N 15-864)

284   1969   C. T. Ruddick, Jr., "Behold, I Send My Messenger," JBL 88:381-417. (N 14-500)

285   1967   F. Mussner, "Gottesherrschaft und Sendung Jesu nach Mk 1,14f.: Zugleich ein Beitrag über die inner Struktur des Markusevangeliums," in Mussner, Praesentia Salutis: Gesammelte Studien zu Fragen und Themen des Neuen Testaments (Düsseldorf: Patmos-Verlag), pp. 81-98. ₍Originally in TTZ 66 (1957):257-275, but much reworked.₎

286   L. F. Rivera, "Una estructura en la redacción de Marcos," RevistB 29:1-21. (N 12-174)

287   1966   I. de la Potterie, "De compositione evangelii Marci," VD 44:135-141. (N 11-718)

288   L. E. Keck, "The Introduction to Mark's Gospel," NTS 12:352-370. (N 11-719)

289 1964 E. Schweizer, "Mark's Contribution to the Quest of the Historical Jesus," <u>NTS</u> 10:421-432.   (N 9-165)

290   "Die theologische Leistung des Markus," <u>EvT</u> 24:337-355.   (N 9-166)
[Republished in Schweizer, <u>Beiträge zur Theologie des Neuen Testaments</u> (Zürich: Zwingli-Verlag, 1970), pp. 21-42; republished again in <u>Das Markus-Evangelium</u> (ed. by R. Pesch; Wege der Forschung 411; Darmstadt: Wissenschaftliche Buchgesellschaft, 1979), pp. 163-189.]

291 1963 W. F. Ryan, "The Preaching Within the Preaching," <u>TBT</u> 1:457-464.   (N 8-589)

292 1961 H. Sawyerr, "The Marcan Framework," <u>SJT</u> 14:279-294.   (N 6-463)

293 1960 T. A. Burkill, "Strain on the Secret: An Examination of Mark 11:1 - 13:37," <u>ZNW</u> 51:31-46.   (N 5-409)

294 1959 A.-M. Denis, "Les richesses du Fils de Dieu selon saint Marc (I-VI,30)," <u>VSpir</u> 41:229-239.   (N 4-394)

295 1958 A. Kuby, "Zur Konzeption des Markus-Evangeliums," <u>ZNW</u> 49:52-64.   (N 3-80)

296 1957 C. E. Faw, "The Outline of Mark," <u>JBR</u> 25:19-23. (N 2-52)

297   G. Schille, "Die Topographie des Markusevangeliums, ihre Hintergründe und ihre Einordnung," <u>ZDPV</u> 73:133-166.

III. <u>MANUSCRIPT EVIDENCE</u>

See also 518, 664, 1066.

298 1981 Larry HURTADO. <u>Text-Critical Methodology and the Pre-Caesarean Text. Codex W in the Gospel of Mark</u>. Grand Rapids: Wm. B. Eerdmans Publishing Company. 112 pp.

299 1979 M. McCormick, "Two Leaves from the Lost Uncial Codex: Mark 4:24-29 and 4:37-41," <u>ZNW</u> 70:238-242.   (N 25-98)

300 1978 D. B. GAIN. <u>Evidence for Supposing That Our Greek Text of the Gospel of St. Mark Is Translated from Latin, That Most of This Latin Still Survives, and That by Following the Latin We Can Recover Words and Actions of Jesus</u>

<u>Which Have Been Falsified in the Greek Translation</u>. Gra-
hamstown, S. Africa: Rhodes University. 21 pp.

301   1976   J. H. Greenlee, "Codex 0269, A Palimpsest Fragment of
             Mark," in <u>Studies in New Testament and Text: Essays in</u>
             <u>Honour of George D. Kilpatrick on the Occasion of his</u>
             <u>Sixty-fifth Birthday</u> (ed. by J. K. Elliott; Supplements
             to Novum Testamentum 44; Leiden: E. J. Brill), pp. 235-
             238.

302   D. W. Palmer, "The Origin, Form, and Purpose of Mark XVI.4
             in Codex Bobbiensis," <u>JTS</u> 27:113-122.   (N 20-806)

303   J. M. Plumley and C. H. Roberts, "An Uncial Text of St.
             Mark in Greek from Nubia," <u>JTS</u> 27:34-45.   (N 20-789)

304   1972   Hans QUECKE (ed.). <u>Das Markusevangelium saïdisch. Text</u>
             <u>der Handschrift PPalau Rib. Inv.-Nr. 182 mit den Variant-</u>
             <u>en der Handschrift M 569</u>. Papyrologica Castroctaviana 4.
             Barcelona: Papyrologica Castroctaviana. xiii-184 pp.

305   "Eine koptische Bibelhandschrift des 5.
             Jahrhunderts (PPalau Rib. Inv.-Nr. 182)," <u>SPap</u> 11:77-81,
             1 plate.   (N 18-117)

306   "Eine neue koptische Bibelhandschrift
             (P. Palau Rib. Inv.-Nr. 182)," <u>Or</u> 41:469-471. (N 18-118)

307   1970   <u>Itala. Das neue Testament in altlateinischer Überliefer-</u>
             <u>ung</u>. Ed. by A. Jülicher. Vol. II: <u>Marcus Evangelium</u>.
             Revised edition. Berlin: de Gruyter. vii-160 pp.

308   1969   J. N. Birdsall, "A Report of the Textual Complexion of the
             Gospel of Mark in Ms 2533," <u>NovT</u> 11:233-239.

309   1968   O. Linton, "Evidences of a Second-Century Revised Edition
             of St. Mark's Gospel," <u>NTS</u> 14:321-355.   (13-183)

310   1966   T. F. Glasson, "An Early Revision of the Gospel of Mark,"
             <u>JBL</u> 85:231-233.   (N 11-235)

311   1959   J. P. Brown, "An Early Revision of the Gospel of Mark,"
             <u>JBL</u> 78:215-227.

312   1955   H. W. Huston, "Mark 6 and 11 in P45 and in the Caesarean
             Text," <u>JBL</u> 74:262-271.   (N Experimental Issue - 31)

IV. PATRISTIC WITNESS

See also 566.

313 1980 G. D. Fee, "The Text of John and Mark in the Writings of Chrysostom," NTS 26:525-547.   (N 25-28)

314 1977 J. L. North, "MARKOS O KOLOBODAKTYLOS: Hippolytus, Elenchus, VII.30," JTS 28:498-507.   (N 22-406)

315 1975 E. R. Kalin, "Early Traditions about Mark's Gospel: Canonical Status Emerges, the Story Grows," CurTM 2:332-341.
                                                                     (N 20-451)

316 1974 F. F. BRUCE. The 'Secret' Gospel of Mark. London: Athlone. 20 pp.

317 1973 Morton SMITH. Clement of Alexandria and a Secret Gospel of Mark. Cambridge, MA: Harvard University Press. x-454 pp.

318   The Secret Gospel. The Discovery and Interpretation of the Secret Gospel According to Mark. New York: Harper & Row. xi-148 pp.

319 1966 A. Weber, "Die Taufe Jesu im Jordan als Anfang nach Eusebius von Cäsarea," TP 41:20-29.

320 1964 L. W. Barnard, "St. Mark and Alexandria," HTR 57:145-150.
                                                                     (N 9-163)

321 1955 C. F. D. Moule and A. M. G. Stephenson, "R. G. Heard on Q and Mark," NTS 2:114-118. (N Experimental Issue - 30)

Papias

322 1980 U. H. J. Körtner, "Markus der Mitarbeiter des Petrus," ZNW 71:160-173.

323 1977 J. Kürzinger, "Die Aussage des Papias von Hierapolis zur literarischen Form des Markusevangeliums," BZ 21:245-264.   (N 22-97)

324 1976 T. Y. Mullins, "Papias and Clement and Mark's Two Gospels," VC 30:189-192.   (N 21-91)

325 1969 H. A. Blair, "Fact and Gospel," in Studia Evangelica 6: Papers Presented to the Fourth International Congress on New Testament Studies held at Oxford, 1969 (ed. by Elizabeth A. Livingstone; Berlin: Akademie Verlag), pp. 14-19.

326   1967   J. Kürzinger, "Formgeschichte im 1. Jahrhundert. Das
             Papiaszeugnis in neuer Interpretation," Theologie der
             Gegenwart 10:157-164.

327   1963   W. C. van Unnik, "Zur Papias-Notiz über Markus (Eusebius
             H. E. III 39,15," ZNW 54:276-277.   (N 8-960)
             ₁Republished in van Unnik, Sparsa collecta: The Col-
             lected Essays of W. C. van Unnik. Part One: Evangel-
             ia--Paulina--Acta (NovT Supplement 29; Leiden: E. J.
             Brill, 1973), pp. 70-71.₁

328   1960   H. E. W. Turner, "Modern Issues in Biblical Studies: The
             Tradition of Mark's Dependence upon Peter," ExpTim 71:
             260-263.   (N 5-88)

329   1956   H. A. Rigg, Jr., "Papias on Mark," NovT 1:161-183.
                                                         (N 1-396)

                    V.   SURVEYS OF LITERATURE

See also 1420.

330   1979   J. D. Kingsbury, "The Gospel of Mark in Current Research,"
             RelSRev 5:101-107.   (N 23-838)

331   1978   J. A. Brooks, "An Annotated Bibliography on Mark," SWJourn-
             Theol 21:75-82.   (N 23-444)

332   H. C. Kee, "Mark's Gospel in Recent Research," Int32:353-
             368.   (N 23-110)

333   W. L. Lane, "The Gospel of Mark in Current Study," SWJourn-
             Theol 21:7-21.   (N 23-450)

334   "From Historian to Theologian: Milestones in
             Markan Scholarship," RevExp 75:601-617.   (N 23-449)

335   "Mark," Bibliographie Biblique 1930 - 1975. Vol. 2. Ed.
             by P.-É. Langevin, S.J.; Québec: Les Presses de l'uni-
             versité Laval. Pp. 654-691.
             ₁Extends bibliography of Catholic authors (see 339)
             from 1970 to 1975 and covers non-Catholic authors
             from 1930 to 1975.₁

336   R. P. Martin, "The Theology of Mark's Gospel," SWJourn-
             Theol 21:23-36.   (N 23-451)

337   1974   É. Trocmé, "Trois critiques au miroir de l'Évangile selon

Marc," RHPR 55:289-295.

338 1973 Günter WAGNER. An Exegetical Bibliography on the Gospel
of Mark. Bibliographical Aids 2. Rüschlikon-Zürich:
Baptist Theological Seminary. 174 pp.

339 1972 "Mark," Bibliographie Biblique 1930 - 1970. Vol. 1. Ed.
by P.-É. Langevin, S.J.; Québec: Les Presses de l'université Laval. pp. 293-308.

340 N. Thien An Vo, "Interpretation of Mark's Gospel in the
Last Two Decades," Studia Biblica et Theologica 2:37-62.

341 1971 H. C. Kee, "Mark as Redactor and Theologian: A Survey of
Some Recent Markan Studies," JBL 90:333-336.(N 16-545)

342 R. Kugelman, "With Today's Biblical Books. With Today's
Mark and John," TBT 9:316-321.

343 1970 B. Corsani, "Il Vangelo secondo Marco. Recenti studi sul-
la interpretazione e esegesi," Protestantesimo 25:136-
154.

344 P. E. Dinter, "Redaction Criticism of the Gospel of Mark:
A Survey," DunRev 10:178-197. (N 15-152)

345 1968 R. S. Barbour, "Recent Study of the Gospel According to
St. Mark," ExpTim 79:324-329. (N 13-575)

346 H.-D. Knigge, "The Meaning of Mark. The Exegesis of the
Second Gospel," Int 22:53-70. (N 12-884)

347 1958 "Studies in the Gospel of Mark," RevExp 55:351-399.
(N 3-589)

VI. TEXTUAL STUDIES

348 1980 J. C. MEAGHER. Clumsy Construction in Mark's Gospel. A
Critique of Form- and Redaktionsgeschichte. Toronto
Studies in Theology 3. New York/Toronto: Edwin Mellen
Press. xiv-165 pp.

Markan Summary Verses

See also 559-561.

349 1976 Wilhelm EGGER. Frohbotschaft und Lehre: Die Sammelberich-

te des Wirkens Jesu im Markusevangelium. Frankfurter
Theologische Studien 19. Frankfurt: Josef Knecht. viii-
184 pp.   (e 57-3737)

Linguistic/Narrative/Structuralist Analyses

See also 263, 465, 496, 499, 510, 694, 697, 700, 704, 705, 741, 963,
    992, 1090, 1091, 1093, 1176, 1178, 1270, 1311, 1372.

350   1979   J. Calloud, "Toward a Structural Analysis of the Gospel of
             Mark," Semeia 16:133-165.

351   1978   Yvan ALMEIDA. L'opérativité sémantique des récits-para-
             boles. Sémiotique narrative et textuelle. Herméneuti-
             que du discours religieux. Bibliothèque des cahiers de
             l'Institut de Linguistique de Louvain 13. Paris: Cerf/
             Louvain:Éditions Peeters. xiv-486 pp.

Pragmatic/Materialist Interpretations

See also 267, 491.

352   1980   Fernando BELO. A Materialist Reading of the Gospel of
             Mark. Maryknoll, NY: Orbis Books.

353   1977   K. Füssel, "Was heisst materialistische Lektüre der Bi-
             bel?" US 32:46-54.

354   1976   Michel CLÉVENOT. Approches Matérialistes de la Bible.
             Paris: Éditions du Cerf. 174 pp.

355   R. Trevijano Etcheverría, "Lecturas materialistas del E-
             vangelio de San Marcos," Burgense 17:477-503.(N 21-392)

356   1975   Fernando BELO. Lecture matérialiste de l'Évangile de
             Marc: récit, pratique, ideologie. 2nd ed., rev. Paris:
             Éditions du Cerf. 415 pp.

Redaction Criticism of Mark

See also 87, 117, 121, 123, 220, 341, 344, 348, 606, 612, 1468, 1556.

357   1979   T. E. Crane, "Redaction-criticism and Mark," Essays in
             Faith and Culture [Sydney] 3:157-172.   (N 25-84)

358   1976   C. L. Mitton, "Some Further Studies in St. Mark's Gospel,"
             ExpTim 87:297-301.   (N 21-90)

359   R. Mohrlang, "Redaction Criticism and the Gospel of Mark:
           An Evaluation of the Work of W. Marxsen," Studia Biblica
           et Theologica 6:18-33.

360   1975 J. C. Meagher, "Die Form- und Redaktionsungeschickliche
           Methoden: The Principle of Clumsiness and the Gospel of
           Mark," JAAR 43:459-472.   (N 20-452)

361   1974 M. SABBE. (ed.) L'Évangile selon Marc. Tradition et ré-
           daction. Bibliotheca ephemeridum theologicarum lovani-
           ensium 34. Leuven/Gembloux: Leuven University Press/
           Éditions J. Duculot. 594 pp.   (E 56-2950)

362   1972 H. Simonsen, "Zur Frage der grundlegenden Problematik in
           form- und redaktionsgeschichtlicher Evangelienforschung,"
           ST 26:1-23.   (N 17-135)

363   1971 E. C. Hobbs, "Norman Perrin on Methodology in the Interpre-
           tation of Mark," in Christology and a Modern Pilgrimage:
           A Discussion with Norman Perrin (ed. by Hans Dieter
           Betz; Claremont, CA: New Testament Colloquium), pp. 79-
           91.

364   N. Perrin, "Towards an Interpretation of the Gospel of
           Mark," in Christology and a Modern Pilgrimage: A Discuss-
           ion with Norman Perrin (ed. by Hans Dieter Betz; Clare-
           mont, CA: New Testament Colloquium), pp. 1-78.

365   R. H. Stein, "The Proper Methodology for Ascertaining A
           Markan Redaction History," NovT 13:181-198. (N 16-169)

366   1954 H. Riesenfeld, "Tradition und Redaktion im Markusevangel-
           ium," in Neutestamentliche Studien für Rudolf Bultmann:
           zu seinem siebzigsten Geburtstag (Beihefte zur ZNW 21;
           Berlin: Alfred Töpelmann), pp. 157-164 [2nd rev. ed,1957]
           [Republished in Das Markus-Evangelium (ed. by R. Pesch;
           Wege der Forschung 411; Darmstadt: Wissenschaftliche
           Buchgesellschaft, 1979), pp. 103-112.]

Problem of History

367   1980 M. E. Glasswell, "St. Mark's Attitude to the Relationship
           between History and the Gospel," in Studia Biblica 1978:
           II. Papers on the Gospels. Sixth International Congress
           on Biblical Studies, Oxford, 3-7 April 1978 (ed. by E. A.
           Livingstone; JSNT Supplement Series 2; Sheffield: JSOT),
           pp. 115-127.

368   1968 E. Haenchen, "Historie und Verkündigung bei Markus und Luk-
           as," in Haenchen, Die Bibel und Wir. Gesammelte Auf-

sätze. <u>Zweiter Band</u>. (Tübingen: J. C. B. Mohr), pp. 156-181.
⌈Republished in <u>Das Lukas-Evangelium</u>. <u>Die redaktions-</u>
<u>und kompositionsgeschichtliche Forschung</u> (ed. by G.
Braumann; Wege der Forschung 280; Darmstadt: Wissen-
schaftliche Buchgesellschaft, 1974), pp. 287-316.⌉

369   1966   O. M. Rao, "The Problem of History in St. Mark's Gospel,"
              <u>Indian Journal of Theology</u> 15:60-66.

370   1965   J. M. Robinson, "The Problem of History in Mark, Reconsid-
              ered," <u>USQR</u> 20:131-147.

371   1957   James M. ROBINSON. <u>The Problem of History in Mark</u>. Stud-
              ies in Biblical Theology 21. London: SCM. 95 pp.
                                                      (E 38-1624)

The Theme of the Whole Gospel

See also 1540.

372   1978   J. R. Donahue, "Jesus as the Parable of God in the Gospel
              of Mark," <u>Int</u> 32:369-386.   (N 23-109)

373   1976   H. H. Graham, "The Gospel According to St. Mark: Mystery
              and Ambiguity," <u>ATR</u> suppl. 7:43-55.   (N 21-736)

374   1963   T. A. BURKILL. <u>Mysterious Revelation</u>. <u>An Examination of</u>
              <u>the Philosophy of St. Mark's Gospel</u>. Ithaca, NY: Cornell
              University Press. xii-337 pp.   (E 44-1594)

The Gospel Text: Mark 1:1 - 16:20

Chs. 1 - 12

See 282.

1:1-28

375   1980   A. Radaelli, "I racconti dell'infanzia nel contesto del
              prologo all'Evangelo," <u>RicBibRel</u> 15:7-26.   (N 25-92)

1:1-15

See 288

376   1978   G. Dautzenberg, "Die Zeit des Evangeliums. Mk 1, 1-15 und
              die Konzeption des Markusevangeliums (Schluss)," <u>BZ</u> 22:
              76-91.   (N 23-114)

377 1977 G. Dautzenberg, "Die Zeit des Evangeliums. Mk 1,1-15 und die Konzeption des Markusevangeliums," BZ 21:219-234. (N 22-100)

378 1973 H. Langkammèr, "Tradycja i redakcja w prologu Ewangelii Marka (1,1-15)," RoczTeolKan 20:37-57. (N 19-101)

379 1971 Rámon TREVIJANO ETCHEVERRÍA. Comienzo del Evangelio. Estudio sobre el Prólogo de San Marcos. Publicaciones de la Facultad de Teológica del Norte de España, Sede de Burgos 26. Burgos: Ediciones Aldecoa. xxiii-273 pp. (E 53-2720)

380 1971 B. van Iersel, "Theology and Detailed Exegesis," in Theology, Exegesis and Proclamation (ed.by Roland Murphy; Concilium 70; New York: Herder and Herder), pp. 80-89.

381 1970 R. Pesch, "Anfang des Evangeliums Jesu Christi: Eine Studie zum Prolog des Markusevangeliums (Mk 1,1-15)," in Die Zeit Jesu: Festschrift für Heinrich Schlier (ed. by Günther Bornkamm and Karl Rahner; Freiburg/Basel/Vienna: Herder), pp. 108-144.
[Republished in Das Markus-Evangelium (ed. by R. Pesch; Wege der Forschung 411; Darmstadt: Wissenschaftliche Buchgesellschaft, 1979), pp. 311-355.]

382 1963 O. J. F. Seitz, "Praeparatio Evangelica in the Markan Prologue," JBL 82:201-206. (N 8-145)

1:1-13

383 1965 J. Willemse, O.P., "God's First and Last Word: Jesus (Mark 1,1-13 and John 1,1-18," (tr. by David T. LeFort) in The Human Reality of Sacred Scripture (ed. by Pierre Benoit, O.P. and Roland E. Murphy, O. Carm.; Concilium 10; New York: Paulist Press), pp. 75-95.

384 1963 Ulrich W. MAUSER. Christ in the Wilderness. The Wilderness Theme in the Second Gospel and Its Basis in the Biblical Tradition. Studies in Biblical Theology 39. Naperville, IL: Allenson. 159 pp. (E 46-1405)

1:1-11

See also 1432 - 1433.

385 1974 Wolfgang FENEBERG. Der Markusprolog: Studien zur Formbestimmung des Evangeliums. Studien zum Alten und Neuen Testament 36. Munich: Kösel. 214 pp. (E 55-2901)

1:1-8

See also 284.

386   1974   S. Fausti, "Mc 1,1-8: exegesi e alcune considerazioni di
                antropologia cristiana," Rivista di Teologia Morale 6:
                193-219.

387   1969   P. Ternant, "Le ministère de Jean, commencement de l'Évan-
                gile, Mc 1,1-8," AsSeign 6:41-53.

1:1-6

388   1972   M. Herranz Marco, "La presentación del Bautista en el evan-
                gelio de S. Marcos (Mc 1,1-6)," in La esperanza en la
                Biblia (Semana Bíblica Española XXX; Madrid: Consejo Su-
                perior de Investigaciones Científicas, Instituto Francis-
                co Suárez), pp. 389-411.

1:1

389   1977   G. Arnold, "Mk 1:1 und Eröffnungswendungen in griechischen
                und lateinischen Schriften," ZNW 68:123-127.(N 22-99)

390   J. Slomp, "Are the Words 'Son of God' in Mark 1.1 Origi-
                nal?" BT 28:143-150.   (N 21-394)

391   1976   M. Bouttier, "Commencement, force et fin de l'évangile,"
                ÉTR 51:465-493.   (N 21-393)

392   1974   M. E. Glasswell, "The Beginning of the Gospel: A Study of
                St. Mark's Gospel with Regard to its First Verse," in
                New Testament Christianity for Africa and the World: Es-
                says in Honour of Harry Sawyerr (ed. by Mark E. Glasswell
                and Edward W. Fasholé-Luke; London: SPCK), pp. 36-43.

393   1970   P. Lamarche, "'Commencement de l'évangile de Jésus, Christ,
                Fils de Dieu' (Mc I,1)," NRT 92:1024-1036. (N 15-867)

1:2-8

394   1972   B. Marconcini, "La predicazione del Battista in Marco e
                Luca confrontata con la redazione di Matteo," RivB 20
                (suppl.): 451-466.   (N 19-102)

1:2-6

See also 160.

395   1966   M.-É. Boismard, "Évangile des Ébionites et problème synop-
                tique (Mc. I,2-6 et par.)," RB 73:321-352. (N 11-1046)

<u>1:2-3</u>

396   1980   K. R. Snodgrass, "Streams of tradition emerging from Isaiah 40:1-5 and their adaptation in the New Testament," <u>JSNT</u> 8:24-45.   (N 25-93)

<u>1:3-4</u>

397   1962   A. Ortega, "Nueva visión de Marcos I, 3-4," <u>Salmanticensis</u> 9:599-607.   (N 8-146)

<u>1:4-5</u>

398   1971   R. Trevijano Etcheverría, "La tradición sobre el Bautista en Mc. 1, 4-5 y par.," <u>Burgense</u> 12:9-39.   (N 16-170)

<u>1:4</u>

399   1975   J. K. Elliott, "Ho baptizōn and Mark i.4," <u>TZ</u> 31:14-15.
                    (N 20-102)

400   1964   H. Thyen, "Baptisma metanoias eis aphesin hamartiōn (Mc 1,4 = Lc 3,3)," in <u>Zeit und Geschichte. Dankesgabe an Rudolf Bultmann zum 80. Geburtstag</u> (ed. by Erich Dinkler in collaboration with Hartwig Thyen; Tübingen: J. C. B. Mohr [Paul Siebeck]), pp. 97-125.

<u>1:7</u>

401   1978   P. Proulx and L. Alonso Schökel, "Las Sandalias del Mesias Esposo," <u>Bib</u> 59:1-37.

402   1966   O. Cullmann, "Ho opisō mou erchomenos," in Cullmann, <u>Vorträge und Aufsätze, 1925 - 1962</u> (ed. by Karlfried Fröhlich; Tübingen/Zürich: J. C. B. Mohr [Paul Siebeck]/Zwingli Verlag), pp. 169-175.

403   1961s   F. L. Andersen, "The Diet of John the Baptist (Mc 1,7)," <u>AbrN</u> 3.

404   1961   W. R. Weeks, "Mark i. 7," <u>ExpTim</u> 73:54.   (N 6-465)

<u>1:8</u>

405   1972   J. D. G. Dunn, "Spirit-and-Fire Baptism," <u>NovT</u> 14:81-92.
                    (N 17-139)

406   1958   J. E. Yates, "The Form of Mark i. 8b. 'I baptized you with water; he will baptize you with the Holy Spirit,'" <u>NTS</u> 4: 334-338.   (N 3-81)

<u>1:9-14</u>

407   1969   P. Zarrella, "Il battesimo di Gesú nei Sinottici (Mc. 1,9-
               14; Mt. 3,13-17; Lc. 3,21-22," <u>ScuolCatt</u> 97:3-29.
                                                        (N 14-156)

<u>1:9-11</u>

See also 149, 1562.

408   1979   A. Feuillet, "Vocation et mission des prophètes, Baptême et
               mission de Jésus. Étude de christologie biblique," <u>Nov-
               Vet</u> 54:22-40.   (N 23-842)

409   1974   G. Richter, "Zu den Tauferzählungen Mk 1:9-11 und Joh 1:32-
               34," <u>ZNW</u> 65:43-56.   (N 19-551)

410   J. Riquelme, "Significación del Bautismo de Jesús," <u>Teol-
               Vida</u> 15:115-139.   (N 19-552)

411   D. O. Wenthe, "The Historical-Critical Interpretation of
               the Baptism of Jesus from the Perspective of Traditional
               Lutheran Exegesis," <u>Springfielder</u> 37:230-240.(N 19-103)

412   1973   A. Vargas-Machuca, "La narración del bautismo de Jesús (Mc
               1,9-11) y la exégesis reciente. ¿Visión real o 'género
               didáctico'?" <u>CB</u> 30:131-141.

413   1972s   L. Hartman, "Dop, ande och barnaskap. Några traditionshis-
               toriska överväganden till Mk 1:9-11 par," in <u>SEÅ</u> 37-38:
               88-106.   (N 18-869)
                 [Republished as "Taufe, Geist und Sohnschaft: Tradi-
                 tionsgeschichtliche Erwägungen zu Mk 1,9-11 par," in
                 <u>Jesus in der Verkündigung der Kirche</u> (ed. by Albert
                 Fuchs; Studien zum Neuen Testament und seiner Umwelt,
                 Ser. A, vol. 1; Linz, Austria: privately published),
                 pp. 89-109.

414   1972   A. Vögtle, "Die sogenannte Taufperikope Mk 1,9-11. Zur
               problematik der Herkunft und des ursprünglichen Sinns,"
               in <u>Evangelisch-Katholischer Kommentar zum Neuen Testa-
               ment: Vorarbeiten 4</u> (Zürich/Einsiedeln/Köln: Benziger and
               Neukirchen: Neukirchener Verlag), pp. 105-139.

415   1968   D. Zeller, "Jesu Taufe -- ein literarischer Zugang zu Mark-
               us 1,9-11," <u>BK</u> 23:90-94.   (N 13-579)

416   1965   L. F. Rivera, "El Bautismo de Jesus en San Marcos," <u>RevistB</u>
               27:140-152.   (N 11-240)

417   1964   A. Feuillet, "Le Baptême de Jésus," <u>RB</u> 71:321-352.(N 9-555)

[Translated and digested as "The baptism of Jesus," <u>TD</u> 14:213-212.   (N 11-1047)

418   1961   A. Legault, "Le baptême de Jésus et la doctrine du Servi-
             teur souffrant," <u>SciEccl</u> 13:147-166.   (N 6-136)

419   1959   A. Feuillet, "Le Baptême de Jésus d'après l'Évangile selon
             Saint Marc (1,9-11)," <u>CBQ</u> 21:468-490.   (N 4-395)

420   1955   C. E. B. Cranfield, "The Baptism of Our Lord--A Study of
             St. Mark 1,9-11," in <u>SJT</u> 8:53-63.

421   1954   H. A. Blair, "Spirit-Baptism in St. Mark's Gospel," <u>CQR</u>
             155:369-377.

1:10-11

422   1960   J. Knackstedt, "Manifestatio S. Trinitatis in Baptismo Dom-
             ini," <u>VD</u> 38:76-91.

1:10

423   1976   S. Gero, "The Spirit as a Dove at the Baptism of Jesus,"
             <u>NovT</u> 18:17-35.   (N 20-791)

424   1975   A. Tosato, "Il battesimo di Gesù e alcuni passi trascurati
             dello Pseudo-Filone," <u>Bib</u> 56:405-409.   (N 20-792)

425   1970   L. E. Keck, "The Spirit and the Dove," <u>NTS</u> 17:41-67.
                                                              (N 15-518)

1:11

See also 146.

426   1969   I. H. Marshall, "Son of God or Servant of Yahweh?--A Recon-
             sideration of Mark i. 11," <u>NTS</u> 15:326-336. (N 13-878)

427   1968   P. G. Bretscher, "Exodus 4:22-23 and the Voice from Heav-
             en," <u>JBL</u> 87:301-311.   (N 13-580)

428   1963   P.-E. Bonnard, "Troil lectures du psaume 2," <u>BVC</u> 53:37-44.
                                                              (N 8-591)

1:12-15

429   1973   F. Smyth-Florentin, "Jésus, le Fils du Père, vainqueur de
             Satan. Mt 4,1-11; Mc 1,12-15; Lc 4,1-13," <u>AsSeign</u> 14:
             56-75.   (N 17-936)

1:12-13

430   1975   A. Vargas-Machuca, "La tentación de Jesús según Mc 1,12-13:
             ¿hecho real o relato de tipo haggadico?" in Homenaje a
             Juan Prado: miscelánea de estudios bíblicos y hebraicos
             (ed. by L. Alvarez Verdes and E. J. Alonso Hernandez;
             Madrid: Instituto "Benito Arias Montano" de Estudios He-
             bráicos, Sefardies y Oriente Próximo, Consejo Superior
             de Investigaciones Cientificas), pp. 301-328.

431   1974   R. F. Collins, "The Temptation of Jesus," MelTheol 26:32-
             45.   (N 19-962)

432   P. Pokorný, "The Temptation Stories and their Intention,"
             NTS 20: 115-127.   (N 18-870)

433   1973   C. Bombo, "As Tentações de Jesus nos Sinóticos," RCB 10:
             83-102.   (N 19-104)

434   A. Vargas-Machuca, "La tentación de Jesús según Mc. 1,12-
             13, ¿Hecho real o relato de tipo haggádico?" EstEcl 48:
             163-190.   (N 18-487)

435   1972   J. P. Comiskey, "Begone, Satan!" TBT 58:620-626.(N 16-873)

436   J. I. González Faus, "Las tentaciones de Jesús y la tenta-
             ción cristiana," EstEcl 47:155-188.   (N 17-140)

437   J. A. Kirk, "The Messianic Role of Jesus and the Temptation
             Narrative: A Contemporary Perspective," EvQ 44:11-29.
                                                        (N 16-874)

438   1971   J. B. Livio, "Face à face dans le désert (Mc 1,12s)," BTS
             127:2-5.

439   1966   J. Dupont, "L'origine du récit des tentations de Jésus au
             désert," RB 73:30-76.

440   1964   H. A. Kelly, "The Devil in the Desert," CBQ 26:190-220.

441   1963   J. Jeremias, "Nachwort zum Artikel von H.-G. Leder," ZNW
             54:278-279.   (N 8-962)

442   H.-G. Leder, "Sündenfallerzählung und Versuchungsgeschich-
             te. Zur Interpretation von Mc 1 12f.," ZNW 54:188-216.
                                                        (N 8-961)

443   1960   A. Feuillet, "L'épisode de la Tentation d'après l'Évangile
             selon Saint Marc (I, 12-13)," EstBíb 19:49-73. (N 5-404)
             [Translated and digested as "The temptation of Jesus
             in Mark," TD 12:79-82.]

1:13

444   1973   W. Stählin, "Und Jesus war bei den Tieren (Mk 1,13)," in
             Stählin, <u>Wissen und Weisheit</u> (Stuttgart: Ev. Verlags-
             werk), pp. 98-100.

445   1965   E. Fascher, "Jesus und die Tiere," <u>TLZ</u> 90:561-570.
                                                           (N 10-528)

446   1955   A. W. Schulze, "Der Heilige und die wilden Tiere. Zur Ex-
             egese von Mk 1,13b," <u>ZNW</u> 46:280-283.

1:14 - 3:6

447   1975   P. Simpson, "Reconciliation in the making: A reading of
             Mark 1,14-3,6," <u>AfricEcclRev</u> 17:194-203.   (N 20-456)

1:14-34

448   1976   E. Fuchs and B. Rordorf, "Mc 1,14-34: L'irruption du Roy-
             aume," <u>Bulletin du Centre Protestant d'Études</u> 28:16-17,
             17-19.

1:14-20

449   1973   J. Brière, "Jésus agit par ses disciples. Mc 1,14-20,"
             <u>AsSeign</u> 34:32-46.   (N 18-871)

1:14-15

See also 285.

450   1977   J. J. A. Kahmann, "Marc. 1,14-15 en hun plaats in het ge-
             heel van het Marcusevangelie," <u>Bijdragen</u> 38:84-98.
                                                           (N 21-743)

451   P. Pokorný, "'Anfang des Evangeliums': Zum Problem des An-
             fangs und des Schlusses des Markusevangeliums," in <u>Die</u>
             <u>Kirche des Anfangs: Festschrift für Heinz Schürmann zum</u>
             <u>65. Geburtstag</u> (ed. by Rudolf Schnackenburg, Josef Ernst
             and Joachim Wanke; Erfurter theologische Studien 38;
             Leipzig: St. Benno, and Freiburg/Basel: Herder (c. 1978)
             pp. 115-132.

452   1972   K.-G. Reploh, "'Evangelium' bei Markus. Das Evangelium des
             Markus als Anruf an die Gemeinde zu Umkehr und Glaube (1,
             14-15)," <u>BK</u> 27:110-114.   (N 17-937)

453   1957   F. Mussner, "Die Bedeutung von Mk 1,14f. für die Reichs-
             gottesverkündigung," <u>TTZ</u> 66:257-275.   (N 2-294)

<u>1:16-20</u>

See also 1514, 1518.

454   1969   R. Pesch, "Berufung und Sendung, Nachfolge und Mission.
             Eine Studie zu Mk 1, 16-20," <u>ZKT</u> 91:1-31.   (N 14-157)

455   1968   F. Agnew, "Vocatio primorum discipulorum in traditione syn-
             optica," <u>VD</u> 46:129-147.   (N 13-581)

<u>1:16-18</u>

456   1967   G. Klein, "Die Berufung des Petrus," <u>ZNW</u> 58:1-44.(N 12-562)

<u>1:17-18</u>

457   1966   J. Crosby, "The Call to Discipleship in Mk 1, 17-18," <u>TBT</u>
             27:1919-1922.

<u>1:16</u>

458   1980   J. D. M. Derrett, "<u>Ēsan gar halieis</u> (Mk. I 16). Jesus'
             Fishermen and the Parable of the Net," <u>NovT</u> 22:108-137.
                                                         (N 24-805)

<u>1:17</u>

459   1978   E.C. B. MacLaurin, "The Divine Fishermen," <u>St. Mark's Re-
             view</u> ₍Canberra₎ 94:26-28.   (N 23-115)

460   1977   J. B. Livio, "Pêcheurs d'hommes," <u>BTS</u> 192:22.

461   1959   C. W. F. Smith, "Fishers of Men. Footnotes on a Gospel
             Figure," <u>HTR</u> 52:187-203.   (N 4-660)

<u>1:21-45</u>

462   1976   D. Dideberg and P. Mourlon Beernaert, "'Jésus vint en Gali-
             lée.' Essai sur la structure de <u>Marc 1</u>, 21-45," <u>NRT</u> 98:
             306-323.   (N 21-93)

<u>1:21-39</u>

463   1968   R. Pesch, "Ein Tag vollmächtigen Wirkens Jesu in Kapharna-
             um (Mk 1, 21-34. 35-39)," <u>BibLeb</u> 9:114-128, 177-195, 261-
             277.   (N 13-189, 582, 897)

<u>1:21-28</u>

464   1980   P. Guillemette, "Un enseignement nouveau, plein d'autori-
             té," <u>NovT</u> 22:222-247.   (N 25-94)

465   1976   M. de Burgos Nuñez, "Le enseñanza liberadora de Jesús des-
             de la Sinagoga. Ensayo de semiótica narrativa en Marcos
             1,21-28," Communio 9:201-219.   (N 21-744)

466   A. Viard, "Quatrième Dimanche (Mc 1,21-28)," EspVie 86:8-
             10.

467   1973   J. Brière, "Le cri et le secret. Signification d'un ex-
             orcisme. Mc 1,21-28," AsSeign 35:34-46.   (N 18-872)

468   1968   R. Pesch, "'Eine neue Lehre aus Macht.' Eine Studie zu Mk
             1,21-28," in Evangelienforschung. Ausgewählte Aufsätze
             Deutscher Exegeten (ed. by Johannes Baptist Bauer; Graz/
             Köln: Verlag Styria), pp. 241-276.

1:21-22

469   1970   R. H. Stein, "The 'Redaktionsgeschichtlich' Investigation
             of a Markan Seam (Mc 1:21f.)," ZNW 61:70-94.(N 15-519)

1:22

470   1973   L. I. J. Stadelmann, "A Autoridade como una Característica
             do Ministério de Jesus. Estudo Exegético de Mc 1,22.27,"
             Perspectiva Teologica 5:173-184.

471   1969   A. W. Argyle, "The Meaning of exousia in Mark I: 22, 27,"
             ExpTim 80: 343.   (N 14:158)

1:24-25

472   1970   R. Trevijano, "El trasfondo apocalíptico de Mc. 1,24.25;
             5, 7.8 y par.," Burgense 11:117-133.   (N 15-160)

1:24

473   1978   P. Guillemette, "Mc 1,24 est-il une formule de défense mag-
             ique?" SciEs 30:81-96.   (N 22-776)

474   1960   F. Mussner, "Ein Wortspiel in Mk 1,24?" BZ 4:285-286.
                                                              (N 5-405)

475   E. Schweizer, "'Er wird Nazoräer heissen' (zu Mc 1,24; Mt
             2,23)," in Judentum, urchristentum, kirche. Festschrift
             für Joachim Jeremias (ed. by Walther Eltester; Beihefte
             ZNW 26; Berlin: Verlag Alfred Töpelmann), pp. 90-93.

1:27

See also 470, 471.

476   1975   A. M. Ambrozic, "New Teaching with Power (Mk 1:27)," in
               Word and Spirit: Essays in Honor of David Michael Stan-
               ley, S.J. on his 60th Birthday (ed. by Joseph Plevnik,
               S.J.; Willowdale, Ont.: Regis College), pp. 113-149.

1:29-39

477   1974   G. Gaide, "De l'admiration à la foi. Mc 1,29-39," AsSeign
               36:39-48.   (N 18-873)

1:29-31

478   1969   M. L. Rigato, "Tradizione e redazione in Mc. 1,29-31 (e
               paralleli). La guarigione della suocera di Simon Pie-
               tro," RivB 17:139-174.   (N 14-503)

479   1965   P. Lamarche, "La guerison de la belle-mère de Pierre," NRT
               87:515-526.
               [Republished in Lamarche, Révélation de Dieu chez Marc
               (Le Point Théologique 20; Paris: Beauchesne, 1976),
               pp. 47-60.]

1:32-34

480   1972   T. W. Kowalski, "Les sources pré-synoptiques de Marc 1,32-
               34 et parallèles. Phénomènes d'amalgame et indépendance
               mutuelle immédiate des évangélistes synoptiques," RSR 60:
               541-573.   (N 17-938)

1:35-39

481   1969   M. Wichelhaus, "Am ersten Tage der Woche. Mk. i 35-39 und
               die didaktischen Absichten des Markus-Evangelisten," NovT
               11:45-66.   (N 14-159)

1:35

482   1978   W. Kirchschläger, "Jesu Gebetsverhalten als Paradigma zu Mk
               1,35," Kairos 20:303-310.   (N 23-843)

1:38

483   1977   D. O. Wretlind, "Jesus' Philosophy of Ministry: A Study of
               a Figure of Speech in Mark 1:38," JournEvangTheolSoc 20:
               321-323.   (N 22-408)

1:40-45

484   1979   C. H. Cave, "The Leper: Mark i. 40-45," NTS 25:245-250.
                                                            (N 23-455)

485   1978   J. K. Elliott, "The Healing of the Leper in the Synoptic
             Parallels," <u>TZ</u> 34:175-176.   (N 23-456)

486   1972   M. Herranz Marco, "La curación de un leproso según San Mar-
             cos (Mc 1,40-45)," <u>EstBíb</u> 31:399-433.   (N 18-488)

487   1970   A. Paul, "La guérison d'un lépreux. Approche d'un récit
             de Marc (1, 40-45)," <u>NRT</u> 92:592-604.   (N 15-520)

<u>1:45</u>

See also 1580.

488   1976   J. K. Elliott, "Is <u>ho exelthōn</u> a Title for Jesus in Mark
             i. 45?" <u>JTS</u> 27:402-405.   (N 21-395)

489   1971   J. K. Elliott, "The Conclusion of the Pericope of the Heal-
             ing of the Leper and Mark i. 45," <u>JTS</u> 22:153-157.
                                                                  (N 16-171)

<u>2:1 - 3:6</u>

See also 119, 166.

490   1979   R. Kernaghan, "History and Redaction in the Controversy
             Stories in Mark 2:1 - 3:6," <u>Studia Biblica et Theologica</u>
             9:23-47.

491   E. Stegemann, "Von Kritik zur Feindschaft. Eine Auslegung
             von Markus 2,1 - 3,6," in <u>Der Gott der kleinen Leute.</u>
             <u>Sozialgeschichtliche Bibelauslegungen. Band 2: Neues</u>
             <u>Testament</u> (ed. by W. Schottroff and W. Stegemann; Munich:
             Kaiser), pp. 39-57.

492   1978   Joanna DEWEY. <u>Markan Public Debate: Literary Technique,</u>
             <u>Concentric Structure and Theology in Mark 2:1 - 3:6.</u>
             Chico, CA: Scholars Press. xii-277 pp.

493   1976   Werner THISSEN. <u>Erzählung der Befreiung: Eine exegetische</u>
             <u>Untersuchung zu Mk 2:1 - 3:6.</u> Forschung zur Bibel 21.
             Würzburg: Echter Verlag. 420 pp.

494   1973   J. Dewey, "The Literary Structure of the Controversy Stor-
             ies in Mark 2:1 - 3:6," <u>JBL</u> 92:394-401.   (N 18-489)

495   P. Mourlon Beernaert, "Jésus controversé. Structure et
             théologie de Marc 2,1 - 3,6," <u>NRT</u> 95:129-149.(N 19-106)

<u>2:1-22</u>

496   1979   J. Calloud, "Toward a Structural Analysis of the Gospel of

Mark," <u>Semeia</u> 16:133-165.   (N 24-806)

<u>2:1-12</u>

See also 116, 183.

497   1977   M. Herránz Marco, "El proceso ante el Sanhedrín (Continua-
             ción)," <u>EstBíb</u> 36:35-55.   (N 24-108)

498   1975   J. Gnilka, "Das Elend vor dem Menschensohn (Mk 2,1-12),"
             in <u>Jesus und der Menschensohn: Für Anton Vögtle</u> (ed. by
             Rudolf Pesch and Rudolf Schnackenburg, with Odilo Kaiser;
             Freiburg/Basel/Vienna: Herder), pp. 196-209.

499   1974   D. Dormeyer, "'Narrative Analyse' von Mk 2, 1-12. Möglich-
             keiten und Grenzen einer Verbindung zwischen 'Generativer
             Poetik' und Didaktik neutestamentlicher Wundererzählung-
             en," <u>LingBib</u> 31:68-88.   (N 19-105)

500   1971   Ingrid MAISCH. <u>Die Heilung des Gelähmten. Eine exege-
             tisch-traditionsgeschichtliche Untersuchung zu Mk 2,1-12.</u>
             Stuttgarter Bibelstudien 52. Stuttgart: Katholische Bi-
             belwerk. 139 pp.   (E 53-2687)

501   1966   G. G. Gamba, "Considerazioni in margine alla poetica di Mc
             2,1-12," <u>Salesianum</u> 28:324-349.

502   1961   R. T. Mead, "The Healing of the Paralytic--a Unit?" <u>JBL</u> 80:
             348-354.   (N 6-787)

503   1957   A. Cabaniss, "A Fresh Exegesis of Mark 2:1-12," <u>Int</u> 11:
             324-327.   (N 2-291)

<u>2:3</u>

504   1969   E. Rasco, "'Cuatro' y 'la fe': quiénes y de quién? (Mc 2,
             3b.5a)," <u>Bib</u> 50:59-67.   (N 14-160)

<u>2:10</u>

See also 1482.

505   1973   K. Kertelge, "Die Vollmacht des Menschensohnes zur Sünden-
             vergebung (Mk 2,10)," in <u>Orientierung an Jesus: Zur The-
             ologie der Synoptiker: Für Josef Schmid</u> (ed. by Paul
             Hoffmann with Norbert Brox and Wilhelm Pesch; Freiburg/
             Basel/Vienna: Herder), pp. 205-213.

506   1971   C. Colpe, "Traditionsüberschreitende Argumentationen zu
             Aussagen Jesu über sich selbst," in <u>Tradition und Glaube:
             das frühe Christentum in seiner Umwelt. Festgabe für</u>

<u>Karl Georg Kuhn zum 65. Geburtstag</u> (ed. by Gert Jeremi-
as, Heinz-Wolfgang Kung and Hartmut Stegemann; Göttingen:
Vandenhoeck & Ruprecht), pp. 230-245.

507   1960   C. P. Ceroke, "Is Mk 2, 10 a Saying of Jesus?" <u>CBQ</u> 22:369-
390.   (N 5-406)

508   1957   J. Duplacy, "Marc 2,10. Note de syntaxe," in <u>Mélanges
bibliques rédigés en l'honneur de André Robert</u> (Travaux
de l'Institut Catholique de Paris 4; Paris: Bloud & Gay),
pp. 420-427.

509   1954   G. H. Boobyer, "Mark 2,10a and the Interpretations of the
Healing of the Paralytic," <u>HTR</u> 47:115-120.

<u>2:13-17</u>

510   1978   M. Theobald, "Der Primat der Synchronie vor der Diachronie
als Grundaxiom der Literarkritik. Methodische Erwägung-
en an Hand von Mk 2,13-17 / Mt 9,9-13," <u>BZ</u> 22:161-186.
                                                   (N 23-457)

511   1976   P. Lamarche, "L'appel de Levi. Marc 2,13-17," <u>Christus</u> 23:
107-118.   (N 20-793)

512   1970   P. Lamarche, "The Call to Conversion and Faith. The Vocation of Levi (Mk, 2,13-17)," <u>LumVit</u> 25:301-312.(N 15-521)

513   1969   G. G. Gamba, "Considerazioni in margine alla redazione di
Mc 2,13-17," <u>DivThom</u> 72:201-226.   (N 14-161)

514   1967   B. M. F. Iersel, "La vocation de Lévi (Mc II,13-17; Mt IX,
9-13; Lc V,27-32)," in <u>De Jésus aux Évangiles: Tradition
et Rédaction dans les Évangiles synoptiques. Donum na-
talicum Iosepho Coppens septuagesimum annum complenti D.
D.D. collegae et amici</u> (ed. by I. de la Potterie; Bibliotheca ephemeridum theologicarum lovaniensium 25; Gem-
bloux/Paris: Duculot/Lethielleux), pp. 212-232.

<u>2:14</u>

See also 1514.

515   1968   R. Pesch, "Levi-Matthäus (Mc 2,14 / Mt 9,9; 10,3): Ein Beitrag zur Lösung eines alten Problems," <u>ZNW</u> 59:40-56.

<u>2:15-17</u>

516   1973   H. Braun, "Gott, die Eröffnung des Lebens für Nonkonform-
isten. Erwägungen zu Markus 2,15-17," in <u>Festschrift für
Ernst Fuchs</u> (ed. by Gerhard Ebeling; Eberhard Jüngel and

Gerd Schunack; Tübingen: J. C.B. Mohr ₍Paul Siebeck₎),
pp. 97-101.

517   1970   R. Pesch, "Das Zöllnergastmahl (Mk 2,15-17)," in Mélanges
               bibliques: en hommage au R. P. Béda Rigaux (ed. by Al-
               bert Descamps and André de Halleux; Gembloux: Éditions J.
               Duculot), pp. 63-87.

2:15-16

518   1980   H.-W. Bartsch, "Zur Problematik eines Monopoltextes des
               Neuen Testaments. Das Beispiel Markus 2, Vers 15 und
               16," TLZ 105:91-96.   (N 25-95)

2:16-17

519   1959   J. Alonso, "La parábola del médico en Mc. 2,16-17," CB 16:
               10-12.   (N 4-87)

2:17

520   1965   G. M. Lee, "'They that are whole need not a physician',"
               ExpTim 76:254.   (N 10-134)

2:18-22

521   1976   L. Fanin, "L'interrogazione sul digiuno: Mc 2,18-22," Mis-
               cellanea Franciscana 76:93-107.

522   1975   J. B. Muddiman, "Jesus and Fasting: Mark ii. 18-22," in Jé-
               sus aux origines de la christologie (ed. by J. Dupont;
               Bibliotheca ephemeridum theologicarum lovaniensium 40;
               Gembloux/Louvain: Duculot/Leuven University), pp. 271-281.

523   1973   J. A. Ziesler, "The Removal of the Bridegroom: A Note on
               Mark ii. 18-22 and Parallels," NTS 19:190-194.(N 17-939)

524   1972   G. Gaide, "Question sur le jeûne. Mc 2,18-22," AsSeign
               39:44-54.   (N 17-530)

525   1967   J. O'Hara, "Christian Fasting. Mk 2,18-22," Scr 19:82-95.
                                                              (N 12-176)

2:18-20

526   1972   T. A. Burkill, "Should Wedding Guests Fast? A Considera-
               tion of Mark 2:18-20," in Burkill, New Light on the Ear-
               liest Gospel: Seven Markan Studies (Ithaca, NY: Cornell
               University), pp. 39-47.

527   1969   A. Kee, "The Question about Fasting," NovT 11:161-173.
                                                              (N 14-504)

528 1968 A. Feuillet, "La controverse sur le jeûne (<u>Mc 2</u>, 18-20; <u>Mt</u> <u>9</u>, 14-15; <u>Lc 5</u>, 33-35)," <u>NRT</u> 90:113-136; 252-277.
(N 13-190)

2:19

529 1967 F. G. Cremer, "'Die Söhne des Brautgemachs' (Mk 2, 19 parr) in der griechischen und lateinischen Schrifterklärung," <u>BZ</u> 11:246-253.
(N 12-563)

2:20

530 1965 Franz Gerhard CREMER. <u>Die Fastenansage Jesu. Mk 2,20 und</u> <u>Parallelen in der Sicht der patristischen und scholas-</u> <u>tischen Exegese.</u> Bonner Biblische Beiträge 23. Bonn: Hanstein. xxx-185 pp.
(E 47-2425)

531 1963 G. Braumann, "'An jenem Tag' Mk 2,20," <u>NovT</u> 6:264-267.
(N 9-168)

2:21-22

532 1975 P. Trudinger, "The Word on the Generation Gap. Reflections on a Gospel Metaphor," <u>BTB</u> 5:311-315. (N 20-458)

533 1974 M. G. Steinhauser, "Neuer Wein braucht neue Schläuche. Zur Exegese von Mk 2,21f. par.," in <u>Biblische Randbemerkung-</u> <u>en: Schülerfestschrift für Rudolf Schnackenburg zum 60.</u> <u>Geburtstag</u> (ed. by Helmut Merklein and Joachim Lange; Würzburg: Echter-Verlag), pp. 113-123.

534 1971 F. Hahn, "Die Bildworte vom neuen Flicken und vom jungen Wein (Mk. 2, 21 f parr)," <u>EvT</u> 31:357-375. (N 16-548)

535 1970 A. Kee, "The Old Coat and the New Wine. A Parable of Re-pentance," <u>NovT</u> 12:13-21. (N 14-867)

2:22

536 1979 D. Flusser, "Do You Prefer New Wine?" <u>Immanuel</u> 9:26-31.

2:23 - 3:6

537 1978 G. G. Gamba, "Struttura letteraria e significato dottrin-ale di Marco 2,23-28 e 3,1-6," <u>Salesianum</u> 40:529-582.
(N 23-458)

537a 1973 C. Hinz, "Jesus und der Sabbat," <u>KD</u> 19:91-108.

538 E. A. Russell, "Mark 2,23 - 3,6--A Judaean Setting," in <u>Studia Evangelica 6: Papers Presented to the Fourth In-</u>

ternational Congress on New Testament Studies held at
Oxford, 1969 (ed. by Elizabeth A. Livingstone; Berlin:
Akademie Verlag), pp. 466-472.

539   1972   A. Duprez, "Deuz affrontements un jour de sabbat. Mc 2,23-
             3:6," AsSeign 40:43-53.   (N 17-940)

540   1958   H. Troadec, "Le Fils de l'Homme est Maître même du sabbat
             (Marc 2,23-3:6)," BVC 21:73-83.   (N 2-538)

2:23-28

541   1979   D. M. Cohn-Sherbok, "An Analysis of Jesus' Arguments con-
             cerning the Plucking of Grain on the Sabbath," JSNT 1979,
             2: 31-41.

542   L. Schottroff and W. Stegemann, "Der Sabbat ist um des
             Menschen willen da. Auslegung von Markus 2,23-28," in
             Der Gott der klein Leute. Sozialgeschichtliche Bibelaus-
             legungen. Band 2: Neues Testament (ed. by W. Schottroff
             and W. Stegemann; Munich: Kaiser), pp. 58-70.

543   1976   H. Aichinger, "Quellenkritische Untersuchung der Perikope
             vom Ährenraufen am Sabbat: Mk 2,23-28 par, Mt 12,1-8 par,
             Lk 6,1-5," in Jesus in der Verkündigung der Kirche (ed.
             by Albert Fuchs; Studien zum Neuen Testament und seiner
             Umwelt, Serie A, Bd. 1; Linz: A. Fuchs), pp. 110-153.

544   1975   J. D. M. Derrett, "Judaica in St. Mark," JRAS 1975:2-15.
             [Republished in Derrett, Studies in the New Testament I:
             Glimpses of the Legal and Social Presuppositions of the
             Authors (Leiden: E. J. Brill, 1977), pp. 85-100.]

545   B. Jay, "Jésus et le sabbat. Simples notes à propos de
             de Marc 2/23-28," ETR 50:65-68.   (N 19-963)

546   1973   H. Braun, "Erwägungen zu Markus 2,23-28 Par.," in Ent-
             scheidung und Solidarität: Festschrift für Johannes Har-
             der. Beiträge zur Theologie, Politik, Literatur und Er-
             ziehung (ed. by Hermann Horn; Wuppertal: Hammer), pp.
             53-56.

547   1972   A. J. Hultgren, "The Formation of the Sabbath Pericope in
             Mark 2:23-28," JBL 91:38-43.   (N 16-875)

548   1966   J. W. Leitch, "Lord Also of the Sabbath," SJT 19:426-433.
                                                            (N 11-1048)

549   1960   F. W. Beare, "'The Sabbath Was Made for Man?'" JBL 79:130-
             136.   (N 5-89)

2:23

550 1975 É. Delebecque, "Les épis 'égrenés' dans les Synoptiques,"
Revue des Études Grecques 88:133-142. (N 21-94)

2:26

551 1979 C. S. Morgan, "'When Abiathar was High Priest' (Mark 2:
26)," JBL 98:409-410. (N 24-434)

2:27

552 1975 F. Neirynck, "Jesus and the Sabbath: Some Observations on
Mark II, 27," in Jésus aux origines de la christologie
(ed. by J. Dupont; Bibliotheca ephemeridum theologicarum
lovaniensium 40; Gembloux/Louvain: Duculot/Leuven University), pp. 227-270.

553 1962 F. Gils, "'Le sabbat a été fait pour l'homme et non l'homme
pour le sabbat' (Mc, II,27). Réflexions à propos de Mc
II, 27-28," RB 69:506-523. (N 7-794)

2:28

See 1482.

3:1-6

554 1978 C. Dietzfelbinger, "Vom Sinn der Sabbatheilungen Jesu,"
EvT 38:281-298. (N 23-459)

555 1976 J. Smit Sibinga, "Text and Literary Art in Mark 3:1-6," in
Studies in New Testament and Text: Essays in Honour of
George D. Kilpatrick on the Occasion of his Sixty-fifth
Birthday (ed. by J. K. Elliott; Supplements to NovT 44;
Leiden: E. J. Brill), pp. 357-365.

556 1970 P. Geoltrain, "La violation du Sabbat. Une lecture de Mc
3:1-6," in Les récits de guérison (Cahiers Bibliques de
Foi et Vie 9; Paris: Foi et Vie, 1970), pp. 70-90, 116-
127.

3:6

557 1975 W. J. Bennett, Jr., "The Herodians of Mark's Gospel," NovT
17:9-14. (N 19-964)

3:7-12

See also 153

558   1976   A. Stöger, "Sohn Gottes im Markusevangelium (II). Medita-
             tion (Mk 3,7-12; 5,1-12)," <u>BLit</u> 49:112-115.

559   1969   W. Egger, "Die Verborgenheit in Mk 3,7-12," <u>Bib</u> 50:466-
             490.   (N 14-868)

560   1968   T. A. Burkill, "Mark 3:7-12 and the Alleged Dualism in the
             Evangelist's Miracle Material," <u>JBL</u> 87:409-417.(N 13-583)

561   1965   L. E. Keck, "Mark 3:7-12 and Mark's Christology," <u>JBL</u> 84:
             341-358.   (N 10-529)

3:13-19

See also 1514, 1526.

562   1972   G. Schmahl, "Die Berufung der Zwölf im Markusevangelium,"
             <u>TTZ</u> 81:203-213.   (N 17-531)

563   1960   W. Burgers, "De instelling van de Twaalf in het Evangelie
             van Marcus," <u>ETL</u> 36:625-654.   (N 6-137)

3:16-19

564   1962   O. Cullmann, "Der zwölfte Apostel," <u>RHPR</u> 42:133-140.
             ₍Republished in <u>Vorträge und Aufsätze, 1925 - 1962</u> (ed.
             by Karlfried Fröhlich; Tübingen/Zürich: J. C. B. Mohr
             (Paul Siebeck)/Zwingli Verlag, 1966), pp. 214-222.₎

3:17

565   1981   R. Buth, "Mark 3:17 <u>BONEREGEM</u> and Popular Etymology," in
             <u>JSNT</u> 1981:29-33.

3:18

566   1975   A. Penna, "La variante de Marco 3,18 secondo Origene," in
             <u>Homenaje a Juan Prado: miscelánea de estudios bíblicos y
             hebraicos</u> (ed. by L. Alvarez Verdes and E. J. Alonso Her-
             nandez; Madrid: Instituto "Benito Arias Montano" de Es-
             tudios Hebráicos, Sefardies y Oriente Próximo, 1975, Con-
             sejo Superior de Investigaciones Cientificas), pp. 329-
             339.

3:19-30

567   1971   L. Cope, "The Beelzebul Controversy, Mk 3:19-30 and Para-
             llels: A Model Problem in Source Analysis," in <u>Society of
             Biblical Literature 1971 Seminar Papers I</u> (Atlanta, GA:
             Society of Biblical Literature), pp. 251-256.

3:20 - 4:34

568 1969 Jan LAMBRECHT. <u>Marcus Interpretator. Stijl en boodschap</u>
<u>in Mc. 3,20 - 4,34.</u> Brugge/Utrecht: Desclée de Brouwer.
148 pp.   (E 51-2388)

3:20-35

569 1978 G. Danieli, "Maria e i fratelli di Gesù nel Vangelo di
Marco," <u>Marianum</u> 40:91-109.   (N 23-460)

570 1976 E. Best, "Mark iii. 20, 21, 31-35," <u>NTS</u> 22:309-319.
(N 21-95)

571 1975 Lorenz OBERLINNER. <u>Historische Überlieferung und christo-</u>
<u>logische Aussage. Zur Frage der "Bruder Jesu" in der</u>
<u>Synopse.</u> Forschung zur Bibel 19. Stuttgart: Katholisch-
es Bibelwerk. xi-396 pp.
  [See "Die Brüder Jesu im Markusevangelium: 3 (20f.)
  31-35; 6:1-6a," pp. 149-350.]

572 1974 J. Lambrecht, "The Relatives of Jesus in Mark," <u>NovT</u> 16:
241-258.   (N 19-965)

573 1973 J. D. Crossan, "Mark and the Relatives of Jesus," <u>NovT</u> 15:
81-113.   (N 18-121)

574 1968 J. Lambrecht, "Ware verwantschap en eeuwige zonde. Ont-
staan en structuur van Mc. 3,20-35," <u>Bijdragen</u> 29:114-
150, 234-258, 369-392, 393s. (N 13-191, 584, 880)

3:20-30

575 1974 Y. Congar, "Blasphemy Against the Holy Spirit," in <u>Experi-</u>
<u>ence of the Spirit</u> (ed. by Peter Huizing and William
Bassett; Concilium 99; New York: Seabury Press), pp. 47-
57.

3:20-21

576 1962 F. Spadafora, "Il greco degli Evangeli, esegesi di Mc 3,
20s," <u>Lateranum</u> 28:126-147.

3:21

577 1975 D. Wenham, "The Meaning of Mark iii. 21," <u>NTS</u> 21:295-300.
(N 19-966)

578 1972 H. Wansbrough, "Mark iii. 21--Was Jesus out of his mind?"
<u>NTS</u> 18:233-235.   (N 16-549)

3:22-27

579   1980   Albert FUCHS. <u>Die Entwicklung der Beelzebulkontroverse
             bei den Synoptikern. Traditionsgeschichtliche und redak-
             tionsgeschichtliche Untersuchung von Mk 3,22-27 und Para-
             llelen, verbunden mit der Rückfrage nach Jesus.</u> Studien
             zum Neuen Testament und seiner Umwelt, B, 5. Linz: SNTU.
             279 pp.

3:23

580   1966   W. Ziffer, "Two Epithets for Jesus of Nazareth in Talmud
             and Midrash," <u>JBL</u> 85:356-357.

3:26-27

581   1977   H. Kruse, "Das Reich Satans," <u>Bib</u> 58:29-61.   (N 22-102)

3:26

See 580.

3:28-29

582   1976   M. E. Boring, "The unforgivable Sin Logion Mark III 28-29/
             Matt XII 31-32/Luke XII 10: Formal Analysis and History
             of the Tradition," <u>NovT</u> 18:258-279.   (N 21-745)

583   1975   T. A. Burkill, "Blasphemy: St. Mark's Gospel as Damnation
             History," in <u>Christianity, Judaism and Other Greco-Roman
             Cults: Studies for Morton Smith at Sixty</u> (ed. by Jacob
             Neusner; Studies in Judaism in Late Antiquity 12; Leiden:
             E. J. Brill), Vol. 1, pp. 51-74.

584   1972   M. E. Boring, "How May We Identify Oracles of Christian
             Prophets in the Synoptic Tradition? Mark 3:28-29 as a
             Test Case," <u>JBL</u> 91:501-521.   (N 17-532)

585   R. Holst, "Reexamining Mk 3:28f. and Its Parallels," <u>ZNW</u>
             63:122-124.   (N 17-941)

586   1970   C. Colpe, "Der Spruch von der Lästerung des Geistes," in
             <u>Der Ruf Jesu und die Antwort der Gemeinde: Exegetische
             Untersuchungen. Joachim Jeremias zum 70. Geburtstag ge-
             widmet von seinen Schülern</u> (ed. by Eduard Lohse in colla-
             boration with Christoph Burchard and Berndt Schaller;
             Göttingen: Vandenhoeck & Ruprecht), pp. 63-79.

587   F. Salvoni, "Bestemmia contro lo Spirito Santo (Mc 3,28s
             par)," <u>RicBibRel</u> 5:365-381.

588 1968 E. LÖVESTAM. <u>Spiritus Blasphemia. Eine Studie zu Mk 3,</u>
<u>28f par Mt 12,31f, Lk 12,10.</u> Scripta Minora Regiae So-
cietatis Humaniorum Litterarum Lundensis, 1966-1967: 1.
Lund: Gleerup. 88 pp.   (E 50-2572)

589   "Logiet om hädelse mot den helige Ande (Mark.
3:28f. par. Matt. 12:31f.; Luk. 12:10)," <u>SEÅ</u> 33:101-117.
                                          (N 14-162)

590 1965 R. Scroggs, "The Exaltation of the Spirit by Some Early
Christians," <u>JBL</u> 84:359-373.   (N 10-530)

591   J. G. Williams, "A Note on the 'Unforgivable Sin' Logion,"
<u>NTS</u> 12:75-77.   (N 10-531)

3:30-31

592 1956 F. Spadafora, "Entusiasmo della folla frenato dagli apos-
toli e proposito energico dei parenti di Gesù (Mc 3,
30s)?" <u>RivB</u> 4:98-113.

3:31-35

593 1974 G. Lafon, "Qui est dedans? Qui est dehors? Une lecture de
Marc 3,31-35," <u>Christus</u> (Paris) 21:41-47.
           [Republished in Lafon, <u>Esquisses pour un christianisme</u>
(Paris: Éditions du Cerf, 1979), pp. 217-224.]

594 1967 G. R. Castellino, "Beata Virgo Maria in Evangelio Marci
(Mc 3,31-35)," in <u>Maria in sacra Scriptura. Acta Con-</u>
<u>gressus mariologicimariani in Republica Dominicana anno</u>
<u>1965 celebrati. Vol. 4: De Beata Virgine Maria in Evan-</u>
<u>geliis Synopticis</u> (Rome: Pontificia Academia mariana in-
ternationalis), pp. 519-528.

Chs. 4 - 8

595 1960 H. Hegermann, "Bethsaida und Gennesar. Eine traditions-
und redaktionsgeschichtliche Studie zu Mc 4 - 8," in <u>Ju-</u>
<u>dentum, urchristentum, kirche. Festschrift für Joachim</u>
<u>Jeremias</u> (ed. by Walther Eltester; Beihefte <u>ZNW</u> 26; Ber-
lin: Verlag Alfred Töpelmann), pp. 130-140.

4:1-34

See also 350, 1537.

596 1980 Vittorio FUSCO. <u>Parola e regno: La sezione delle parabole</u>
<u>(Mc. 4,1-34) nella prospettiva marciana</u>. Aloisiana 13.
Brescia: Morcelliana. ix-421 pp.

597   1978   P. R. Jones, "The Seed Parables of Mark," RevExp 75:519–
             538.   (N 23-462)

598   1977   É Trocmé, "Why Parables? A Study of Mark IV," BJRL 59:
             458-471.   (N 21-746)

599   1976   D. A. Losada, "Las parábolas de crecimiento en el Evangel-
             io de Marcos," RevistB 38:113-125.   (N 21-397)

600   1975   J. Lambrecht, "Parabels in Mc. 4," TijdTheol 15:26-43.
                                                      (N 19-970)

601   R. P. Merendino, "Ohne Gleichnisse redete er nicht zu Ihn-
             en (Zu Mk 4,1-34)," in Homenaje a Juan Prado: miscelánea
             de estudios bíblicos y hebraicos (ed. by L. Alvarez Ver-
             des and E. J. Alonso Hernandez; Madrid: Instituto "Beni-
             to Arias Montano" de Estudios Hebráicos, Sefardies y Or-
             iente Próximo, 1975, Consejo Superior de Investigaciones
             Cientificas), pp. 341-371.

602   1974   B. Englezakis, "Markan Parable: More than Word Modality, a
             Revelation of Contents," DeltBibMel 2:349-357.(N 19-969)

603   J. Lambrecht, "Redaction and Theology in Mk. IV," in L'é-
             vangile selon Marc: Tradition et rédaction (ed. by M.
             Sabbe; Bibliotheca ephemeridum theologicarum lovaniensi-
             um 34; Gembloux/Louvain: Duculot/Leuven University), pp.
             269-307.

604   P. Merendino, "Gleichnisrede und Wortliturgie. Zu Mk 4,1-
             34," Archiv für Liturgiewissenschaft 16:7-31.(N 20-794)

605   1973   S. Pedersen, "Is Mark 4,1-34 a Parable Chapter?" in Studia
             Evangelica 6: Papers presented to the Fourth Internation-
             al Congress on New Testament Studies held at Oxford, 1969
             (ed. by Elizabeth A. Livingstone; Berlin: Akademie Ver-
             lag), pp. 408-416.

606   Heikki RÄISÄNEN. Die Parabeltheorie im Markusevangelium.
             Schriften der Finnischen Exegetischen Gesellschaft 26.
             Helsinki/Leiden: Finnish Exegetical Society/E. J. Brill.
             173 pp.   (E 55-2916)

607   1972   J. W. Pryor, "Markan Parable Theology. An Inquiry into
             Mark's Principles of Redaction," ExpTim 83:242-245.
                                                      (N 17-141)

608   D. Wenham, "The Synoptic Problem Revisited: Some New Sug-
             gestions about the Composition of Mark 4:1-34," TynBull
             23:3-38.   (N 17-942)

609 1971 M. Morlet, "Le chapitre des paraboles dans l'Évangile de
            Marc," EspVie 81:513-520.   (N 16-550)

610 1970 S. Pedersen, "Er Mark 4 et 'lignelseskapitel'?" DTT 33:20-
            30.   (N 15-162)

611 1968 J. Lambrecht, "De vijf parabels van Mc. 4, Structuur en
            theologie van de parabelrede," Bijdragen 29:25-53.
                                                   (N 12-887)

612 1967 K. Weinholt Petersen, "Messiashemmelighed og lignelsesfor-
            kyndelse i Markusevangeliet," DTT 30:1-25. (N 12-175)

613 1961 G. H. Boobyer, "The Redaction of Mark iv. 1-34," NTS 8:59-
            70.   (N 6-466)

614 1959 M. Miguens, "La predicazione di Gesù in parabole (Mc 4;
            Lc 8,4-18; Mt 13)," BeO 1:35-39.

4:1-20

See also 115.

615 1980 P. B. Payne, "The Authenticity of the Parable of the Sower
            and Its Interpretation," in Gospel Perspectives: Studies
            of History and Tradition in the Four Gospels, Vol. 1 (ed.
            by R. T. France and David Wenham; Sheffield: JSOT), pp.
            163-207.

616 1979 F. Hahn, "Das Gleichnis von der ausgestreuten Saat und
            seine Deutung (Mk iv. 3-8, 14-20)," in Text and Interpre-
            tation: Studies in the New Testament Presented to Matthew
            Black (ed. by Ernest Best and R. Mcl. Wilson; New York/
            London: Cambridge University Press), pp. 133-142.

617 1975 E. Schweizer, "From the New Testament Text to the Sermon.
            Mk 4:1-20," RevExp 72:181-188.   (N 19-968)

618 1974 J. W. Bowker, "Mystery and Parable: Mark iv. 1-20," JTS 25:
            300-317.   (N 19-967)

619 1973 J. Drury, "The Sower, the Vineyard, and the Place of Alle-
            gory in the Interpretation of Mark's Parables," JTS 24:
            367-379.   (N 18-874)

620 1972 T. K. Seim, "Apostolat og forkynnelse. En studie til Mk.
            4.1-20," DTT 35:206-222.   (N 18-490)

621 1969 M. Didier, "La parabole du semeur," in Au service de la
            parole de Dieu. Mélanges offerts à Monseigneur André-
            Marie Charue (Gembloux:Éditions J. Duculot), pp. 21-41.

622   C. F. D. Moule, "Mark 4:1-20 Yet Once More," in <u>Neotesta-
             mentica et Semitica: Studies in honour of Matthew Black</u>
             (ed. by E. Earle Ellis and Max Wilcox; Edinburgh: T & T
             Clark), pp. 95-113.

623   1968 E. Schweizer, "Marc 4,1-20," <u>ÉTR</u> 43:256-264. (N 14-163)

<u>4:1-2a</u>

See 153.

<u>4:2-9</u>

624   1964 K. D. White, "The Parable of the Sower," <u>JTS</u> 15:300-307.
                                                          (N 9-556)

<u>4:3-9</u>

625   1979 J. Horman, "The Source of the Version of the Parable of the
             Sower in the Gospel of Thomas," <u>NovT</u> 21:326-343.
                                                          (N 24-435)

626   T. J. Weeden, "Recovering the Parabolic Intent in the Para-
             ble of the Sower," <u>JAAR</u> 47:97-120.   (N 24-109)

627   1978 H.-J. Geischer, "Verschwenderische Güte. Versuch über
             Markus 4,3-9," <u>EvT</u> 38:418-427.   (N 23-464)

628   1975 R. Bultmann, "Die Interpretation von Mk 4,3-9 seit Jülich-
             er," in <u>Jesus und Paulus: Festschrift für Werner Georg
             Kümmel zum 70. Geburtstag</u> (ed. by E. Earle Ellis and
             Erich Grässer; Göttingen: Vandenhoeck & Ruprecht), pp.
             30-34.

629   1974 A. N. Wilder, "The Parable of the Sower: Naiveté and Method
             in Interpretation," <u>Semeia</u> 2:134-151.   (N 19-971)

630   1970 C. Dietzfelbinger, "Das Gleichnis vom ausgestreuten Samen,"
             in <u>Der Ruf Jesu und die Antwort der Gemeinde: Exegetische
             Untersuchungen. Joachim Jeremias zum 70. Geburtstag ge-
             widmet von seinen Schülern</u> (ed. by Eduard Lohse in colla-
             boration with Christoph Burchard and Berndt Schaller;
             Göttingen: Vandenhoeck & Ruprecht), pp. 80-93.

631   1959 A. George, "Le sens de la parabole des semailles (Mc., 4,
             3-9 et parallèles)," in <u>Sacra Pagina. Miscellanea bibli-
             ca Congressus Internationalis Catholici de re Biblica</u>
             (ed. by J. Coppens et al.; Bibliotheca ephemeridum theo-
             logicarum lovaniensium 12-13; Gembloux/Paris: Éditions J.
             Duculot/J. Gabalda), pp. 163-169.

4:3-8

632 1978 P. B. Payne, "The Order of Sowing and Ploughing in the Parable of the Sower," <u>NTS</u> 25:123-129.   (N 23-463)

633 1966 J. Jeremias, "Palästinakundliches zum Gleichnis vom Säemann (Mark. IV. 3-8 Par.)," <u>NTS</u> 13:48-53.   (N 11-1050)

634 1965 W. Neil, "Expounding the Parables: II. The Sower (Mk 4:3-8)," <u>ExpTim</u> 77:74-77.   (N 10-923)

4:9

635 1977 C. Roggenbuck, "Mk 4:9: eine Weck-Formel?" <u>Biblische Notizen</u> 3:27-32.

4:10-12

636 1980 F. C. Synge, "A Plea for the Outsiders: Commentary on Mark 4,10-12," <u>JournTheolSAfric</u> 30:53-58.   (N 25-96)

637 1977 J. R. Kirkland, "The Earliest Understanding of Jesus' Use of Parables: Mark IV 10-12 In Context," <u>NovT</u> 19:1-21.   (N 21-747)

638 1974 P. Lampe, "Die markinische Deutung des Gleichnisses vom Sämann Markus 4:10-12," <u>ZNW</u> 65:140-150.   (N 19-554)

639 K. H. Schelkle, "Der Zweck der Gleichnisreden (Mk 4,10-12)," in <u>Neues Testament und Kirche: Für Rudolf Schnackenburg</u> (ed. by Joachim Gnilka; Freiburg im Br./Basel/Vienna: Herder), pp. 71-75.

640 1964 J. Coutts, "'Those Outside' (Mk 4:10-12)," in <u>Studia Evangelica II: Papers Presented to the Second International Congress on New Testament Studies held at Christ Church, Oxford, 1961</u> (ed. by F. L. Cross; Texte und Untersuchungen zur Geschichte der altchristlichen Literatur 87; Berlin: Akademie-Verlag), pp. 155-157.

641 1961 E. F. Siegman, "Teaching in Parables (Mk 4, 10-12; Lk 8, 9-10; Mt 13, 10-15)," <u>CBQ</u> 23:161-181.   (N 6-138)

642 1957 W. Manson, "The Purpose of the Parables: A Re-Examination of St. Mark iv. 10-12," <u>ExpTim</u> 68:132-135.   (N 1-395)
    ₍Republished in Manson, <u>Jesus and the Christian</u> (London: J. Clarke, 1967), pp. 48-66.₎

643 1956 T. A. Burkill, "The Cryptology of Parables in St. Mark's Gospel," <u>NovT</u> 1:246-262.   (N 2-290)

644   P. H. Igarashi, "The Mystery of the Kingdom (Mark 4,
               10ss)," JBR 24:83-89.

645   1955   W. Marxsen, "Redaktionsgeschichtliche Erklärung der soge-
               nannte Parabeltheorie des Markus," ZTK 52:255-271.

4:10

646   1974   D. E. Dozzi, "Chi sono 'Quelli attorno a Lui' di Mc 4,
               10?" Marianum 36:153-183.   (N 19-553)

647   1964   R. P. Meye, "Mk 4:10; 'Those about Him with the Twelve',"
               in Studia Evangelica II: Papers Presented to the Second
               International Congress on New Testament Studies held at
               Christ Church, Oxford, 1961 (ed. by F. L. Cross; Texte
               und Untersuchungen zur Geschichte der altchristlichen
               Literatur 87; Berlin: Akademie-Verlag), pp. 211-218.

4:11-12

648   1974   M. Hubaut, "Le 'mystère' révélé dans les paraboles (Mc 4,
               11-12)," RTL 5:454-461.   (N 19-972)

649   1972   G. Haufe, "Erwägungen zum Ursprung der sogenannten Parabel-
               theorie Markus 4,11-12," EvT 32:413-421.   (N 17-944)

650   1967   A. M. Ambrozic, "Mark's Concept of the Parable," CBQ 29:
               220-227.   (N 12-179)

4:11

651   1973   S. Brown, "'The Secret of the Kingdom of God' (Mark 4:11),"
               JBL 92:60-74.   (N 17-943)

652   1972   K. Haacker, "Erwägungen zu Mc IV 11," NovT 14:219-225.
                                                                (N 17-533)

653   1957   J. A. Baird, "A Pragmatic Approach to Parable Exegesis:
               Some New Evidence on Mark 4:11, 33-34," JBL 76:201-207.
                                                                (N 2-534)

4:12

654   1974   C. A. Moore, "Mark 4:12: More Like the Irony of Micaiah
               than Isaiah," in A Light unto my Path: Old Testament
               Studies in honor of Jacob M. Meyers (ed. by Howard N.
               Bream, Ralph D. Heim and Carey A. Moore; Gettysburg The-
               ological Studies IV; Philadelphia: Temple University
               Press), pp. 335-344.

655   1968   C. H. Peisker, "Konsekutives hina in Markus 4:12," ZNW 59:
               126-127.   (N 13-192)

656 1955   A. Soldatelli, "Ne quando convertantur, Mc 4,12," <u>PalCler</u>
            34:534-543.

4:14-20

657 1980   P. B. Payne, "The Seeming Inconsistency of the Interpreta-
            tion of the Parable of the Sower," <u>NTS</u> 26:564-568.
                                                          (N 25-97)

658 1978   G. O'Mahony, "Mark's Gospel and the Parable of the Sower,"
            <u>TBT</u> 98:1764-1768.   (N 23-465)

659 1974   D. Wenham, "The Interpretation of the Parable of the Sow-
            er," <u>NTS</u> 20:299-319.   (N 19-107)

4:21

660 1971   J. D. M. Derrett, "The Lamp Which Must Not be Hidden (Mk
            iv. 21)," in Derrett, <u>Law in the New Testament</u> (London/
            New York: Darton, Longman & Todd/Fernhill House), pp.
            189-207.

661 1970   G. Schneider, "Das Bildwort von der Lampe. Zur Traditions-
            geschichte eines Jesus-Wortes," <u>ZNW</u> 61:183-209.(N 15-868)

662 1966   W. G. Essame, "<u>kai elegen</u> in Mark iv. 21, 24, 26, 30,"
            <u>ExpTim</u> 77:121.   (N 10-924)

663 1954   J. M. Bover, "'Nada hay encubierto que no se descubra'
            (Mc 4,21 par)," <u>EstBib</u> 13:319-323.

4:22-24

664 1971   J. O'Callaghan, "Posible identificación de P44 C <u>recto</u> b
            como Mc 4, 22-24," <u>Bib</u> 52:398-400.   (N 16-551)

4:24-29

See also 299.

665 1955   F. Mussner, "Gleichnisauslegung und Heilsgeschichte. Dar-
            getan am Gleichnis von der wachsenden Saat (Mc 4,24-29),"
            <u>TTZ</u> 64:257-266.

4:26-29

666 1975   J. Dupont, "Encore la parabole de la Semence, qui pousse
            toute seule (Mc 4,26-29)," in <u>Jesus und Paulus: Fest-
            schrift für Werner Georg Kümmel zum 70. Geburtstag</u> (ed.
            by E. Earle Ellis and Erich Grässer; Göttingen: Vanden-
            hoeck & Ruprecht), pp. 96-108.

667   1973   W. G. Kümmel, "Noch einmal: Das Gleichnis von der selbst-
                wachsende Saat. Bemerkungen zur neutestamentlichen Dis-
                kussion um die Auslegung der Gleichnisse Jesu," in Ori-
                entierung an Jesu. Zur Theologie der Synoptiker. Für
                Josef Schmid (ed. by Paul Hoffmann with Norbert Brox and
                Wilhelm Pesch; Freiburg: Herder), pp. 220-237.
                    ₍Republished in Heilsgeschehen und Geschichte. Band 2.
                Gesammelte Aufsätze 1965 - 1977 (ed. by Erich Grässer
                and Otto Merk; Marburger Theologische Studien 16;
                Marburg: N. G. Elwert Verlag, 1978), pp. 143-156.₎

668   R. Stuhlmann, "Beobachtungen und Überlegungen zu Markus iv.
                26-29," NTS 19:153-162.   (N 17-945)

669   1971   W. G. Doty, "An Interpretation: Parable of the Weeds and
                Wheat," Int 25:185-193.   (N 16-176)

670   1967   H. Baltensweiler, "Das Gleichnis von der selbstwachsenden
                Saat (Markus 4,26-29) und die theologische Konzeption
                des Markusevangelisten," in Oikonomia: Heilsgeschichte
                als Thema der Theologie. O. Cullmann zum 65. Geburtstag
                gewidmet (ed. by Felix Christ; Hamburg-Bergstedt: Reich),
                pp. 69-75.

671   J. Dupont, "La parabole de la semence qui pousse toute
                seule (Marc 4, 26-29)," RSR 55:367-392.   (N 12-564)

4:30-32

672   1980   J. A. Sproule, "The Problem of the Mustard Seed," Grace
                Theological Journal (Winona Lake, IN) 1:37-42.(N 25-76)

673   1978   A. Casalegno, "La parabola del granello di senape (Mc. 4,
                30-32)," RivB 26:139-161.   (N 23-466)

674   1973   R. W. Funk, "The Looking-Glass Tree Is for the Birds. Ezek-
                iel 17:22-24; Mark 4:30-32," Int 27:3-9.   (N 17-946)

675   1971   K.-P. Hertzsch, "Jésus herméneute. Une étude de Mc 4,30-
                32," in Reconnaissance à Suzanne de Dietrich (Cahiers
                Bibliques de Foi et Vie; Paris: Foi et Vie), pp. 109-116.

676   H. K. McArthur, "The Parable of the Mustard Seed," CBQ 33:
                198-210.   (N 15-869)

4:30

677   1959   H.-W. Bartsch, "Eine bisher übersehene Zitierung der LXX
                in Mark 4, 30," TZ 15:126-128.   (N 4-396)

4:33-34

See 653.

678 1970 E. Molland, "Zur Auslegung von Mc 4,33 <u>kathōs ēdunato</u>
akouein," in Molland, <u>Opuscula Patristica</u> (Oslo: Uni-
versitets-förlaget), pp. 1-8.
[Originally in <u>Symbolae Osloenses</u> 8 (1929): 83-91.]

4:35 - 9:49

See 26.

4:35 - 8:30

679 1971 L. F. Rivera, "La liberación en el éxodo. El éxodo de
Marcos y la revelación del líder (4,35-8,30)," <u>RevistB</u>
33:13-26. (N 16-177)

4:35 - 8:26

See also 167, 169.

680 1978 R. Meye, "Psalm 107 as 'Horizon' for Interpreting the Miracle Stories of Mark 4:35 - 8:26," in <u>Unity and Diversity
in New Testament Theology: Essays in Honor of George E.
Ladd</u> (ed. by Robert A.Guelich; Grand Rapids: William B.
Eerdmans), pp. 1-13.

4:35 - 6:6a

681 1970 Walter SCHMITHALS. <u>Wunder und Glaube. Eine Auslegung von
Markus 4,35 - 6,6a</u>. Biblische Studien 59. Neukirchen-
Vluyn: Neukirchener Verlag. 99 pp. (E 52-2592)

4:35 - 5:43

682 1981 K. M. Fisher and U. C. von Wahlde, "The Miracles of Mark
4:35 - 5:43: Their Meaning and Function in the Gospel
Framework," <u>BTB</u> 11:13-16.

4:35 - 5:20

683 1967 E. Hilgert, "Symbolismus und Heilsgeschichte in den Evangelien. Ein Beitrag zu den Seesturm- und Gerasenererzähl-
ungen," in <u>Oikonomia: Heilsgeschichte als Thema der Theologie. O. Cullmann zum 65. Geburtstag gewidmet</u> (ed. by
Felix Christ; Hamburg-Bergstedt: Reich), pp. 51-56.

4:35-41

See also 153, 299.

684   1979   G. M. Soares Prabhu, "And There Was a Great Calm. A
             'Dhvani' Reading of the Stilling of the Storm (Mk 4,35-
             41)," Biblebhashyam 5:295-308.   (N 24-807)

685   1978   U. Ruegg, H. Stotzer-Kloo, and M. Voser, "Zum Vertrauen be-
             freit, Jesus mit seinen Jüngern im Sturm (Markus 4,35-
             41). Ein Rettungswunder," in Wunder Jesu (ed. by Anton
             Steiner; Bibelarbeit in der Gemeinde 2; Basel/Zürich:
             Reinhardt/Benziger), pp. 113-126.

686   B. M. F. van Iersel and A. J. M. Linmans, "The Storm on the
             Lake, Mk iv 35-41 and Mt viii 18-27 in the Light of Form
             Criticism, 'Redaktionsgeschichte' and Structural Analy-
             sis," in Miscellanea Neotestamentica vol. 2 (ed. by T.
             Baarda, A. F. J. Klihn and W. C. van Unnik; NovT Supple-
             ment 48; Leiden: E. J. Brill), pp. 17-48.

687   1975   T. M. Suriano, "'Who Then Is This?'...Jesus Masters the
             Sea," TBT 79:449-456.   (N 20-459)

688   1969   P. Lamarche, "La tempête apaisée," AsSeign 43:43-53.
             [Republished in Lamarche, Révélation de Dieu chez Marc
             (Le Point Théologique 20; Paris: Beauchesne, 1976), pp.
             61-77.]

689   1965   G. Schille, "Die Seesturmerzählung Markus 4:35-41 als Bei-
             spiel neutestamentlicher Aktualisierung," ZNW 56:30-40.
                                                          (N 10-532)

690   1962   P. Achtemeier, "Person and Deed. Jesus and the Storm-Toss-
             ed Sea," Int 16:169-176.   (N 7-150)

5:1-20

See also 153.

691   1980   J. D. M. Derrett, "Legend and Event: The Gerasene Demoniac:
             An Inquest into History and Liturgical Projection," in
             Studia Biblica 1978: II. Papers on the Gospels. Sixth
             International Congress on Biblical Studies, Oxford, 3-7
             April 1978 (ed. by E. A. Livingstone; JSNT Supplement
             Series 2; Sheffield: JSOT), pp. 63-73.

692   1979   J. D. M. Derrett, "Contributions to the Study of the Gera-
             sene Demoniac," JSNT 3:2-17.   (N 23-844)

693   1977   J.-N. Aletti, "Une lecture en questions," in Les miracles
             de Jésus selon le Nouveau Testament (ed. by Xavier Léon-
             Dufour; Parole de Dieu; Paris:Éditions du Seuil), pp.
             189-208.

694   T. Aurelio, "Mistero del regno e unione con Gesù: Mc 5:1-
           21," BeO 19:59-68.   (N 22-103)

695   O. Bächli, "'Was habe ich mit Dir zu schaffen?'. Eine for-
           melhafte Frage im Alten Testament und Neuen Testament,"
           TZ 33:69-80.

696   L. Beirnaert, "Approche psychanalytique," in Les miracles
           de Jésus selon le Nouveau Testament (ed. by Xavier Léon-
           Dufour; Parole de Dieu; Paris: Éditions du Seuil), pp.
           183-188.

697   J. Calloud, G. Bombet, and J. Delorme, "Essaie d'analyse
           sémiotique," in Les miracles de Jésus selon le Nouveau
           Testament (ed. by Xavier Léon-Dufour; Parole de Dieu;
           Paris: Éditions du Seuil), pp. 151-181.

698   H. Harsch, "Psychologische Interpretation biblischer Texte.
           Ein Versuch zu Mk 5,1-20: Die Heilung des Besessenen von
           Gerasa," US 32:39-45.   (N 21-748)

699   1976 Franz ANNEN. Heil für die Heiden: Zur Bedeutung und Ge-
           schichte der Tradition vom Besessenen Gerasener (Mk 5,1-
           20 parr.). Frankfurter Theologische Studien 20. Frank-
           furt: Josef Knecht. viii-253 pp.   (E 57-3830)

700   1974 A. Paul, "Le récit (biblique) comme surface. Éléments thé-
           oriques pour une sémantique narrative," RSPT 58:584-598.

701   1973 M. de Burgos, "El poseso de Gerasa (Mc 5,1-20): Jesús por-
           tador de una existencia liberadora," Communio 6:103-118.
                                                          (N 18-875)

702   1972 F. J. Leenhardt, "Essai exégétique: Mc 5,1-20," in Analyse
           structurale et exégèse biblique: Essais d'interprétation
           (ed. by Roland Barthes et al.; Neuchâtel: Delachaux &
           Niestlé), pp. 95-121.
              [Republished as "An Exegetical Essay: Mark 5:1-20," in
              Structural Analysis and Biblical Exegesis: Interpreta-
              tional Essays (ed. by R. Barthes et al.; tr. by Alfred
              M. Johnson, Jr.; Pittsburgh Theological Monograph Ser-
              ies; Pittsburgh: Pickwick, 1974), pp. 85-109.]

703   Rudolf PESCH. Der Besessene von Gerasa. Entstehung und
           Überlieferung einer Wundergeschichte. Stuttgarter Bibel-
           studien 56. Stuttgart: Katholisches Bibelwerk. 70 pp.

704   J. Starobinski, "The Struggle with Legion: A Literary Ana-
           lysis of Mark 5:1-20," New Literary History 4:331-356.

705   "Le démoniaque de Gérasa. Analyse de Mc

5,1-20," in <u>Analyse structurale et exégèse biblique</u> (ed.
by Roland Barthes et al.; Neuchâtel: Delachaux & Niest-
lé), pp. 63-94.
ɾRepublished as "The Gerasene Demoniac: A Literary
Analysis of Mark 5:1-20," in <u>Structural Analysis and
Biblical Exegesis: Interpretational Essays</u> (ed. by
R. Barthes, et al.; tr. by Alfred M. Johnson, Jr.;
Pittsburgh Theological Monograph Series; Pittsburgh:
Pickwick, 1974), pp. 57-84.ɺ

706   1971   M. de Mello, "The Gerasene Demoniac. The Power of Jesus
Confronts the Power of Satan," <u>EcumRev</u> 23:409-418.
(N 16-877)

707   R. Pesch, "The Markan Version of the Healing of the Gerasene Demoniac," <u>EcumRev</u> 23:349-376.   (N 16-878)

708   J. Starobinski, "An Essay in Literary Analysis--Mark 5,1-
20," <u>EcumRev</u> 23:377-397.   (N 16-879)

709   1969   J. Bligh, "The Gerasene Demoniac and the Resurrection of
Christ," <u>CBQ</u> 31:383-390.   (N 14-505)

710   1968   J. F. Craghan, "The Gerasene Demoniac," <u>CBQ</u> 30:522-536.
(N 13-585)

711   P. Lamarche, "Le possédé de Gérasa," <u>NRT</u> 90:581-597.
ɾRepublished in Lamarche, <u>Révélation de Dieu chez Marc</u>
(Le Point Théologique 20; Paris: Beauchesne, 1976),
pp. 79-103.ɺ

712   J. Lambrecht, "Le possédé et le troupeau (Mc 5,1-20),"
<u>Revue du Clergé Africain</u> 33:557-569.

713   1964   C. H. Cave, "The Obedience of Unclean Spirits," <u>NTS</u> 11:93-
97.   (N 9-557)

714   H. Sahlin, "Die Perikope vom gerasenischen Besessenen und
der Plan des Markusevangeliums," <u>ST</u> 18:159-172.(N 9-937)

715   1958   J. Louw, "De bezetene en de kudde, Marc. 5:1-20. Een hy-
pothese," <u>NedTTs</u> 13:59-61.   (N 3-591)

716   1957   T. A. Burkill, "Concerning Mk 5,7 and 5,18-20," <u>ST</u> 11:159-
166.   (N 3-592)

<u>5:7-8</u>

See 472.

5:10

717 1976 G. Schwarz, "'Aus der Gegend' (Markus v. 10b)," NTS 22: 214-215.   (N 20-795)

5:21-43

718 1971 L. Dambrine, "Guérison de la femme hémorroïsse et résur-rection de la fille de Jaïre. Un aspect de la lecture d'un texte: Mc 5:21-43; Mt 9:18-26; Lc8:40-56," in Re-connaissance à Suzanne de Dietrich (Cahiers Bibliques de Foi et Vie; Paris: Foi et Vie), pp. 75-81.

5:22

719 1970 R. Pesch, "Jaïrus (Mk 5,22/Lk 8,41)," BZ 14:252-256.
                                                               (N 15-524)

5:24b-34

720 1980 J. T. Cummings, "The Tassel of his Cloak: Mark, Luke, Matthew--and Zechariah," in Studia Biblica 1978: II. Papers on the Gospels. Sixth International Congress on Biblical Studies, Oxford, 3-7 April 1978 (ed. by E. A. Livingstone. JSNT Supplement Series 2; Sheffield: JSOT), pp. 47-61.

5:41

721 1964 E. López-Dóriga, "Y cogiendo la mano de la niña le dice: Talitha koumi (Mc 5,41). Nota exegético-filológica," EstEcl 39:377-381.

722 1961 J. C. Hindley, "Our Lord's Aramaic--A Speculation," ExpTim 72:180-181.   (N 6-139)

5:43

723 1972 J. E. Efird, "Note on Mark 5:43," in The Use of the Old Testament in the New and Other Essays: Studies in Honor of William Franklin Stinespring (ed. by James M. Efird; Durham, NC: Duke University), pp. 307-309.

Ch. 6

724 1957 G. F. Dowden, "The Significance of Mark 6," CQR 158:39-48.

6:1-6a

See also 571, 573.

725 1978 B. Mayer, "Überlieferungs- und redaktionsgeschichtliche

Überlegungen zu Mk 6, 1–6a," BZ 22:187–198. (N 23–467)

726   1974   C. Perrot, "Jésus à Nazareth. Mc 6,1–6," AsSeign 45:40–
              49.   (N 19–108)

727   1969   E. Grässer, "Jesus in Nazareth, (Mark VI. 1–6a). Notes
              on the Redaction and Theology of St. Mark," NTS 16:1–23.
                                                           (N 14–869)
              ₍Republished as "Jesus in Nazareth (Mk 6,1–6a): Bemerk-
              ungen zur Redaktion und Theologie des Markus," in
              Jesus in Nazareth (ed. by Walther Eltester; Beiheft
              ZNW 40; Berlin/New York: de Gruyter, 1972), pp. 1–37,
              and again in Grässer, Text und Situation: Gesammelte
              Aufsätze zum Neuen Testament (Gütersloh: G. Mohn,
              1973), pp. 13–49, including a brief supplementary
              note.₎

6:3

728   1977   A. Salas, "Jesús 'Ben Myriam' (Mc 6,3). Anotaciones cri-
              ticas sobre el origen de Jesús en la tradición sinópti-
              ca," Estudio Agustiniano 12:87–97.

729   1973   H. K. McArthur, "'Son of Mary,'" NovT 15:38–58.(N 17–947)

730   1969   E. Stauffer, "Jeschu ben Mirjam. Kontroversgeschichtliche
              Anmerkungen zu Mk 6:3," in Neotestamentica et Semitica:
              Studies in honour of Matthew Black (ed. by E. Earle
              Ellis and Max Wilcox; Edinburgh: T & T Clark), pp. 119–
              128.

6:6b–13

731   1972   G. Testa, "Studio di Mc 6,6b–13 secondo il metodo della
              storia della tradizione," DivThom 75:177–191.(N 17–534)

6:7–13

See also 1514, 1526.

732   1974   J. Delorme, "La mission des Douze en Galilée. Mc 6,7–13,"
              AsSeign 46:43–50.   (N 19–109)

6:8–9

733   1979   L. Legrand, "Bare foot Apostles? The shoes of St. Mark
              (Mk. 6:8–9 and parallels)," IndTheolStud 16:201–219.
                                                           (N 24–436)
6:10

734   1976   G. M. Lee, "Two Notes on St. Mark," NovT 18:36.(N 20–796)

6:11

735 1969 G. B. Caird, "Uncomfortable Words II. Shake off the Dust
      from Your Feet (Mk 6:11)," ExpTim 81:40-43. (N 14-506)

6:14-8:30

See 267.

6:14-17, 17-20

See 301.

6:15

See 1454.

6:17-29

736 1977 D. Losada, "La muerte de Juan el Bautista. Mc 6,17-29,"
      RevistB 39:143-154.   (N 22-777)

737 1973 J. Gnilka, "Das Martyrium Johannes' des Täufers (Mk 6,17-
      29)," in Orientierung an Jesus: Zur Theologie der Syn-
      optiker: Für Josef Schmid (ed. by Paul Hoffmann in col-
      laboration with Norbert Brox and Wilhelm Pesch; Frei-
      burg/Basel/Vienna: Herder), pp. 78-92.

738 1966 I. de la Potterie, "Mors Johannis Baptistae (Mc 6,17-29),"
      VD 44:142-151.   (N 11-722)

739 1965 J. D. M. Derrett, "Herod's Oath and the Baptist's Head
      (With an Appendix on Mk IX. 12-13, Mal III. 24, Micah
      VII. 6)," BZ 9:49-59, 233-246.   (N 10-135,533)
      [Republished in Derrett, Law in the New Testament
      (London: Darton, Longman & Todd, 1970/New York: Fern-
      hill House, 1971), pp. 339-362.]

6:17

740 1970 W. A. A. Wilson, "Who Married Herodias? (And Other Ques-
      tions from the Gospel of Mark)," BT 21:138-140.
                                              (N 15-517)

6:30 - 8:26

741 1978 C. Combet-Galland, "Analyse structurale de Marc 6,30 à 8,
      26," in Marc 6:30 - 8:26: Lectures en Dialogue (Cahiers
      Bibliques 17 of Foi et Vie; Paris: Foi et Vie 77), pp.
      34-46.

742   1968   A.-M. Denis, "La section des pains selon S. Marc (6,30 -
             8,26), une théologie de l'Eucharistie," in Studia Evan-
             gelica 4,1: Papers Presented to the Third International
             Congress on New Testament Studies held at Christ Church,
             Oxford, 1965: Part I. The Scriptures (ed. by F. L. Cross;
             Berlin: Akademie Verlag), pp. 171-179.

743   1966   T. A. Burkill, "Mk 6,31-8,26. The Context of the Story of
             the Syrophoenician Woman," in The Classical Tradition:
             Literary and Historical Studies in Honor of Harry Caplan
             (ed. by Luitpold Wallach; Ithaca, NY: Cornell University
             Press), pp. 329-344.

744   1959   A.-M. Denis, "Une théologie de la vie chrétienne chez saint
             Marc (VI, 30 - VIII,27)," VSpir 41:416-427. (N 4-397)

6:30 - 8:21

745   1972   F. C. Synge, "Common Bread. The Craftsmanship of a Theo-
             logian," Theology 75:131-135.   (N 16-881)

6:30 - 7:30

746   1978   P. Bonnard, "La méthode historico-critique appliquée à
             Marc 6,30 à 7,30," in Marc 6:30 - 8:26: Lectures en Di-
             alogue (Cahiers Bibliques 17 of Foi et Vie; Paris: Foi
             et Vie 77), pp. 6-18.

6:30-56

See 263.

6:30-53

747   1979   G. Pace, "La prima moltiplicazione dei pani. Topografia,"
             BeO 21:85-91.   (N 24-110)

747a 1977   Groupe d'Entrevernes, "'Ils n'avaient pas compris au sujet
             des pains...' Plusieurs épisodes, un récit, Mc 6,30-53,"
             in Signes et Paraboles: sémiotique et texte évangélique
             (Paris: Seuil), pp. 53-91.
                 [The book is available in English as Signs and Para-
                 bles. Semiotics and Gospel Texts, by the Entrevernes
                 Group. Tr. by G. Phillips. Pittsburgh Theological
                 Monograph Series 23. Pittsburgh: Pickwick Press,
                 1978.)

748   1963   J. O'Hara, "Two Bethsaidas or One?" Scr 15:24-27.(N 8-147)

6:30-46

749   1976   R. Trevijano Etcheverría, "Historia de milagro y cristolo-

gía en la multiplicación de los panes," Burgense 17:9-
38.   (N 21-96)

750   1975   R. Trevijano Etcheverría, "Crisis mesiánica en la multiplicación de los panes (Mc 6,30-46 y Jn 6,1-15)," Burgense 16:413-439.   (N 20-797)

751   1974   R. Trevijano Etcheverría, "La multiplicación de los panes
(Mc 6,30-46; 8,1-10 y par.)," Burgense 15:435-465.
                                                          (N 19-555)

6:30-44

See also 284.

752   1979   R. M. Fowler, "The Feeding of the Five Thousand: A Markan
Composition," in Society of Biblical Literature 1979
Seminar Papers I (ed. by Paul J. Achtemeier; Missoula,
MT: Scholars Press), pp. 101-104.

753   1976   J. Hug and C. Devaud, "Mc 6:30-44: La multiplication des
pains," Bulletin du Centre Protestant d'Études 28:20-21,
21-24.

754   L. Williamson, Jr., "An Exposition of Mark 6:30-44," Int
30:169-173.

755   1975   Jean Marie VAN CANGH. La multiplication des pains et
l'Eucharistie. Lectio Divina 86. Paris: Éditions du
Cerf. 197 pp.   (E 57-3834)

756   1972   T. Suriano, "Eucharist Reveals Jesus: The Multiplication
of the Loaves," TBT 58:642-651.   (N 16-880)

757   1969   R. Dross, "Die Bedeutung didaktischer Konzeptionen für die
Interpretation biblischer Texte, dargestellt an Mk 6,30-
44," in Theologie und Unterricht: über die Repräsentanz
des Christlichen in der Schule. Festgabe für Hans Stock
zu seinem 65. Geburtstag (ed. by Klaus Wegenast; Gütersloh: Gütersloher Verlagshaus Gerd Mohn), pp. 65-78.

758   1960   G. Ziener, "Die Brotwunder im Markusevangelium," BZ 4:282-
285.   (N 5-407)

6:30-32

759   1962   H. Montefiore, "Revolt in the Desert? (Mark vi. 30ff.),"
NTS 8:135-141.   (N 6-788)

6:31-44

760   1964   G. Friedrich, "Die beiden Erzählungen von der Speisung in

Mark. 6,31-44; 8,1-9," <u>TZ</u> 20:10-22.   (N 9-938)

6:32 - 15:47

See 192.

6:32-44

See also 153.

761 1976   R. H. Hiers and C. A. Kennedy, "The Bread and Fish Euchar-
            ist in the Gospels and Early Christian Art," <u>PerspRel-</u>
            <u>Stud</u> 3:20-47.   (N 20-798)

762 1974   J.-M. van Cangh, "La multiplication des pains dans l'évan-
            gile de Marc: Essai d'exégèse globale," in <u>L'évangile</u>
            <u>selon Marc: Tradition et rédaction</u> (ed. by M. Sabbe; Bib-
            liotheca ephemeridum theologicarum lovaniensium 34; Gem-
            bloux/Louvain: Duculot/Leuven University), pp. 309-346.

6:34-44

763 1969   A. Heising, "Das Kerygma der wunderbaren Fischvermehrung
            (Mk 6,34-44 parr)," <u>BibLeb</u> 10:52-57.   (N 14-164)

764 1961   A. Shaw, "The Marcan Feeding Narratives," <u>CQR</u> 162:268-278.
                                                           (N 6-467)

765 1955   E. Stauffer, "Zum apokalyptischen Festmahl in Mk 6,34ff.,"
            <u>ZNW</u> 46:264-266.   (N 1-44)

6:35-44

766 1971   G. Ory, "Des pains, des poissons et des hommes," <u>CahCerc-</u>
            <u>ErnRen</u> 18:21-28.   (N 16-179)

767   J.-M. van Cangh, "Le thème des poissons dans les récits
            évangéliques de la multiplication des pains," <u>RB</u> 78:71-
            83.   (N 16-178)

768 1964   B. van Iersel, "Die wunderbare Speisung und das Abendmahl
            in der synoptischen Tradition (Mk vi 35-44 par., viii 1-
            20 par.)," <u>NovT</u> 7:167-194.   (N 10-136)

6:37

769 1978   J. A. Grassi, "'You yourselves give them to eat.' An easi-
            ly forgotten command of Jesus (Mk 6:37; Mt. 14:16; Lk.
            9:13)," <u>TBT</u> 97:1704-1709.   (N 23-116)

6:38

770 1978 E. Repo, "Fünf Brote und zwei Fische," in Probleme der Forschung (ed. by Albert Fuchs; Studien zum Neuen Testament
und seiner Umwelt, Ser. A:3; Vienna/Munich: Herold), pp.
99-113.
[Originally appeared in Finnish in Teologinen Aikakaus-
kirja 73 (1968):331-342, with the German version somewhat expanded.]

6:40

771 1975 J. D. M. Derrett, "Leek-beds and Methodology," BZ 19:101-
103.   (N 19-973)
[Republished in Derrett, Studies in the New Testament
2: Midrash in Action and as a Literary Device (Leiden:
E. J. Brill, 1978), pp. 1-3.

6:41-42

772 1975 I. de la Potterie, "Le sens primitif de la multiplication
des pains," in Jésus aux origines de la christologie (ed.
by J. Dupont; Bibliotheca ephemeridum theologicarum lovaniensium 40; Gembloux/Leuven: Duculot/Louvain University), pp. 303-329.

6:45-52

773 1979 H. Ritt, "Der 'Seewandel Jesu' (Mk 6,45-52 par). Literar-
ische und theologische Aspekte," BZ 23:71-84.(N 23-847)

774 1976 D. Losada, "Jesús camina sobre las aguas. Un relato apocalíptico," RevistB 38:311-319.   (N 21-749)

775 1969 J. Kremer, "Jesu Wandel auf dem See nach Mk 6,45-52. Auslegung und Meditation," BibLeb 10:221-232. (N 14-507)

776 1968 Thierry SNOY. La Rédaction Marcienne de la Marche sur les
Eaux. Mc. VI, 45-52. Analecta Lovaniensia Biblica et
Orientalia, Ser. IV, Fasc. 44. Brugges--Paris/Gembloux:
Desclée de Brouwer/Éditions J. Duculot).
[Originally published as a two-part article with the
same title in ETL 44:205-241, 433-481.(N 13-194,881)]

6:48

777 1974 T. Snoy, "Marc 6,48: '...et il voulait les dépasser': Pro-
position pour la solution d'une énigme," in L'évangile
selon Marc: Tradition et rédaction (ed. by M. Sabbe; Bibliotheca ephemeridum theologicarum lovaniensium 34; Gem-
bloux/Leuven: Duculot/Louvain University), pp. 347-363.

6:52

778   1969   Quentin QUESNELL, S.J.   The Mind of Mark.   Interpretation
               and Method through the Exegesis of Mk 6,52.   Analecta
               Biblica 38.   Rome: Pontifical Biblical Institute.   xxiv-
               327 pp.   (E 51-2405)

6:53-56

See 153.

6:53

779   1975   G. Rinaldi, "Traversata del lago e sbarco a Genezaret in
               'Marco' 6,53," BeO 17:43-46.   (N 20-799)

7:1-23

780   1977   J. Lambrecht, "Jesus and the Law.   An Investigation of Mk
               7,1-23," ETL 53:24-82.   (N 22-104)

781   1976   H. Hübner, "Mark vii. 1-23 und das 'Jüdisch-Hellenistische'
               Gesetzesverständnis," NTS 22:319-345.   (N 21-97)

782   1972   N. J. McEleney, "Authenticating Criteria and Mark 7:1-23,"
               CBQ 34:431-460.   (N 17-535)

783   1970   R. Pesch, "Pur et impur: Précepte humain et commandement
               divin, Mc 7,1-8.14-15.21-23," AsSeign 53:50-59.

7:3

784   1976   W. D. McHardy, "Mark 7:3--A Reference to the Old Testa-
               ment?" ExpTim 87:119.   (N 20-800)

785   J. M. Ross, "'With the Fist,'" ExpTim 87:374-375.(N 21-98)

786   1971   S. M. Reynolds, "A Note on Dr. Hengel's Interpretation of
               pygmē in Mark 7:3," ZNW 62:295-296.   (N 16-882)

787   1969   M. Hengel, "Mc 7:3 pygmē: Die Geschichte einer exegetisch-
               en Aporie und der Versuch ihrer Lösung," ZNW 60:182-
               198.   (N 14-870)

788   1966   S. M. Reynolds, "PYGMHI (Mark 7:3) as 'Cupped Hand'," JBL
               85:87-88.   (N 10-925)

789   1957   P. R. Weis, "A Note on Pygmei," NTS 3:233-236.(N 2-54)

7:6-13

See 144.

7:11

790   1970   J. D. M. Derrett, "KORBAN, HO ESTIN DŌRON," NTS 16:364–
            368.   (N 15-163)
            [Republished in Derrett, Studies in the New Testament
            I: Glimpses of the Legal and Social Presuppositions
            of the Authors (Leiden: E. J. Brill, 1977), pp. 112–
            117.]

791   1968   S. Zeitlin, "Korban: A Gift," JQR 59:133-135. (N 13-882)

792   1964   J. Bligh, "'Qorban!'," HeyJ 5:192-193.   (N 9-169)

793   1962   S. Zeitlin, "Korban," JQR 53:160-163.   (N 8-148)

794   1959   J. A. Fitzmyer, "The Aramaic Qorbān Inscription from Jebel
            Hallet et-Ṭûri and Mark 7:11/Matt 15:5," JBL 78:60-65.
                                                                (N 4-88)
            [Republished in Fitzmyer, Essays on the Semitic Back-
            ground of the New Testament (London: Geoffrey Chap-
            man, 1971), pp. 93-100.]

7:14-23

See 115, 183.

7:14

795   1968   C. Carlston, "The Things that Defile (Mark vii. 14) and
            the Law in Matthew and Mark," NTS 15:75-96. (N 13-883)

7:15-23

796   1975   J. D. M. Derrett, "Marco VII 15-23: il vero significato di
            'purificare'," Conoscenza Religiosa 1975,2:125-130.
            [Republished in Derrett, Studies in the New Testament
            I: Glimpses of the Legal and Social Presuppositions
            of the Authors (Leiden: E. J. Brill, 1977), pp. 176–
            183.]

7:15

797   1970   J. Domon, "Du texte au sermon: Mc 7,15," ÉTR 45:349-354.

798   1968   H. Merkel, "Markus 7,15 – das Jesuswort über die innere
            Verunreinigung," ZRGG 20:340-363.   (N 14-165)

7:24-30(31)

799   1977   A. Dermience, "Tradition et rédaction dans la péricope de
            la Syrophénicienne: Marc 7,24-30," RTL 8:15-29.
                                                                (N 21-750)

800   1973   J. D. M. Derrett, "Law in the New Testament: The Syrophoe-
             nician Woman and the Centurion of Capernaum," NovT 15:
             161-186.   (N 18-876)
                 [Republished in Derrett, Studies in the New Testament
                 I: Glimpses of the Legal and Social Pre-suppositions
                 of the Authors (Leiden: E. J. Brill, 1977), pp. 143-
                 169.]

801   1968   T. A. Burkill, "The Syrophoenician Woman: Mark 7,24-31,"
             in Studia Evangelica 4,1: Papers Presented to the Third
             International Congress on New Testament Studies held at
             Christ Church, Oxford, 1965: Part I. The Scriptures (ed.
             by F. L. Cross; Berlin: Akademie Verlag), pp. 166-170.

802   B. Flammer, "Die Syrophoenizerin. Mk 7,24-30," TQ 148:
             463-478.   (N 14-166)
                 [Translated and digested as "The Syro-Phoenician Woman
                 (Mk 7:24-30)," TD 18 (1970):19-24.]

803   1967   T. A. Burkill, "The historical development of the story of
             the Syrophoenician woman (Mark vii: 24-31)," NovT 9:161-
             177.   (N 12-565)
                 [Republished as "The Life History of Mark 7:24-31,"
                 in Burkill, New Light on the Earliest Gospel: Seven
                 Markan Studies (Ithaca, NY: Cornell University, 1972),
                 pp. 96-120. This title combines the NovT 9 (1967)
                 article with the one that appeared in Studia Evangeli-
                 ca 4,1 (1968).]

804   1966   T. A. Burkill, "The Syrophoenician Woman: The Context of
             Mark 7:24-31," in The Classical Tradition: Literary and
             Historical Studies in Honor of Harry Caplan (ed. by L.
             Wallach; Ithaca, NY: Cornell University), pp. 329-344.
                 [Republished in Burkill, New Light on the Earliest Gos-
                 pel: Seven Markan Studies (Ithaca, NY: Cornell Uni-
                 versity, 1972), pp. 48-70.]

805   T. A. Burkill, "The Syrophoenician Woman: The congruence
             of Mark 7:24-31," ZNW 57:23-37.   (N 11-241)
                 [Republished as "The Congruence of Mark 7:24-31," in
                 Burkill, New Light on the Earliest Gospel: Seven Mark-
                 an Studies (Ithaca, NY: Cornell University, 1972), pp.
                 71-95.]

806   1963   J. Alonso Díaz, "Cuestión sinóptica y universalidad del
             mensaje cristiano en el pasaje evangélico de la mujer ca-
             nanea (Mc 7,24-30; Mt 15,21-28)," CB 20:274-279.(N 8-963)

7:25-30

See 1526.

7:28

807   1970   W. Storch, "Zur Perikope von der Syrophönizierin. Mk 7,28
und Ri 1,7," BZ 14:256-257.   (N 15-525)

7:31-37

808   1978   U. Ruegg, H. Stotzer-Kloo, and M. Voser, "Zur Kommunika-
tion befreit. Jesus heilt einen Taubstummen (Markus 7,
31-37). Ein Heilungswunder," in Wunder Jesu (ed. by Anton Steiner; Bibelarbeit in der Gemeinde 2; Basel/Zürich:
Reinhardt/Benziger), pp. 59-76.

809   1976   I. Paci, "Simbologia o storia? A proposito d'un testo di
S. Mc 7,31-37," PalCler 55:1204-1206.

810   1963   L. Leloir, "L'Évangile," ⌜du 11e Dimanche après la Pente-
côte⌝ AsSeign 65:31-41.

7:31

811   1978   F. G. Lang, "'Über Sidon mitten ins Gebiet der Dekapolis,'
Geographie und Theologie in Markus 7,31," ZDPV 94:145-
160.   (N 23-848)

7:34

812   1972   S. Morag, "Ephphatha (Mark vii. 34): Certainly Hebrew, not
Aramaic?" JSS 17:198-202.   (N 17-536)

813   1971   I. Rabinowitz, "Ephphatha (Mark vii. 34): Certainly Hebrew,
Not Aramaic," JSS 16:151-156.   (N 16-883)

814   1962   I. Rabinowitz, "'Be Opened' = Ephphatha (Mark 7:34): Did
Jesus Speak Hebrew?" ZNW 53:229-238.   (N 7-795)

8:1-10

See also 751, 755, 756, 758, 760, 765, 766, 767.

815   1969   E. S. English, "A Neglected Miracle," BS 126:300-305.
        (N 14-508)

816   1963   J. Comblin, "L'Évangile" ⌜du 6e Dimanche après la Pente-
côte⌝ AsSeign 60:28-39.

8:3

817   1963   F. W. Danker, "Mark 8:3," JBL 82:215-216.   (N 8-149)

8:10

See also 216.

818   1971   F. Pili, "Dalmanutha (Mc 8,10)," BeO 13:227-230.

8:11-12

819   1974   A. Ambrozic, "Die Zeichenforderung und der christliche Di-
alog mit der Welt," in Biblische Randbemerkungen: Schülerfestschrift für Rudolf Schnackenburg zum 60. Geburtstag (ed. by Helmut Merklein and Joachim Lange; Würzburg:
Echter-Verlag), pp. 273-282.

820   1972   D. Merli, "Il segno di Giona," BeO 14:61-77.   (N 18-491)

821   1965   O. Linton, "The Demand for a Sign from Heaven. (Mk 8,11-
12 and Parallels)," ST 19:112-129.   (N 11-242)

8:14-21

See also 115.

822   1981   N. A. Beck, "Reclaiming a Biblical Text: The Mark 8:14-21
Discussion about Bread in the Boat," CBQ 43:49-56.

823   1978   F. McCombie, "Jesus and the Leaven of Salvation," NewBlack-
fr 59:450-462.   (N 23-468)

824   1964   J. Mánek, "Mark viii 14-21," NovT 7:10-14.   (N 9-939)

8:15

825   1967   A. Negōitā and C. Daniel, "L'énigme du levain. Ad Mc. viii
15; Mt. xvi 6; et Lc. xii 1," NovT 9:306-314.(N 12-888)

826   1958   G. Ziener, "Das Bildwort vom Sauerteig Mk 8,15," TTZ 67:
247-248.   (N 3-360)

8:18

827   1966   A. J. Jewell, "Did St. Mark 'Remember'?" LondQuartHolRev
35:117-120.   (N 11-243)

8:22 - 10:52

828   1980   J. F. O'Grady, "Reflections on The Passion in Mark," BTB
10:83-87.   (N 24-808)

829   1970   E. Best, "Discipleship in Mark: Mark 8.22-10.52," SJT 23:
323-337.   (N 15-526)

8:22-26

830 1979 E. S. Johnson, "Mark viii. 22-26: The Blind Man from Bethsaida," NTS 25:370-383. (N 23-849)

831 1975 G. Walker, "The Blind Recover Their Sight," ExpTim 87:23.
(N 20-460)

832 1968 R. Beauvery, "La guérison d'un aveugle à Bethsaïde (Mc 8,
22-26)," NRT 90:1083-1091. (N 13-884)

8:24

833 1978 G. M. Lee, "Mark viii 24," NovT 20:74. (N 23-117)

8:27 - 10:52

See also 1439, 1519, 1592.

834 1978 Wilhelm EGGER. Glaube und Nachfolge. Ein Arbeitsheft zum
Markusevangelium. Gespräche zur Bibel 5. Klosterneu-
burg: Österreichisches Katholisches Bibelwerk. 36 pp.

835 1974 D. C. Duling, "Interpreting the Markan 'Hodology': Biblical Criticism in Preaching and Teaching," Nexus 17:2-11.
(N 19-110)

836 1972 H.-J. Venetz, "Widerspruch und Nachfolge. Zur Frage des
Glaubens an Jesus nach Mk 8,27 - 10,52," FreibZeitPhil-
Theol 19:111-119. (N 17-143)

837 1964 H. Simonsen, "Mark. 8,27 - 10,52 i Markusevangeliets komposition," DTT 27:83-99. (N 9-558)

838 1956 C. E. Faw, "The Heart of the Gospel of Mark," JBR 24:77-
82. (N 1-394)

8:27 - 10:45

See 262.

8:27 - 9:13

See 1447.

839 1973 Maria HORSTMANN. Studien zur markinischen Christologie:
Mk 8:27 - 9:13 als Zugang zum Christus bild des zweiten
Evangeliums. 2nd ed. [1rst ed.: 1969] Neutestamentliche
Abhandlungen, N.F. Band 6. Münster: Aschendorff. vi-
150 pp. (E 55-2931)

840   1969   R. Lafontaine and P. Mourlon Beernaert, "Essai sur la
             structure de Marc, 8,27 - 9,13," RSR 57:543-561.
                                                   (N 14-871)

8:27 - 9:1

841   1976   J. L. Mays, "An Exposition of Mark 8,27 - 9:1," Int 30:174-
             178.

842   1975   D. A. Koch, "Zum Verhältnis von Christologie und Eschatolo-
             gie im Markusevangelium: Beobachtungen auf Grund von 8,
             27 - 9,1," in Jesus Christus in Historie und Theologie:
             neutestamentliche Festschrift für Hans Conzelmann zum 60.
             Geburtstag (ed. by Georg Strecker; Tübingen: Mohr), pp.
             395-408.

843   1963   E. Haenchen, "Die Komposition von Mk viii 27 - ix 1 und
             Par.," NovT 6:81-109.   (N 8-964)
               [Republished as "Leidens-nachfolge. Eine Studie zu Mk
               8,27 - 9,1 und den kanonischen Parallelen" in Haenchen
               Die Bibel und Wir (Tübingen: Mohr, 1968), pp. 102-
               134.]

8:27-35

844   1974   A. Denaux, "La confession de Pierre et la première annonce
             de la Passion. Mc 8,27-35," AsSeign 55:31-39.(N 19-557)

8:27-33

See also 1590.

845   1978   J. Ernst, "Petrusbekenntnis--Leidensankündigung--Satans-
             wort (Mk 8,27-33). Tradition und Redaktion," Catholica
             32:46-73.   (N 23-118)

846   1969   A. Denaux, "Petrusbelijdenis en eerste lijdensvoorspelling.
             Een exegese van Mc. 8,27-33 par. Lc. 9, 18-22," CollBrug-
             Gand 15:188-220.   (N 14-509)

847   1967   C. M. Martini, "La confessione messianica di Pietro a Cae-
             sarea e l'inizio del nuovo popolo di Dio secondo il Van-
             gelo di S. Marco (8, 27-33)," CivCatt 118:544-551.
                                                          (N 12-180)

8:27-30

848   1974   R. Pesch, "Das Messiasbekenntnis des Petrus (Mk 8,27-30).
             Neuverhandlung einer alten Frage (Schluss)," BZ 18:20-31.
                                                          (N 19-556)

849   1973   R. Pesch, "Das Messiasbekenntnis des Petrus (Mk 8,27-30).
             Neuverhandlung einer alten Frage," BZ 17:178-195(N18-492)

850   1962s   K. Schubert, "Die Juden und die Römer," <u>BLit</u> 36:235-242.

<u>8:28</u>

See 1454.

<u>8:29</u>

851   1978   H. Frankemölle, "Jüdische Messiaserwartung und christlicher
             Messiasglaube. Hermeneutische Anmerkungen im Kontext des
             Petrusbekenntnisses Mk 8,29," <u>Kairos</u> 20:97-109.(N 23-469)

852   1977   J. Althaisen, "Wer sagt denn ihr, dass ich sei? (Mk 8,
             29)," <u>Lutherische Rundschau</u> 27:89-100.

<u>8:31 - 11:10</u>

See 1590, 1596.

<u>8:31-38</u>

853   1974   J. B. Metz, "Messianische Geschichte als Leidensgeschichte:
             Meditation zu Mk 8,31-38," in <u>Neues Testament und Kirche:
             Für Rudolf Schnackenburg</u> (ed. by Joachim Gnilka; Frei-
             burg/Basel/Vienna: Herder), pp. 63-70.

854   Johann Baptist METZ and Jürgen MOLTMANN. <u>Leidensgeschicht-
             e: Zwei Meditationen zu Markus 8,31-38.</u> Freiburg/Basel/
             Vienna: Herder. 58 pp.   (E 55-2934)

<u>8:31</u>

See also 1594 - 1599.

855   1976   A. Pérez Gordo, "Notas sobre los anuncios de la Pasión,"
             <u>Burgense</u> 17:251-270.   (N 21-99)

856   1975   W. J. Bennett, Jr., "'The son of man must...,'" <u>NovT</u> 17:
             113-129.   (N 20-103)

857   1973   P. Hoffmann, "Mk 8,31. Zur Herkunft und markinischen Re-
             zeption einer alten Überlieferung," in <u>Orientierung an
             Jesus: Zur Theologie der Synoptiker: Für Josef Schmid</u>
             (ed. by Paul Hoffmann in collaboration with Norbert Brox
             and Wilhelm Pesch; Freiburg/Basel/Vienna: Herder), pp.
             170-204.

858   1971   O. Michel, "Der Umbruch: Messianität = Menschensohn: Frag-
             en zu Markus 8,31," in <u>Tradition und Glaube: Das frühe
             Christentum in seiner Umwelt: Festgabe für Karl Georg
             Kuhn zum 65. Geburtstag</u> (ed. by Gert Jeremias, Heinz-

Wolfgang Kuhn, and Hartmut Stegemann; Göttingen: Vandenhoeck & Ruprecht), pp. 310-316.

859   1964   D. Meyer, "POLLA PATHEIN," ZNW 55:132.   (N 9-559)

8:33

See also 1531.

860   1974   C. Kazmierski, "Mk 8,33--Eine Ermahnung an die Kirche?"
             in Biblische Randbemerkungen: Schülerfestschrift für Ru-
             dolf Schnackenburg zum 60. Geburtstag (ed. by Helmut
             Merklein and Joachim Lange; Würzburg: Echter-Verlag), pp.
             103-112.

861   1973   B. A. E. Osborne, "Peter: Stumbling-Block and Satan," NovT
             15:187-190.   (N 18-878)

862   1963s T. Arvedson, "Lärjungaskapets 'demoni.' Några reflexioner
             till Mk 8,33 par.," SEÅ 28-29:54-63.   (N 10-137)

8:34-38

863   1961   A. Kahmann, "Het volgen van Christus door zelfverloochen-
             ing en kruisdragen volgens Mark. 8,34-38 par.," TijdTheol
             1:205-226.   (N 6-789)

864   1957   H. Kahlefeld, "Jünger des Herrn," GeistLeb 30:1-6.(N 2-53)

8:34-35

865   1955   J. J. Vincent, "The Evangelium of Jesus," JBR 23:266-271.

8:34

866   1975   G. Schwarz, "'...aparnēsasthō heauton...'? (Markus viii 34
             Parr.)," NovT 17:109-112.   (N 20-104)

867   1970   J. G. Griffiths, "The Disciple's Cross," NTS 16:358-364.
                                                           (N 15-164)

868   1964   D. R. Fletcher, "Condemned to Die. The Logion on Cross-
             bearing: What Does It Mean?" Int 18:156-164.(N 9-170)

8:35

869   1979   W. A. Beardslee, "Saving One's Life By Losing It," JAAR
             47:57-72.   (N 24-111)

870   1967   J. Sudbrack, "'Wer sein Leben um meinetwillen verliert...'
             (Mk 8,35). Biblische Überlegungen zur Grundlegung

christlicher Existenz," GeistLeb 40:161-170.(N 12-182)

871   1963   J. B. Bauer, "'Wer sein Leben retten will...' (Mk 8,35
Parr.)," in Neutestamentliche Aufsätze: Festschrift für
Prof. Josef Schmid zum 70. Geburtstag (ed. by J. Blinz-
ler, O. Kuss, and F. Mussner; Regensburg: Friedrich Pus-
tet), pp. 7-10.
[Republished in Bauer, Scholia biblica et patristica
(Graz: Akademische Druck- u. Verlagsanstalt, 1972),
pp. 41-46.]

8:37

872   1974   M. Herranz, "' ¿Qué dará el hombre a cambio de su alma?'
(Mc 8,37)," CB 31:23-26.

8:38

See also 1480.

873   1980   B. Lindars, "Jesus as Advocate: A Contribution to the
Christology Debate," BJRL 62:476-497.

874   1975   W. G. Kümmel, "Das Verhalten Jesus gegenüber und das Verhalten des Menschensohns. Markus 8,38 par. und Lukas
12,8f. par. Matthäus 10,32f.," in Jesus und den Menschensohn: Für Anton Vögtle (ed. by Rudolf Pesch and Rudolf
Schnackenburg, with Odilo Kaiser; Freiburg/Vienna/Basel:
Herder), pp. 210-224.
[Republished in Heilsgeschehen und Geschichte. Band
2. Gesammelte Aufsätze 1965 - 1977 (ed. by Erich
Grässer and Otto Merk; Marburger Theologische Studien
16; Marburg: N. G. Elwert Verlag, 1978), pp. 201-214.]

9:1

See also 1534.

875   1980   K. Brower, "Mark 9:1. Seeing the Kingdom in Power," JSNT
6:17-41.   (N 24-809)

876   1978   B. D. Chilton, "An evangelical and critical approach to the
sayings of Jesus," Themelios 3:78-85.   (N 23-119)

877   1977   H. Greeven, "Nochmals Mk ix. 1 in Codex Bezae (D,05)," NTS
23:305-308.   (N 21-751)

878   Martin KÜNZI. Das Naherwartungslogion Markus 9,1 par: Geschichte seiner Auslegung, mit einem Nachwort zur Ausle-
gungsgeschichte von Markus 13,30 par. Beiträge zur Geschichte der biblischen Exegese 21. Tübingen: J. C. B.

Mohr (Paul Siebeck). viii-247 pp.   (E 58s-4924)

879 1973 I. A. Moir, "The Reading of Codex Bezae (D-05) at Mark ix.
           1," NTS 20:105.   (N 18-493)

880 1969 N. Perrin, "The Composition of Mark ix, 1," NovT 11:67-
           70.   (N 14-167)

881 1964 É. Trocmé, "Mc 9:1: prédiction ou réprimande?" in Studia
           Evangelica II: Papers Presented to the Second Interna-
           tional Congress on New Testament Studies held at Christ
           Church, Oxford, 1961 (ed. by F. L. Cross; Texte und Un-
           tersuchungen zur Geschichte der altchristlichen Litera-
           tur 87; Berlin: Akademie Verlag), pp. 259-265.

9:2-29

882 1959 A.-M. Denis, "Une théologie de la Rédemption. La Trans-
           figuration chez saint Marc," VSpir 41:136-149.(N 4-398)

9:(1)2-13

883 1977 Enrique NARDONI. La transfiguración de Jesús y el diálogo
           sobre Elías según el Evangelio de San Marcos. Teología,
           Estudios y Documentos 2. Buenos Aires: Ediciones de la
           Facultad de Teología de la Universidad Católica Argen-
           tina/Editora Patria Grande. 254 pp.   (E 58s-4923)

884 1970 F. C. Synge, "The Transfiguration Story," ExpTim 82:82-83.
                                                     (N 15-873)

885 1964 C. Masson, "La transfiguration de Jésus (Marc 9:2-13),"
           RTP 97:1-14.   (N 9-171)

9:(1)2-10

886 1980 M. Smith, "The Origin and History of the Transfiguration
           Story," USQR 36:39-44.

887 1977 A. Fuchs, "Die Verklärungserzählung des Mk-Ev in der Sicht
           moderner Exegese," TPQ 125:29-37.   (N 22-105)

888 1975 L. Soubigou, "A Transfiguração de Cristo Segundo São Mar-
           cos (9,1-10)," RCB 12:59-72.   (N 21-100)

889 1974 B. Trémel, "Des récits apocalyptiques: Baptême et Trans-
           figuration," LumVie 23:70-83.   (N 19-974)

890 1973 M. Coune, "Radieuse Transfiguration. Mt 17,1-9; Mc 9,2-
           10; Lc 9,28-36," AsSeign 15:44-84.   (N 17-948)

891   Johannes M. NÜTZEL. <u>Die Verklärungserzählung im Markus-evangelium. Eine redaktionsgeschichtliche Untersuchung</u>. Forschung zur Bibel 6. Würzburg: Echter Verlag. v plus viii-327 pp.   (E 55-2942)

892   1972   S. Gennarini, "Le principali interpretazioni postliberali della pericope della trasfigurazione di Gesù," <u>Rivist-StorLettRel</u> 8:80-132.   (N 17-537)

893   H. C. Kee, "The Transfiguration in Mark: Epiphany or Apocalyptic Vision?" in <u>Understanding the Sacred Text: Essays in Honor of Morton S. Enslin on the Hebrew Bible and Christian Beginnings</u> (ed. by John Reumann; Valley Forge, PA: Judson Press), pp. 135-152.

894   1970   M. E. Thrall, "Elijah and Moses in Mark's account of the Transfiguration," <u>NTS</u> 16:305-317.   (N 15-166)

895   J. A. Ziesler, "The Transfiguration Story and the Markan Soteriology," <u>ExpTim</u> 81:263-268.   (N 15-167)

896   1969   L. F. Rivera, "El relato de la Transfiguración en la redacción del evangelio de Marcos," <u>RevistB</u> 31:143-158, 229-243.   (N 14-872)

897   1968   L. F. Rivera, "Interpretatio Transfigurationis Jesu in redactione evangelii Marci," <u>VD</u> 46:99-104.   (N 13-588)

898   1967   W. Gerber, "Die Metamorphose Jesu, Mark. 9, 2f. par.," <u>TZ</u> 23:385-395.   (N 12-889)

899   1965   R. Silva, "El relato de la transfiguración. Problemas de crítica literaria y motivos teológicos en Mc 9,2-10; Mt 17,1-9; Lc 9,28-37," <u>Compostellanum</u> 10:5-26.

<u>9:2-8</u>

900   1979   A. A. Trites, "The Transfiguration of Jesus: The Gospel in Microcosm," <u>EvQ</u> 51:67-79.   (N 23-850)

901   1976   R. H. Stein, "Is the Transfiguration (Mark 9:2-8) a Misplaced Resurrection-Account?" <u>JBL</u> 95:79-96. (N 20-801)

902   1973   U. B. Müller, "Die christologische Absicht des Markusevangeliums und die Verklärungsgeschichte," <u>ZNW</u> 64:159-193.   (N 19-111)

903   1960   H.-P. Müller, "Die Verklärung Jesu. Eine motivgeschichtliche Studie," <u>ZNW</u> 51:56-64.   (N 5-408)

9:2-3

904   1966   L. F. Rivera, "El misterio del Hijo del Hombre en la trans-
             figuración (Mr 9,2-3)," RevistB 28:19-34.   (N 11-244)

9:2

905   1980   E. L. Schnellbächer, "KAI META HĒMERAS HEX (Markus 9,2),"
             ZNW 71:252-257.

906   1974   F. R. McCurley, Jr., "'And after Six Days' (Mark 9:2): A
             Semitic Literary Device," JBL 93:67-81.   (N 18-879)

9:4-5

See 1454.

9:4

907   1970   D. Baly, "The Transfiguration Story, ExpTim 82:83.
                                                      (N 15-874)
9:7-13

908   1966   L. F. Rivera, "El misterio del Hijo del hombre en la Trans-
             figuración," RevistB 28:79-89.   (N 11-723)

9:11-13

See also 1454.

909   1967   A. Ragot, "Le retour d'Élie," Bulletin du Cercle Ernest
             Renan 15:15-16.

9:12b

See 1594.

9:12-13

See 739.

9:14-29

See also 1548, 1586.

910   1978   H. Aichinger, "Zur Traditionsgeschichte der Epileptiker-
             Perikope Mk 9,14-29 par Mt 17,14-21 par Lk 9,37-43a,"
             in Probleme der Forschung (ed. by Albert Fuchs; Studien
             zum Neuen Testament und seiner Umwelt, Ser. A:3; Vienna/
             Munich: Herold), pp. 114-143.

911   V. Weymann and H. Busslinger, "Zum Standhalten befreit.
        Jesus heilt einen besessenen Knaben (Markus 9,14-29).
        Eine Dämonenaustreibung," in Wunder Jesu (ed. by Anton
        Steiner; Bibelarbeit in der Gemeinde 2; Basel/Zürich:
        Reinhardt/Benziger), pp. 89-112.

912 1977 W. Schmithals, "Die Heilung des Epileptischen (Mk 9,14-
        29): Ein Beitrag zur notwendigen Revision der Formge-
        schichte," Theologia Viatorum 13 (1975s): 211-233.

913 1976 G. Petzke, "Die historische Frage nach den Wundertaten
        Jesu. Dargestellt am Beispiel des Exorzismus Mark. ix.ﬨ
        14-29 par," NTS 22:180-204.   (N 20-803)

914 1972 W. Schenk, "Tradition und Redaktion in der Epileptiker-
        Perikope Mk 9:14-29," ZNW 63:76-94.   (N 17-949)

915 1970 G. Bornkamm, "Pneuma alalon. Eine Studie zum Markusevan-
        gelium," in Das Altertum und jedes neue Gute. Für Wolf-
        gang Schadewaldt zum 15 März 1970 (ed. by Konrad Gaiser;
        Stuttgart/Berlin/Köln/Mainz: Kohlhammer), pp. 369-385.
            ₍Republished in Bornkamm, Geschichte und Glaube II
            (Beiträge zur evangelischen Theologie 53; Munich: Chr.
            Kaiser Verlag, 1971), pp. 21-36.₎

916 1957s H. Riesenfeld, "De fientlige andarna (Mk 9:14-29)," SEÅ
        22-23:64-74.   (N 3-593)

9:30-37

917 1976 P. J. Achtemeier, "An Exposition of Mark 9:30-37," Int 30:
        178-182.

918 1974 J. Brière, "Le Fils de l'homme livré aux hommes. Mc 9,30-
        37," AsSeign 56:42-52.   (N 19-559)

9:31

See 1594 - 1599.

9:33 - 10:31

919 1974 P. Mourlon Beernaert, "Accueillir le royaume comme fait un
        enfant. Lecture de Mc 9,33 - 10,31," La Foi et le Temps
        4:186-208.

9:33-50

920 1981 H. Fleddermann, "The Discipleship Discourse (Mark 9:33-
        50)," CBQ 43:57-75.

921 1980 J. I. H. McDonald, "Mark 9:33-50: Catechetics in Mark's

Gospel," in Studia Biblica 1978: II. Papers on the Gos-
pels. Sixth International Congress on Biblical Studies,
Oxford, 3-7 April 1978 (ed. by E. A. Livingstone; JSNT
Supplement Series 2; Sheffield: JSOT), pp. 171-177.

922   1971   R. Schnackenburg, "Mk 9,33-50," in Schnackenburg, Schrift-
en zum Neuen Testament: Exegese in Fortschritt und Wandel (München: Kösel-Verlag), pp. 129-155.
             [Originally published in Synoptische Studien: Fest-
             schrift für A. Wikenhauser (München: Karl Zink, 1953),
             pp. 184-206.]

923   1966   F. Neirynck, "The Tradition of the Sayings of Jesus: Mark
             9,33-50," (translated by Theodore L. Westow) in The Dyna-
             mism of the Biblical Tradition (Concilium 20; ed. by
             Pierre Benoit, O.P. and Roland E. Murphy, O. Carm.; New
             York: Paulist Press), pp. 62-74.

9:33-37

924   1972   A. Strus, "Mc. 9,33-37. Problema dell'autenticità e dell'
             interpretazione," RivB 20 (supplement):589-619.
                                                        (N 19-112)
9:37-39

925   1968   A. Calmet, "Pour nous...Contre nous? Marc 9,37-39," BVC
             79:52-53.   (N 12-890)

9:38-39

926   1967   H. Kosmala, "'In my name'," ASTI 5:87-109.
             [Republished in Kosmala, Studies, Essays and Reviews II
             (Leiden: E. J. Brill, 1978), pp. 25-47.]

9:40

927   1971   T. Horvath, "Is hēmōn in Mk 9,40 Authentic?" JES 8:385-
             386.   (N 16-180)

928   1956   S. Garofalo, "Mark 9,40 'apertura ecumenica'?" Euntes Do-
             cete 9:343-349.

9:42-50

929   1973   J. D. M. Derrett, "Salted with Fire. Studies in Texts:
             Mark 9:42-50," Theology 76:364-368.   (N 18-122)

9:42

930   1973   J. D. M. Derrett, "Law in the New Testament: Si scandaliz-

averit te manus tua, abscinde eam (Mk 9,42) and Comparative Legal History," Revue Internationale des Droits de l'Antiquité 20:11-36.
 ₍Republished in Derrett, Studies in the New Testament I: Glimpses of the Legal and Social Presuppositions of the Authors (Leiden: E. J. Brill, 1977), pp. 4-31.₎

9:43-47

931 1978   H. Koester, "Mark 9:43-47 and Quintilian 8.3.75," HTR 71: 151-153.
 ₍Abbreviated and republished as "Using Quintilian to Interpret Mark," Biblical Archaeology Review 6 (1980): 44-45.₎

9:49(-50)

932 1959   T. J. Baarda, "Mark ix. 49," NTS 5:318-321.   (N 4-399)

933   H. Zimmermann, "'Mit Feuer gesalzen werden.' Eine Studie zu Mk 9:49," TQ 139:28-39.   (N 4-89)

934 1957   O. Cullmann, "Que signifie le sel dans la parabole de Jésus (Mc 9,49s par.)," RHPR 37:36-43.
 ₍Republished as "Das Gleichnis vom Salz. Zur frühesten Kommentierung eines Herrenworts durch die Evangelien," in Cullmann, Vorträge und Aufsätze, 1925 - 1962 (ed. by Karlfried Fröhlich; Tübingen/Zürich: J. C. B. Mohr₍₍Paul Siebeck₎₎/Zwingli Verlag, 1966), pp. 192-201.₎

10:1 - 16:8

See 27.

10:1-12

See 144.

10:2-16

935 1974   J. Delorme, "Le mariage, les enfants et les disciples de Jésus. Mc 10, 2-16," AsSeign 58:42-51.   (N 19-560)

10:2-12

936 1978   A.-L. Descamps, "Les textes évangéliques sur le mariage," RTL 9:259-286.   (N 23-470)

937   B. Hemelsoet, "Créé à l'image de Dieu: la question du divorce dans Marc X," in Miscellanea Neotestamentica, vol.

2 (ed. by T. Baarda, A. F. J. Klihn and W. C. van Unnik; NovT Supplement 48; Leiden: E. J. Brill), pp. 49-57.

938   E. Lövestam, "De synoptiska Jesus-orden om skilsmässa och omgifte: referensramar och implikationer," SEÅ 43:65-73. (N 23-471)

939   1977   E. Lövestam, "Die funktionale Bedeutung der synoptischen Jesusworte über Ehescheidung und Wiederheirat," in Theologie aus dem Norden (ed. by Albert Fuchs; Studien zum Neuen Testament und seiner Umwelt A,2; Linz:SNTU), pp. 19-28.

940   1977   R. Trevijano Etcheverría, "Matrimonio y divorcio en Mc 10, 2-12 y par.," Burgense 18:113-151.   (N 22-106)

941   1974   D. R. Catchpole, "The Synoptic Divorce Material As A Traditio-Historical Problem," BJRL 57:92-127.   (N 20-105)

10:2(10)

942   1979   P. Ellingworth, "Text and Context in Mark 10:2, 10," JSNT 5:63-66.   (N 24-438)

10:5

943   1970   K. Berger, "Hartherzigkeit und Gottes Gesetz. Die Vorgeschichte des antijüdischen Vorwurfs in Mc 10:5," ZNW 61: 1-47.   (N 15-527)

10:6

944   1968   F. Vattioni, "A propos de Marc 10,6," SciEs 20:433-436. (N 13-885)

10:8

945   1971   T. A. Burkill, "Two into One: The Notion of Carnal Union in Mark 10:8; 1 Cor. 6:16; Eph. 5:31," ZNW 62:115-120. (N 16-181)

10:11-12

946   1973   J. P. M. Sweet, "A Saying, a Parable, a Miracle," Theology 76:125-133.

947   1970   E. Bammel, "Markus 10:11f. und das jüdische Eherecht," ZNW 61:95-101.   (N 15-528)

948   B. Schaller, "Die Sprüche über Ehescheidung und Wiederheirat in der synoptischen Überlieferung," in Der Ruf Jesu und die Antwort der Gemeinde: Exegetische Untersuchungen. Joachim Jeremias zum 70. Geburtstag gewidmet von

seinen Schülern (ed. by Eduard Lohse in collaboration
with Christoph Burchard and Berndt Schaller; Göttingen:
Vandenhoeck & Ruprecht), pp. 226-246.

10:11

949 1979 R. H. Stein, "'Is It Lawful for a Man to Divorce His
Wife?'" JournEvangTheolSoc 22:115-121.   (N 24-113)

950 1972 B. Schaller, "'Commits adultery with her', not 'against
her', Mk 10:11," ExpTim 83:107-108.   (N 16-885)

951 1960 P. Katz, "Mk 10,11 Once Again," BT 11:152.

952 1956 G. Delling, "Das Logion Mark. x 11 [und seine abwandlung-
en] im Neuen Testament," NovT 1:263-274.   (N 2-293)
[Republished in Delling, Studien zum Neuen Testament
und zum hellenistischen Judentum: Gesammelte Aufsätze
1950 - 1968 (ed. by Ferdinand Hahn, Traugott Holtz,
and Nikolaus Walter; Göttingen: Vandenhoeck & Ruprecht, 1970), pp. 226-235.]

10:13-16

953 1980 B. Vrijdaghs, "Werden wie Kinder...Die Seligpreisung der
Kinder durch Jesus," Der Evangelische Erzieher [Frank-
furt/M.] 32:170-181.   (N 25-99)

954 1976 E. Best, "Mark 10:13-16: The Child as Model Recipient," in
Biblical Studies: Essays in honour of William Barclay
(ed. by Johnston R. McKay and James F. Miller; London:
Collins), pp. 119-134.

955 1973 Gerhard KRAUSE, ed. Die Kinder im Evangelium. Praktische
Schriftauslegung 10. Stuttgart/Göttingen: Klotz. 112
pp.

956 1972 C. Perrot, "La lecture d'un texte évangelique. Essai
méthodologique à partir de Marc X, 13-16," in Le Point
Théologique 2 (Paris: Beauchesne), pp. 51-130.

10:14

957 1978 J. P. Lewis, "Mark 10:14, Koluein, and Baptizein," Restor-
Quart 21:129-134.   (N 23-472)

958 1969 J. Blinzler, "Kind und Königreich Gottes (Mk 10,14f.),"
in Blinzler, Aus der Welt und Umwelt des Neuen Testaments. Gesammelte Aufsätze 1 (Stuttgarter Biblische
Beiträge; Stuttgart: Katholisches Bibelwerk), pp. 41-53.
[Originally published in Klerusblatt 38 (1944):90-96.]

10:15

959 1973 J. I. H. McDonald, "Receiving and Entering the Kingdom: A
           Study of Mark 10:15," in Studia Evangelica 6: Papers Pre-
           sented to the Fourth International Congress on New Testa-
           ment Studies held at Oxford, 1969 (ed. by Elizabeth A.
           Livingstone; Berlin: Akademie Verlag), pp. 328-332.

960 1965 F. A. Schilling, "What Means the Saying about Receiving the
           Kingdom of God as a Little Child (tēn basileian tou theou
           hōs paidion)? Mk x. 15; Lk xviii. 17," ExpTim 77:56-58.

10:17-(30)31

See also 1586.

961 1980 W. Egger, "Nachfolge Jesu und Verzicht auf Besitz. Mk 10,
           17-31 aus der Sicht der neuesten exegetischen Methoden,"
           TPQ 128:127-136.   (N 25-100)

962 1979 Wilhelm EGGER. Nachfolge als Weg zum Leben. Chancen neuer
           exegetischer Methoden dargelegt an Mk 10,17-31. Öster-
           reichische Biblische Studien 1. Klosterneuburg: Öster-
           reichisches Katholisches Bibelwerk. vi-319 pp.

963 1978 J. M. R. Tillard, "Le propos de pauvreté et l'exigence é-
           vangélique," NRT 100:207-232.   (N 22-778)

964 1977 S. Légasse, "The Call of the Rich Man," in Gospel Poverty:
           Essays in Biblical Theology (Tr. ₍from French: 1971 ed.₎
           by Michael D. Quinan O.F.M.; Chicago: Franciscan Herald
           Press), pp. 53-80.

965 1974 S. Légasse, "Tout quitter pour suivre le Christ. Mc 10,17-
           30," AsSeign 59:43-54.   (N 19-561)

966 1972 M. Mees, "Das Paradigma vom reichen Mann und seiner Beruf-
           ung nach den Synoptikern und dem Nazaräerevangelium,"
           VetChrist 9:245-265.   (N 18-494)

967 1971 E. P. Sanders, "Mark 10:17-31 and Parallels," in Society of
           Biblical Literature 1971 Seminar Papers I (Atlanta, GA:
           Society of Biblical Literature), pp. 257-270.

968 1969 B. Celada, "Problemas acerca de la riqueza y seguimiento de
           Jesús en Mc 10:17-31," CB 26:218-222.

969 1966 S. LÉGASSE. L'appel du riche (Mc 10, 17-31 et parallèles).
           Contribution à l'étude des fondements scripturaires de
           l'état religieux. Verbum Salutis, collection annexe 1.
           Paris: Beauchesne. 294 pp.   (E 48-2432)

970   1962   N. Walter, "Zur Analyse von Mc 10:17-31," <u>ZNW</u> 53:206-218.
                                                                    (N 7-796)

971   1959   W. Zimmerli, "Die Frage des Reichen nach dem Ewigen Leben
             (Mc 10, 17-31 par.)," <u>EvT</u> 19:90-97.

10:17-27

972   1978   B. Jay, "Le jeune homme riche.   Notes homilétiques sur Marc
             10:17-27," <u>ÉTR</u> 53:252-258.

973   1973   W. Harnisch, "Die Berufung des Reichen.   Zur Analyse von
             Markus 10,17-27," in <u>Festschrift für Ernst Fuchs</u> (ed. by
             Gerhard Ebeling; Eberhard Jüngel and Gerd Schunack; Tü-
             bingen: J. C. B. Mohr [Paul Siebeck]), pp. 161-176.

10:17-22

See also 144.

974   1977   M. L. O'Hara, "Jesus' Reflections on a Psalm," <u>TBT</u> 90:1237-
             1240.   (N 21-752)

975   1975   J. Galot, "Le fondement évangélique du voeu religieux de
             pauverté," <u>Greg</u> 56:441-467.   (N 20-461)

976   1974   J. J. Degenhardt, "Was muss ich tun, um das ewige Leben zu
             gewinnen?   Zu Mk 10,17-22," in <u>Biblische Randbemerkungen:
             Schülerfestschrift für Rudolf Schnackenburg zum 60. Ge-
             burtstag</u> (ed. by Helmut Merklein and Joachim Lange; Würz-
             burg: Echter-Verlag), pp. 159-168.

977   1973   P. J. Riga, "Poverty as Counsel and as Precept," <u>TBT</u> 65:
             1123-1128.   (N 17-950)

978   J. M. van Cangh, "Fondement évangélique de la vie religi-
             euse," <u>NRT</u> 95:635-647.

979   1969   H. Troadec, "La vocation de l'homme riche," <u>VSpir</u> 120:138-
             148.   (N 13-886)

10:18

980   1969   B. Celada, "'Nadie es bueno sino sólo Dios' (Mc 10:18),"
             <u>CB</u> 26:106-108.

981   1967   G. M. Lee, "Studies in Texts: Mark 10:18," <u>Theology</u> 70:167-
             168.   (N 12-183)

10:23-31

982   1979   D. Malone, "Riches and Discipleship: Mark 10:23-31," BTB 9:
               78-88.   (N 23-851)

10:23-27

983   1964   S. Légasse, "Jésus a-t-il annoncé la Conversion Finale d'
               Israël? (A propos de Marc x. 23-7)," NTS 10:480-487.
                                                                  (N 9-172)
10:24-27

984   1974   R. Blachère, "Regards sur un passage parallèle des Évan-
               giles et du Coran," in Mélanges d'Islamologie: volume dé-
               dié à la memoire de Armand Abel par ses collègues, ses é-
               lèves et ses amis (ed. by Pierre Salmon; Leiden: E. J.
               Brill), pp. 69-73.

10:25

985   1972   R. Köbert, "Kamel und Schiffstau: Zu Markus 10,25 (Par.)
               und Koran 7,40/38," Bib 53-229-233.   (N 17-538)

986   1970   E. Best, "Uncomfortable Words: VII. The Camel and the
               Needle's Eye (Mk 10:25)," ExpTim 82:83-89.   (N 15-875)

10:28

987   1977   G. Theissen, "'Wir haben alles verlassen' (Mc. X. 28):
               Nachfolge und soziale Entwurzelung in der jüdisch-paläs-
               tinischen Gesellschaft des 1. Jahrhunderts n. Ch.," NovT
               19:161-196.   (N 22-409)
                 [Republished in Theissen, Studien zur Soziologie des
                 Urchristentums (Tübingen: Mohr [[Siebeck]], 1979), pp.
                 106-141.]

10:29-30

988   1978   J. García Burillo, "El ciento por uno (Mc 10,29-30 par).
               Historia de las interpretaciones y exégesis," EstBíb 37:
               29-55.   (N 25-101)

989   1977   H. Fürst, "Verlust der Familie--Gewinn einer neuen Familie
               (Mk 10,29f parr.)," in Studia Historico-Ecclesiastica:
               Festgabe für Luchesius G. Spätling (ed. by Isaac Vazquez;
               Rome: Pontificium Athenaeum Antonianum), pp. 17-48.

990   1977   J. García Burillo, "El ciento por uno (Mc 10,29-30 par).
               Historia de las interpretaciones y exégesis," EstBíb 36:
               173-203.   (N 24-114)

991   1956   J. Martin, "'Avec des persécutions'," <u>Revue des Études</u>
               <u>Grecques</u> 69:35-40.

10:32-52

992   1979   D. O. Via, "Mark 10,32-52--A Structural, Literary and The-
               ological Interpretation," in <u>Society of Biblical Litera-</u>
               <u>ture 1979 Seminar Papers 2</u> (ed. by Paul J. Achtemeier;
               Missoula, MT: Scholars Press), pp. 187-203.

10:32-34

993   1976   R. McKinnis, "An Analysis of Mark X 32-34," <u>NovT</u> 18:81-100.
                                                          (N 21-398)

10:33-34

See 1594 - 1599.

10:35-45

994   1975   J. Radermakers, "Revendiquer ou servir? Mk 10,35-45," <u>As-</u>
               <u>Seign</u> 60:28-39.   (N 20-106)

995   1959   A. George, "Le Service du Royaume (Marc 10,35-45)," <u>BVC</u> 25:
               15-19.   (N 3-594)

996   H. Urner, "Der Dienst Jesu Christi. Markus 10,35-45,"
               <u>CommViat</u> 2:287-290.   (N 4-400)

10:35-40

997   1974   S. Légasse, "Approche de l'Épisode préévangélique des Fils
               de Zébédée (Marc x.35-40 par.)," <u>NTS</u> 20:161-177.
                                                          (N 18-880)

998   1967   A. Feuillet, "La coupe et le baptême de la Passion (<u>Mc</u>, x,
               35-40; cf. <u>Mt</u>, xx, 20-23; <u>Lc</u>, xii, 50)," <u>RB</u> 74:356-391.
                                                          (N 12-566)

10:38-39

999   1977   V. Howard, "Did Jesus Speak about His Own Death?" <u>CBQ</u> 39:
               515-527.   (N 22-410)

1000   1965   G. Braumann, "Leidenskelch und Todestaufe (Mc 10:38f.),"
               <u>ZNW</u> 56:178-183.   (N 10-926)

10:38

1001   1957   G. Delling, "<u>baptisma baptisthēnai</u>," <u>NovT</u> 2:92-115.
                                                          (N 3-361)

10:42

1002   1976   K. W. Clark, "The Meaning of ₍kata₎kyrieyein," in Studies
                in the New Testament and Text: Essays in Honour of George
                D. Kilpatrick on the Occasion of his Sixty-fifth Birthday
                (ed. by J. K. Elliott; NovT Supplement 44; Leiden: E. J.
                Brill), pp. 100-105.

10:45

See also 1594.

1003   1980   S. H. T. Page, "The Authenticity of the Ransom Logion (Mark
                10:45b)," in Gospel Perspectives: Studies of History and
                Tradition in the Four Gospels, Vol. 1 (ed. by R. T.
                France and David Wenham; Sheffield: JSOT), pp. 137-161.

1004   1979   M. Adinolfi, "Il servo di Jhwh nel logion del servizio e
                del riscatto (Mc. 10,45)," BeO 21:43-61.   (N 24-115)

1005   1977   W. J. Moulder, "The Old Testament Background and the Inter-
                pretation of Mark x. 45," NTS 24:120-127.   (N 22-411)

1006   1975   K. Kertelge, "Der dienende Menschensohn (Mk 10,45)," in
                Jesus und der Menschensohn: Für Anton Vögtle (ed. by Ru-
                dolf Pesch and Rudolf Schnackenburg, in collaboration
                with Odilo Kaiser; Freiburg/Basel/Vienna: Herder), pp.
                225-239.

1007   1972   C. K. Barrett, "Mark 10,45: A Ransom for Many," in Barrett,
                New Testament Essays (London: S.P.C.K.), pp. 20-26.

1008   J. Roloff, "Anfänge der soteriologischen Deutung des Todes
                Jesu (Mk. x. 45 und Lk. xxii. 27)," NTS 19:38-64.
                                                            (N 17-951)

1009   1968   H. J. B. COMBRINK. Die diens van Jesus. 'n Eksegetiese
                beskouing oor Markus 10:45. Groningen: V.R.B.--Offset-
                drukkerij. 201 pp.   (E 50-2560)

1010   1967   A. Feuillet, "Le logion sur la rançon," RSPT 51:365-402.
                                                            (N 12-891)

1011   1966   J. Jeremias, "Das Lösegeld für Viele (Mk 10,45)," in Jere-
                mias, Abba: Studien zur neutestamentlichen Theologie und
                Zeitgeschichte (Göttingen: Vandenhoeck & Ruprecht), pp.
                216-229.   ₍Originally published in 1947.₎

1012   1960   J. A. Emerton, "The Aramaic Background of Mk 10,45," JTS
                11:334-335.

1013   1959   C. K. Barrett, "The Background of Mark 10,45," in <u>New Tes-tament Essays: Studies in memory of Thomas Walter Manson, 1893 - 1958</u> (ed. by A. J. B. Higgins; Manchester: Man-chester University Press), pp. 1-18.

<u>10:46 - 13:37</u>

1014   1978   C. J. den HEYER. <u>Exegetische methoden in discussie. Een analyse van Markus 10,46 - 13,37.</u> Kampen: J. H. Kok. 222 pp.

<u>10:46 - 12:40</u>

1015   1978   P. J. FARLA. <u>Jezus' oordeel over Israel. Een form- en re-daktionsgeschichtliche analyse van Mc 10,46 - 12,40.</u> Kamp-en: J. H. Kok. xi-581 pp.

<u>10:46-52</u>

1016   1978   P. J. Achtemeier, "'And he followed him': Miracles and Dis-cipleship in Mark 10:46-52," <u>Semeia</u> 11:115-145.
                                                                (N 23-473)

1017   E. S. Johnson, Jr., "Mark 10:46-52: Blind Bartimaeus," <u>CBQ</u> 40:191-204.   (N 22-779)

1018   1976   I. L. Stoffel, "An Exposition of Mk 10:46-52," <u>Int</u> 30:288-292.

1019   1973   V. K. Robbins, "The Healing of Blind Bartimaeus (10:46-52) in the Marcan Theology," <u>JBL</u> 92:224-243.   (N 18-123)

1020   1972   A. Paul, "Guérison de Bartimée. Mc 10,46-52," <u>AsSeign</u> 61: 44-52.   (N 17-539)

<u>10:46</u>

1021   1975   A. Ródenas, "La entrada de Jesús en Jericó (Mc 10,46)," <u>Naturaleza y Gracia</u> 22:225-264.

<u>Chs. 11 - 16</u>

See 142, 145.

<u>11:1 - 13:37</u>

See 293.

<u>Chs. 11 - 12</u>

1022   1978   K. Stock, "Gliederung und Zusammenhang in Mk 11-12," <u>Bib</u> 59:481-515.   (N 23-852)

Ch. 11

1023   1976   J. Christensen, "Indtog og tempeldom. En studie i Markus
              kap. 11," DTT 39:1-9.   (N 21-101)

1024   1976   W. Bauer, "Der Palmesel," in Bauer, Aufsätze und kleine
              Schriften (ed. by Georg Strecker; Tübingen:J.C.B. Mohr
              [Paul Siebeck]), pp. 109-121.
              [From the English article in JBL 72 (1953):220-229.]

1025   1964   V. Eppstein, "The Historicity of the Gospel Account of the
              Cleansing of the Temple (Mc 11, Mt 21, Lc 19)," ZNW 55:
              42-58.

11:1-11

1026   1978   V. MARIADASAN. Le triomphe messianique de Jésus et son en-
              trée à Jérusalem. Étude critico-littéraire des tradi-
              tions évangéliques (Mc 11:1-11; Mt 21:1-11; Lc 19:28-38;
              Jn 12:12-16. Tindivanam, India: Catechetical Centre.
              x-66 pp.

1027   1973   R. Bartnicki, "Mesjański charakter perykopy Marka o wjeźd-
              zie Jezusa do Jerozolimy (Mk 11, 1-11)," RoczTeolKan 20:
              5-16.   (N 19-113)

11:1-10

1028   1979   R. JACOB. Les péricopes de l'entrée à Jérusalem et de la
              préparation de la cène. Contribution a l'étude du prob-
              lème synoptique. Église nouvelle - Église ancienne,
              Études bibliques 2. Paris: Beauchesne. 162 pp.

1029   1977   R. Bartnicki, "Teologia ewangelistów w perykopach o wjeźd-
              zie Jezusa do Jerozolimy," StudTheolVars 15:55-76.
                                                                 (N 22-412)

1030   "Il carattere messianico delle pericopi di
              Marco e Matteo sull'ingresso di Gesù in Gerusalemme (Mc.
              11,1-10; Mt. 21,1-9)," RivB 25:5-27.   (N 23-853)

1031   1971   J. D. M. Derrett, "Law in the New Testament: The Palm Sun-
              day colt," NovT 13:241-258.   (N 16-886)
              [Republished in Derrett, Studies in the New Testament
              2: Midrash in Action and as a Literary Device (Leiden:
              E. J. Brill, 1978), pp. 165-183.]

1032   H. Patsch, "Der Einzug Jesu in Jerusalem. Ein historischer
              Versuch," ZTK 68:1-26.   (N 16-182)

11:2-7

1033 1959 H.-W. Kuhn, "Das Reittier Jesu in der Einzugsgeschichte des Markusevangeliums," ZNW 50:82-91.   (N 4-90)

1034 O. Michel, "Eine philologische Frage zur Einzugsgeschichte," NTS 6:81-82.

11:9-10

1035 1972 J. D. Crossan, "Redaction and Citation in Mark 11:9-10 and 11:17," BR 17:33-50.   (N 17-952).

1036 "Redaction and Citation in Mk 11:9-10, 17 and 14:27," in Society of Biblical Literature 1972 Seminar Papers I (ed. by Lane C. McGaughy; Los Angeles, CA: Society of Biblical Literature), pp. 17-60.

1037 1963 E. Lohse, "Hosianna," NovT 6:113-119.   (N 8-965) [Republished in Lohse, Die Einheit des Neuen Testaments: exegetische Studien zur Theologie des Neuen Testaments (Göttingen: Vandenhoeck & Ruprecht, 1973), pp. 104-110.]

11:11-15

1038 1960 G. W. Buchanan, "An Additional Note to 'Mark 11,11-15: Brigands in the Temple'," HUCA 31:103-105.

11:12-25

1039 1978 A. Radaelli et al., "Lettura 'di un' miracolo (Mc 11,12-25) come introduzione all'intendimento 'del' miracolo," Ric-BibRel 13:115-185.   (N 23-854)

1040 1967 R. Hull, "The Cursing of the Fig Tree. A study in social change and the theology of hope," ChristCent 84:1429-1431.   (N 12-567)

11:12-14, 20-25

1041 1980 W. R. TELFORD. The Barren Temple and the Withered Tree. A redaction-critical analysis of the Cursing of the Fig-Tree pericope in Mark's Gospel and its relation to the Cleansing of the Temple tradition. JSNT Supplement 1. Sheffield: JSOT Press. xvi-319 pp.

1042 1977 L. A. Loslie, "The Cursing of the Fig Tree: Tradition Criticism of a Marcan Pericope (Mark 11:12-14, 20-25)," Studia Biblica et Theologica 7:3-18.

1043 1971 H. Cousin, "Le figuier désséche. Un exemple de l'actuali-

sation de la geste évangélique: Mc 11,12-14,20-25; Mt 21,
18-22," in Reconnaissance à Suzanne de Dietrich (Cahiers
Bibliques de Foi et Vie; Paris: Foi et Vie), pp. 82-93.

1044   J. G. Kahn, "La parabole du figuier stérile et les arbres
            récalcitrants de la Genèse," NovT 13:38-45. (N 16-183)

1045   1962 A. de Q. Robin, "The Cursing of the Fig Tree in Mark xi. A
            Hypothesis," NTS 8:276-281.   (N 7-152)

1046   1960 C. W. F. Smith, "No Time for Figs," JBL 79:315-327.

1047   1958 V. Anzalone, "Il fico maledetto (Mc. XI, 12-14 e 20-25),"
            PalCler 37:257-264.   (N 3-82)

11:12-14, 20-21(22)

1048   1976 H. Giesen, "Der verdorrte Feigenbaum--Eine symbolische Aus-
            sage? Zu Mk 11,12-14.20f," BZ 20:95-111.   (N 21-102)

1049   1969 E. Cortés, "El secamiento de la higuera a la luz de los
            profetas de AT y de sus targumim (Mc 11,12-14.20-21),"
            Estudios Franciscanos 70:5-23.

1050   1968 E. Cortés, "El secamiento de la higuera según Mc 11,12-14.
            20," Estudios Franciscanos 69:41-68.

1051   1962 J. N. Birdsall, "The Withering of the Fig-Tree (Mark xi.
            12-14, 20-22)," ExpTim 73:191.   (N 7-151)

11:12-14

1052   1975 K. Romaniuk, "'Car ce n'était pas la saison des figues...'
            (Mk 11:12-14 parr)," ZNW 66:275-278.   (N 20-804)

1053   1973 J. D. M. Derrett, "Figtrees in the New Testament," HeyJ 14:
            249-265.
                [Republished in Derrett, Studies in the New Testament
                2: Midrash in Action and as a Literary Device (Leiden:
                E. J. Brill, 1978), pp. 148-164.]

1054   1963 G. Münderlein, "Die Verfluchung des Feigenbaumes (Mk. xi.
            12-14)," NTS 10:89-104.   (N 8-966)

11:13

1055   1976 C. J. den Heyer, "'Want het was de tijd niet voor vijgen'
            (Mk 11,13)," GerefTheolTijd 76:129-140.   (N 21-399)

1056   1968 R. H. Hiers, "'Not the Season for Figs,'" JBL 87:394-400.
                                                           (N 13-589)

11:15-19

1057   1980   R. A. Culpepper, "Mark 11:15-19," Int 34:176-181.

1058   1977   J. D. M. Derrett, "The Zeal of the House and the Cleansing of the Temple," DownRev 95:79-94.   (N 22-413)

1059   1975   C. K. Barrett, "The House of Prayer and the Den of Thieves," in Jesus und Paulus: Festschrift für Werner Georg Kümmel zum 70. Geburtstag (ed. by E. Earle Ellis and Erich Grässer; Göttingen: Vandenhoeck & Ruprecht), pp. 13-20.

1060   1959   G. W. Buchanan, "Mark 11.15-19: Brigands in the Temple," HUCA 30:169-177.   (N 5-90)

11:15-17

1061   1972   N. M. Flanagan, "Mark and the Temple Cleansing," TBT 63: 980-984.   (N 17-540)

1062   1971   R. H. Hiers, "Purification of the Temple: Preparation for the Kingdom of God," JBL 90:82-90.   (N 15-876)

1063   1968   C. J. Bjerkelund, "En tradisjons- og redaksjonshistorisk analyse av perikopene om tempelrenselsen," NorTT 69:206-218.   (N 14-168)

1064   1961   S. Jérôme, "La violence de Jésus," BVC 41:13-17.(N 6-468)

1065   1960   C. Roth, "The Cleansing of the Temple and Zechariah xiv 21," NovT 4:174-181.   (N 6-140)

11:15

1066   1961   K. Treu, "Zur vermeintlichen Kontraktion von hierosolyma in 0188, Berlin P. 13416," ZNW 52:278-280.   (N 6-790)

11:16

1067   1976   J. M. Ford, "Money 'bags' in the Temple (Mk 11, 16)," Bib 57:249-253.   (N 21-400)

11:17

See 1035, 1036.

11:23-25

1068   1979   G. Biguzzi, "Mc. 11,23-25 e il Pater," RivB 27:57-68.   (N 24-811)

11:25

1069   1980   C. A. Wanamaker, "Mark 11:25 and the Gospel of Matthew,"
                 in Studia Biblica 1978: II. Papers on the Gospels. Sixth
                 International Congress on Biblical Studies, Oxford, 3-7
                 April, 1978 (ed. by E. A. Livingstone; JSNT Supplement 2;
                 Sheffield: JSOT), pp. 339-350.

11:27-33

1070   1974   G. S. Shae, "The Question on the Authority of Jesus," NovT
                 16:1-29.   (N 19-114)

1071   1971   R. Schnackenburg, "Die Vollmacht Jesu. Zu Mk 11,27-33,"
                 KathGed 27:105-109.   (N 16-554)

1072   1968   J. Kremer, "Jesu Antwort auf die Frage nach seiner Voll-
                 macht. Eine Auslegung von Mk 11,27-33," BibLeb 9:128-
                 136.   (N 13-196)

12:1-12

See also 350.

1073   1979   P. van Ginneken, "Au-delà de l'oedipe? La parabole des
                 vignerons homicides d'un point de vue psychanalytique,"
                 La Foi et le Temps 9:360-383.

1073a   1977   A. Strus, "Funkcja obrazu w przekazie biblijnym: obraz win-
                 nicy w Iz 5, 1-7 i w Ewangelii," StudTheolVars 15:25-54.
                                                             (N 22-414)

1074   1974   J. Blank, "Die Sendung des Sohnes: Zur christologischen Be-
                 deutung des Gleichnisses von den bösen Winzern Mk 12,1-
                 12," in Neues Testament und Kirche: Für Rudolf Schnacken-
                 burg (ed. by Joachim Gnilka; Freiburg im Br./Basel/Vien-
                 na: Herder), pp. 11-41.

1075   B. Dehandschutter, "La parabole des vignerons homicides
                 (Mc., XII, 1-12) et l'évangile selon Thomas," in L'évan-
                 gile selon Marc: Tradition et rédaction (ed. by M. Sabbe;
                 Bibliotheca ephemeridum theologicarum lovaniensium 34;
                 Gembloux/Louvain: Duculot/Leuven University), pp. 203-
                 219.

1076   J. D. M. Derrett, "Allegory and the Wicked Vinedressers,"
                 JTS 25:426-432.   (N 19-975)
                 [Republished in Derrett, Studies in the New Testament
                 2: Midrash in Action and as a Literary Device (Leiden:
                 E. J. Brill, 1978), pp. 92-98.]

1077   K. R. Snodgrass, "The Parable of the Wicken Husbandmen: Is
               the Gospel of Thomas Version the Original?" NTS 21:142-
               144.   (N 19-562)

1078   1973   D. Merli, "La parabola dei vignaioli infedeli (Mc. 12,1-
               12)," BeO 15:97-108.   (N 18-495)

1079   1972   J. E. and R. R. Newell, "The Parable of the Wicked Ten-
               ants," NovT 14:226-237.   (N 17-541)

1080   1971   J. D. Crossan, "The Parable of the Wicked Husbandmen," JBL
               90:451-465.   (N 16-887)

1081   1970   H.-J. Klauck, "Das Gleichnis vom Mord im Weinberg (Mk 12,
               1-12; Mt 21,33-46; Lk 20,9-19)," BibLeb 11:118-145.
                                                             (N 15-529)

1082   1968   M. Hengel, "Das Gleichnis von den Weingärtnern Mc 12:1-12
               im Lichte der Zenonpapyri und der rabbinischen Gleich-
               nisse," ZNW 59:1-39.   (N 13-197)

1083   1966   H. Dombois, "Juristische Bemerkungen zum Gleichnis von den
               bösen Weingärtnern (Mk 12,1-12)," Neue Zeitschrift für
               systematische Theologie und Religionsphilosophie 8:360-
               373.

1084   1959   W. Bammel, "Das Gleichnis von den bösen Winzern und das
               jüdische Erbrecht," Revue Internationale des Droits de
               de l'Antiquité 6:11-17.

12:1-11

1085   1976   Michel HUBAUT. La parabole des vignerons homicides. Cah-
               iers de la Revue Biblique 16. Paris: Gabalda. 155 pp.

12:1-9

1086   1965   W. G. Kümmel, "Das Gleichnis von den bösen Weingärtnern
               (Mk 12,1-9)," Marburger Theologische Studien 3:207-217.

12:10-11

1087   1968   J. D. M. Derrett, "'The Stone that the Builders Rejected',"
               in Studia Evangelica IV (Texte und Untersuchungen zur Ge-
               schichte der altchristlichen Literatur 102; Berlin: Akad-
               emie Verlag), pp. 180-186.
                 ₍Republished in Derrett, Studies in the New Testament
                 2: Midrash in Action and as a Literary Device (Leiden:
                 E. J. Brill, 1978), pp. 60-67.

1088   1964   L. W. Barnard, "The Testimonium Concerning the Stone in the

New Testament and in the Epistle of Barnabas," in <u>Studia</u>
<u>Evangelica 3: Papers Presented to the Second International</u>
<u>al Congress on New Testament Studies held at Christ</u>
<u>Church, Oxford, 1961</u> (Berlin: Akademie Verlag), pp. 306-
313.

<u>12:13-17</u>

1089   1978   A. B. Ogle, "What Is Left for Caesar? A Look at Mark 12:
              13-17 and Romans 13:1-7," <u>TToday</u> 35:254-264.(N 23-475)

1090   1977   E. Güttgemanns, "Narrative Analyse des Streitgesprächs über
              den 'Zinsgroschen,'" <u>LingBib</u> 41-42:88-105. (N 22-781)

1091   H. Jason, "Der Zinsgroschen: Analyse der Erzählstruktur,"
              <u>LingBib</u> 41-42:49-87.   (N 22-780)

1092   1975   G. Petzke, "Der historische Jesus in der sozialethischen
              Diskussion, Mk 12,13-17 par.," in <u>Jesus Christus in His-</u>
              <u>torie und Theologie: neutestamentliche Festschrift für</u>
              <u>Hans Conzelmann zum 60. Geburtstag</u> (ed. by Georg Streck-
              er; Tübingen: Mohr), pp. 223-235.

1093   1972   R. Breymayer, "Zur Pragmatik des Bildes. Semiotische Be-
              obachtungen zum Streitgespräch Mk 12,13-17 ('Der Zins-
              groschen') unter Berücksichtigung der Spieltheorie,"
              <u>LingBib</u> 13-14:19-51.   (N 17-144)

1094   A. Stock, "'Render to Caesar,'" <u>TBT</u> 62:929-934.(N 17-542)

1095   1971   K. Tagawa, "Jésus critiquant l'idéologie théocratique. Une
              étude de Mc 12,13-17," in <u>Reconnaissance à Suzanne de</u>
              <u>Dietrich</u> (Cahiers Bibliques de <u>Foi et Vie</u>; Paris: <u>Foi et</u>
              <u>Vie</u>), pp. 117-125.

<u>12:14</u>

1096   1967   G. Wormser, "'Rendez à César...' (Mc 12,14 par.)," <u>Nouveaux</u>
              <u>Cahiers</u> 3:43-53.

<u>12:17</u>

1097   1964   L. Goppelt, "The Freedom to Pay the Imperial Tax (Mk 12,
              17)," in <u>Studia Evangelica II: Papers Presented to the</u>
              <u>Second International Congress on New Testament Studies</u>
              <u>held at Christ Church, Oxford, 1961</u> (ed. by F. L. Cross;
              Texte und Untersuchungen zur Geschichte der altchrist-
              lichen Literatur 87; Berlin: Akademie-Verlag), pp. 183-
              194.

1098   1962   J. N. Sevenster, "Geeft den keizer wat des keizers is, en

Gode wat Gods is," NedTTs 17:21-31.   (N 8-150)

1099 1961 L. Goppelt, "Die Freiheit zur Kaisersteuer. Zu Mk. 12,17
            und Röm. 13,1-7," in Ecclesia und res publica. Kurt Die-
            trich Schmidt zum 65. Geburtstag (ed. by Georg Kretschmar
            and Bernhard Lohse; Göttingen: Vandenhoeck & Ruprecht),
            pp. 40-50.
               ⌜Republished in Goppelt, Christologie und Ethik. Auf-
            sätze zum Neuen Testament (Göttingen: Vandenhoeck &
            Ruprecht, 1968), pp. 208-219.⌟

12:18-27

1100 1973 A. Ammassari, "Gesù ha veramente insegnato la risurrezi-ˋ
            one!" BeO 15:65-73.   (N 18-496)

1101 1964 E. E. Ellis, "Jesus, the Sadducees and Qumran," NTS 10:274-
            279.   (N 8-967)

1102 1959 G. Carton, "Comme des anges dans le ciel (Marc 12,18-27),"
            BVC 28:46-52.   (N 4-91)

12:24-27

1103 1968 D. H. van Daalen, "Some Observations on Mark 12,24-27," in
            Studia Evangelica 4,1: Papers Presented to the Third In-
            ternational Congress on New Testament Studies held at
            Christ Church, Oxford, 1965: Part I. The Scriptures (ed.
            by F. L. Cross; Berlin: Akademie Verlag), pp. 241-245.

12:26-27

1104 1959 F. Dreyfus, "L'argument scripturaire de Jésus en faveur de
            la résurrection des morts (Marc, XII, 26-27)," RB 66:213-
            225.   (N 4-402)

12:28-34

See also 144.

1105 1978 W.Diezinger, "Zum Liebesgebot Mk xii, 28-34 und Parr,"
            NovT 20:81-83.   (N 23-120)

1106 1970 J.Ernst, "Die Einheit von Gottes- und Nächstenliebe in der
            Verkündigung Jesu," TheolGlaub 60:3-14.   (N 15-169)

1107   M. Miguéns, "Amour, alpha et omega de l'existence, Mc 12,
            28-34," AsSeign 62:53-62.

12:28

1108 1965 N. Lohfink, "Il 'comandamento primo' nell'Antico Testamen-
            to," BeO 7:49-60.   (N 10-139)

1109   1963   N. Lohfink, "Das Hauptgebot im Alten Testament," GeistLeb
                36:271-281.   (N 8-592)

12:30-31

1110   1973   R. L. Pavelsky, "The Commandment of Love and the Christian
                Clinical Psychologist," Studia Biblica et Theologica 3:
                57-65.

12:31

1111   1962   H. Montefiore, "Thou Shalt Love Thy Neighbour as Thyself,"
                NovT 4:157-170.

12:35-37

1112   1979   B. Moriconi, "Chi è Gesù? Mc 12,35-37 momento culminante
                di rivelazione," EphCarm 30:23-51.   (N 24-439)

1113   1974   F. Neugebauer, "Die Davidssohnfrage (Mark xii. 35-7 parr.)
                und der Menschensohn," NTS 21:81-108.   (N 19-563)

1114   1972   G. Schneider, "Die Davidssohnfrage (Mk 12,35-37)," Bib 53:
                65-90.   (N 17-145)

1115   1962   E. Lövestam, "Die Davidssohnsfrage," SEÅ 27:72-82.

12:38

1116   1963   K. H. Rengstorf, "Die stolai der Schriftgelehrten. Eine
                Erläuterung zu Mark. 12,38," in Abraham unser Vater: Jud-
                en und Christen in Gespräch über die Bibel: Festschrift
                für Otto Michel zum 60. Geburtstag (ed. by Otto Betz,
                Martin Hengel, and Peter Schmidt; Leiden/Köln: E. J.
                Brill), pp. 383-404.

12:40

1117   1972   J. D. M. Derrett, "'Eating up the Houses of Widows': Jesus'
                Comment on Lawyers?" NovT 14:1-9.   (N 16-888)
                [Republished in Derrett, Studies in the New Testament
                I: Glimpses of the Legal and Social Presuppositions of
                the Authors (Leiden: E. J. Brill, 1977), pp. 118-127.]

12:41-44

1118   1971   G. M. Lee, "The Story of the Widow's Mite," ExpTim 82:344.
                                                                 (N 16-555)

1119   1969   L. Simon, "Le sou de la veuve. Marc 12/41-44," ÉTR 44:
                115-126.   (N 14-510)

<u>12:42</u>

1120 1967 D. Sperber, "Mark xii 42 and its metrological background.
A study in ancient Syriac versions," <u>NovT</u> 9:178-190.
(N 12-568)

<u>Ch. 13</u>

See also 176, 277, 1532.

1121 1980 A. Feuillet, "La signification fondamentale de Marc XIII.
Recherches sur l'eschatologie des Synoptiques," <u>RevThom</u>
80:181-215.   (N 25-102)

1122 1977 C. Combet-Galland, "Marc 13. Les saisons du monde," in
<u>L'Apocalyptique, littérature du passé?</u> (Cahiers Bibliques
16; Paris: <u>Foi et Vie</u> 76), pp. 45-66.   (N 24-116)

1123   J. Dupont, "La ruine du Temple et la fin des temps dans le
discours de Marc 13," in <u>Apocalypses et théologie de l'es-
pérance: Congrès de Toulouse (1975)</u> (ed. by Louis Monlou-
bou; Lectio Divina 95; Paris: Éditions du Cerf), pp. 207-
269.

1124   D. Lanz, "Lecture écologique de Marc 13 et lecture évangélique d'un texte écologique," in <u>L'Apocalyptique, littérature du passé?</u> (Cahiers Bibliques 16; Paris: <u>Foi et Vie</u>
76), pp. 107-109.

1125   K. Tagawa, "Marc 13. La tâtonnement d'un homme réaliste
éveillé face à la tradition apocalyptique," in <u>L'Apocalyptique, littérature du passé?</u> (Cahiers Bibliques 16;
Paris: <u>Foi et Vie</u> 76), pp. 11-44.   (N 24-117)

1126 1975 S. Laws, "Can Apocalyptic be Relevant?" in <u>What About the
New Testament? Essays in honour of Christopher Evans</u>
(ed. by Morna Hooker and Colin Hickling; London: SCM
Press), pp. 89-102.

1127   D. Wenham, "Recent study of Mark 13," <u>TSFBull</u> 71:6-15; 72:
1-9.   (N 20-108)

1128 1974 K. Grayston, "The Study of Mark XIII," <u>BJRL</u> 56:371-387.
(N 19-564)

1129   H. Langkammer, "Paruzja syna człowieczego (Mk 13)," <u>Rocz-
TeolKan</u> 21:61-74.   (N 20-107)

1130 1973 R. Lapointe, "Actualité de l'apocalyptique," <u>Église et Thé-
ologie</u> 4:197-211.

1131 1970 C. B. Cousar, "Eschatology and Mark's <u>Theologia Crucis</u>. A

Critical Analysis of Mark 13," Int 24:321-335.(N 15-170)

1132   F. Flückiger, "Die Redaktion der Zukunftsrede in Mark. 13,"
        TZ 26:395-409.   (N 15-877)

1133 1968s P. Raymond, "Le discours eschatologique de Marc 13," Bulle-
        tin du Centre Protestant d'Études 1968,8 and 1969,1:35-
        41.

1134 1968 Rudolf PESCH. Naherwartungen. Tradition und Redaktion in
        Mk 13. Kommentare und Beiträge zum Alten und Neuen Tes-
        tament. Düsseldorf: Patmos. 275 pp.   (E 49-2634)

1135 1967 Jan LAMBRECHT. Die Redaktion der Markus-Apokalypse: Liter-
        arische Analyse und Strukturuntersuchung. Analecta Bib-
        lica 28. Rome: Pontifical Biblical Institute. xxix-
        319 pp.   (E 48-2429)

1136   "La structure de Mc. XIII," in De Jésus aux
        Évangiles: Tradition et Rédaction dans les Évangiles syn-
        optiques. Donum natalicum Iosepho Coppens septuagesimum
        annum complenti D.D.D. collegae et amici (ed. by I. de la
        Potterie; Bibliotheca ephemeridum theologicarum lovanien-
        sium 25; Gembloux/Paris: Duculot/Lethielleux), pp. 141-164.

1137 1966 Lars HARTMAN. Prophecy Interpreted. The Formation of Some
        Jewish Apocalyptic Texts and of the Eschatological Dis-
        course, Mark 13 par. Tr. by Neil Tomkinson and Jean Gray.
        Coniectanea Biblica, New Testament Series 1. Lund: C. W.
        K. Gleerup. 299 pp.   (E 48-2422)

1138   I. Hermann, "Die Gefährdung der Welt und ihre Erneuerung.
        Auslegung von Mk 13,1-37," BibLeb 7:305-309.

1139   J. K. Howard, "Our Lord's Teaching Concerning His Parousia:
        A Study in the Gospel of Mark," EvQ 38:68-75, 150-157.
                                                    (N 11-237,245)

1140   N. Walter, "Tempelzerstörung und synoptische Apokalypse,"
        ZNW 57:38-49.   (N 11-246)

1141 1965 J. Lambrecht, "Redactio Sermonis Eschatologici," VD 43:278-
        287.   (N 10-927)

1142   Franz MUSSNER. Christ and the End of the World. A Bibli-
        cal Study in Eschatology. Tr. (from the German: 1958
        1rst ed) by Maria von Eroes. Contemporary Catechetics
        Series 2. Notre Dame, Ind.: University of Notre Dame
        Press. 70 pp.   (E 47-2448)

1143 1964 Franz MUSSNER. Was lehrt Jesus über das Ende der Welt?

<u>Eine Auslegung von Markus 13</u>. 2nd ed. Freiburg/Vienna: Herder. 76 pp.   (E 46-1407)

1144   1962   J. Bligh, "Eschatology and Social Doctrine," <u>HeyJ</u> 3:262-267.   (N 7-516)

1145   1961   G. NEVILLE. <u>The Advent Hope. A Study of the Context of Mark 13</u>. London: Darton, Longman & Todd. 122 pp.
                                                       (E 44-1606)

1146   1960   G. R. Beasley-Murray, "The Eschatological Discourse of Jesus," <u>RevExp</u> 57:153-166.   (N 5-91)

1147   1959   H. Conzelmann, "Geschichte und Eschaton nach Mc 13," <u>ZNW</u> 50:210-221.   (N 4-661)
                ₍Republished in Conzelmann, <u>Theologie als Schriftauslegung: Aufsätze zum Neuen Testament</u> (Beiträge zur evangelischen Theologie 65; Munich: Kaiser, 1974), pp. 62-73.₎

1148   C. Perrot, "Essai sur le Discours eschatologique (<u>Mc. XIII</u>, 1-37; <u>Mt. XXIV</u>, 1-36; <u>Lc. XXI</u>, 5-36)," <u>RSR</u> 47:481-514.
                                                       (N 4-662)

1149   1958   T. F. Glasson, "Mark xiii and the Greek Old Testament," <u>ExpTim</u> 69:213-215.   (N 3-83)

1150   1957   G. R. BEASLEY-MURRAY. <u>A Commentary on Mark 13</u>. London/New York: Macmillan/St. Martin's Press. vii-124 pp.
                                                       (E 39-1653)

1151   1954   G. R. BEASLEY-MURRAY. <u>Jesus and the Future: An examination of the criticism of the eschatological discourse, Mark 13, with special reference to the little apocalypse theory</u>. London/New York: Macmillan/St. Martin's Press. xi-287 pp.   (E 36-1469)

<u>13:2</u>

1152   1971   J. Dupont, "Il n'en sera pas laissé pierre sur pierre (Marc 13,2; Luc 19,44)," <u>Bib</u> 52:301-320.   (N 16-556)

<u>13:9-11</u>

1153   1977   J. Dupont, "La persécution comme situation missionaire (Marc 13,9-11)," in <u>Die Kirche des Anfangs: Festschrift für Heinz Schürmann zum 65. Geburtstag</u> (ed. by Rudolf Schnackenburg, Josef Ernst and Joachim Wanke; Leipzig: St. Benno, 1977 and Freiburg/Basel: Herder, 1978), pp. 97-114.

1154   1955   G. D. Kilpatrick, "The Gentile Missions in Mark and Mk 13,
               9-11," in Studies in the Gospels: Essays in Memory of R.
               H. Lightfoot (ed. by D. E. Nineham; Oxford: B. Blackwell),
               pp. 145-158.

13:9-10

1155   1958   G. D. Kilpatrick, "Mark XIII 9-10," JTS 9:81-86.(N 3-84)

13:9

1156   1968   F. W. Danker, "Double entendre in Mark XIII 9," NovT 10:
               162-163.   (N 13-590)

13:10

1157   1971   J. W. Thompson, "The Gentile Mission As an Eschatological
               Necessity," RestorQuart 14:18-27.   (N 16-184)

1158   1956   A. Farrer, "An Examination of Mark XIII. 10," JTS 7:75-
               79.   (N 1-45)

13:14-20

1159   1960   H.-J. Schoeps, "Ebionitische Apokalyptik im Neuen Testa-
               ment," ZNW 51:101-111.   (N 5-410)

13:14

1160   1965   R. H. Shaw, "A Conjecture on the Signs of the End," ATR 47:
               96-102.   (N 9-940)

1161   1959   B. Rigaux, "Bdelygma tēs erēmōseōs (Mc 13,14; Mt 24,15),"
               Bib 40:675-683.   (N 4-663)

13:24-32

1162   1976   W. S. Towner, "An Exposition of Mk 13:24-32," Int 30:92-96.

1163   1966   F. Mussner, "Christus und das Ende der Welt," in Mussner,
               Christus vor uns: Studien zur christlichen Eschatologie
               (Theologische Brennpunkte, Bd 8/9; Bergen-Enkheim bei
               Frankfurt am Main: Verlag Gerhard Kaffke), pp. 8-18.

13:24-27

See 1159.

1164   1961   F. Mussner, "Die Wiederkunft des Menschensohnes nach Mark-
               us 13, 24-27 und 14, 61-62," BK 16:105-107. (N 6-791)

13:26-27

See 1480, 1531.

13:28-32

See 1053.

13:28-29

1165 1968 J. Dupont, "La parabole du figuier qui bourgeonne (<u>Mc</u>, xiii,
28-29 et par.)," <u>RB</u> 75:526-548. (N 13-890) ,.

13:28

1166 1968 M. Pérez Fernández, "'prope est aestas' (Mc 13,28; Mt 24,
32; Lc 21,29)," <u>VD</u> 46:361-369. (N 14-170)

13:30

1167 1963s E. Lövestam, "En problematisk eskatologisk utsaga: Mark.
13:30 par.," <u>SEÅ</u> 28-29:64-80. (N 10-140)

13:32

1168 1968 E. Fascher, "Probleme der Zukunfterwartung nach Mk 13,32
und Mt 24,36," in Fascher, <u>Frage und Antwort: Studien zur
Theologie und Religionsgeschichte</u> (Berlin-Ost: Evangelische Verlagsanstalt), pp. 68-84.

1169 J. Winandy, "Le logion de l'ignorance (<u>Mc</u>, XIII, 32; <u>Mt</u>.,
XXIV, 36)," <u>RB</u> 75:63-79. (N 13-205)

1170 1964 E. Fascher, "'Von dem Tage aber und von der Stunde weiss
niemand...' Der Anstoss in Mark. 13,32 (Matth. 24,36).
Eine exegetische Skisse zum Verhältnis von historisch-
kritischer und christologischer Interpretation," in <u>Ruf
und Antwort: Festgabe für Emil Fuchs zum 90. Geburtstag</u>
(Leipzig: Koehler and Amelang), pp. 475-483.

1171 1959 S. Pezzella, "Marco 13, 32 e la scienza di Cristo," <u>RivB</u>
7:147-152. (N 4-403)

13:33-37

1172 1971 A. Weiser, "Von der Predigt Jesu zur Erwartung der Parusie.
Überlieferungsgeschichtliches zum Gleichnis vom Türhüter,"
<u>BibLeb</u> 12:25-31. (N 16-557)

1173 1969 E. Lövestam, "Le portier qui veille la nuit, Mc 13,33-37,"
<u>AsSeign</u> 2:44-53.

<u>13:34-36</u>

1174   1970   J. Dupont, "La parabole du maître qui rentre dans la nuit
                (Mc 13,34-36," in <u>Mélanges bibliques: en hommage au R. P.
                Béda Rigaux</u> (ed. by Albert Descamps and André de Halleux;
                Gembloux: Éditions J. Duculot), pp. 89-116.

<u>Chs. 14 - 16</u>

See also 170, 171.

1175   1980   J. Ernst, "Die passionserzählung des Markus und die Aporien
                der Forschung," <u>TheolGlaub</u> 70:160-180.

1176   1979   D. DORMEYER. <u>Der Sinn des Leidens Jesu. Historisch-krit-
                ische und textpragmatische Analysen zur Markuspassion</u>.
                Stuttgarter Bibelstudien 96. Stuttgart: Katholisches
                Bibelwerk. 118 pp.

1177   P. Lamarche, "L'humiliation du Christ," <u>Christus</u> ₍Paris₎
                26:461-470.   (N 24-440)

1178   D. Zeller, "Die Handlungsstruktur der Markuspassion. Der
                Ertrag strukturalistischer Literaturwissenschaft für die
                Exegese," <u>TQ</u> 59:213-227.   (N 24-441)

1179   1976   J. R. Donahue, "Introduction: From Passion Traditions to
                Passion Narrative," in <u>The Passion in Mark: Studies on
                Mark 14 - 16</u> (ed. by Werner H. Kelber; Philadelphia: For-
                tress), pp. 1-20.

1180   Werner H. KELBER, ed. <u>The Passion in Mark. Studies on Mk
                14 - 16</u>. Philadelphia: Fortress. xvii-203 pp.
                                                              (E 58s-4960)

1181   W. H. Kelber, "Conclusion: From Passion Narrative to Gos-
                pel," in <u>The Passion in Mark: Studies on Mark 14 - 16</u>
                (ed. by Werner H. Kelber; Philadelphia: Fortress), pp.
                153-180.

1182   G. O'Collins, "The Crucifixion," <u>DocLife</u> 26:247-263.
                                                              (N 21-103)

1183   1974   Detlev DORMEYER. <u>Die Passion Jesu als Verhaltensmodell:
                literarische und theologische Analyse der Traditions- und
                Redaktionsgeschichte der Markuspassion</u>. Neutestament-
                liche Abhandlungen, Neue Folge, 11. Münster: Verlag
                Aschendorff. viii-338 pp.   (E 57-3871)

1184   W. SCHENK. <u>Der Passionsbericht nach Markus. Untersuchung-
                en zur Überlieferungsgeschichte der Passionstraditionen</u>.
                Gütersloh: Mohn. 285 pp.

1185   W. Schenk, "Die gnostisierende Deutung des Todes Jesu und
              ihre kritische Interpretation durch den Evangelisten
              Markus," in Gnosis und Neues Testament: Studien aus Reli-
              gionswissenschaft und Theologie (ed. by Karl-Wolfgang
              Tröger; Gütersloh: Gütersloher Verlagshaus Gerd Mohn),
              231-243.

1186   Heinrich SCHLIER. Die Markuspassion. Kriterien 32. Ein-
              siedeln: Johannes-Verlag. 96 pp.   (E 56-3053)

1187 1973   R. H. Smith, "Darkness at Noon: Mark's Passion Narrative,"
              CTM 44:325-338.   (N 18-497)

1188 1970   Eta LINNEMANN. Studien zur Passionsgeschichte. Forschung-
              en zur Religion und Literatur des Alten und Neuen Testa-
              ments 102. Göttingen: Vandenhoeck & Ruprecht. 187 pp.

1189 1969   Jacob KREMER. Das Ärgernis des Kreuzes. Eine Hinführung
              zum Verstehen der Leidensgeschichte nach Markus. Stutt-
              gart: Katholisches Bibelwerk. 91 pp.   (E 50-2590)

1190   Johannes SCHREIBER. Die Markuspassion. Wege zur Erfor-
              schung der Leidensgeschichte Jesu. Hamburg: Furche-Ver-
              lag. 72 pp.   (E 51-2416)

1191 1967   F. H. Milling, "History and Prophecy in the Marcan Passion
              Narrative," Indian Journal of Theology 16:42-53.

1192 1962   H.-W.Bartsch, "Historische Erwägungen zur Leidensge-
              schichte," EvT 22:449-459.   (N 7-517)

1193 1958   T. A. Burkill, "St. Mark's Philosophy of the Passion," NovT
              2:245-271.   (N 4-86)

1194 1955   O. A. Piper, "God's Good News. The Passion Story according
              to Mark," Int 9:165-182.

14:1-42

1195 1971   Ludger SCHENKE. Studien zur Passionsgeschichte des Markus.
              Tradition und Redaktion in Markus 14,1-42. Forschung
              zur Bibel 4. Würzburg/Stuttgart: Echter-Verlag/Katho-
              lisches Bibelwerk. xxvii-570 pp.   (E 54-3193)

14:1-25

1196 1966   F. W. Danker, "The Literary Unity of Mark 14:1-25," JBL 85:
              467-472.   (N 11-725)

14:1-9

1197 1977   E. E. Platt, "The Ministry of Mary of Bethany," TToday 34:
              29-39.   (N 21-753)

14:3-9

1198   1974   J. K. Elliott, "The Anointing of Jesus," ExpTim 85:105-107.
                                                        (N 18-881)

1199   1973   R. Pesch, "Die Salbung Jesu in Bethanien (Mk 14,3-9): Eine
               Studie zur Passionsgeschichte," in Orientierung an Jesus:
               Zur Theologie der Synoptiker: Für Josef Schmid (ed. by
               Paul Hoffmann in collaboration with Norbert Brox and Wil-
               helm Pesch; Freiburg/Basel/Vienna: Herder), pp. 267-285.

1200   1966   J. Jeremias, "Die Salbungsgeschichte Mk 14,3-9," in Jere-
               mias, Abba: Studien zur neutestamentlichen Theologie und
               Zeitgeschichte (Göttingen: Vandenhoeck & Ruprecht), pp.
               107-115.
                  [Originally published in ZNW 35 (1936):75-82.]

1201   1959   A. Meli, "'Sempre i poveri avete con voi, ma non sempre
               avete me' (Mc 14, 3.9 par)," Humanitas 14:338-343.

14:4-5

1202   1970   R. Storch, "'Was soll diese Verschwendung?', Bemerkungen
               zur Auslegungsgeschichte von Mk 14,4f.," in Der Ruf Jesu
               und die Antwort der Gemeinde: Exegetische Untersuchungen.
               Joachim Jeremias zum 70. Geburtstag gewidmet von seinen
               Schülern (ed. by Eduard Lohse in collaboration with
               Christoph Burchard and Berndt Schaller; Göttingen: Vanden-
               hoeck & Ruprecht), pp. 247-258.

1203   1959   J. Bauer, "Ut Quid Perditio Ista?--zu Mk 14,4f. und Parr.,"
               NovT 3:54-56.   (N 4-404)
                  [Republished in Bauer, Scholia biblica et patristica
                  (Graz, Austria: Akademische Druck- und Verlagsanstalt,
                  1972), pp. 47-50.]

14:9

1204   1966   J. Jeremias, "Mk 14:9," in Jeremias, Abba: Studien zur neu-
               testamentlichen Theologie und Zeitgeschichte (Göttingen:
               Vandenhoeck & Ruprecht), pp. 115-120.
                  [Originally published in ZNW 44 (1952s): 103-107, re-
                  worked.]

14:11

1205   1973   T. Baarda, "Markus 14,11: epēggeilanto. 'Bron' of 'Redak-
               tie'?" GerefTheolTijd 73:65-75.   (N 19-115)

14:12-25

See also 1560.

1206   1976   V. K. Robbins, "Last Meal: Preparation, Betrayal and Ab-
                sence (Mk 14:12-25)," in The Passion in Mark: Studies on
                Mark 14 - 16 (ed. by Werner H. Kelber; Philadelphia: For-
                tress), pp. 21-40.

14:12-16

See 1028.

14:17-52

1207   1974   P. Mourlon Beernaert, "Structure littéraire et lecture thé-
                ologique de Marc 14, 17-52," in L'évangile selon Marc:
                Tradition et rédaction (ed.by M. Sabbe; Bibliotheca e-
                phemeridum theologicarum lovaniensium 34; Gembloux/Lou-
                vain: Duculot/Louvain University), pp. 241-267.

14:17(18)-25(26)

1208   1980   K. Kertelge, "Das Abendmahl Jesu im Markusevangelium," in
                Begegnung mit dem Wort: Festschrift für Heinrich Zimmer-
                mann (ed. by Josef Zmifewski and Ernst Nellessen; Bonner
                biblische Beiträge 53; Bonn: Peter Hanstein), pp. 67-80.

1209   1973   F. C. Synge, "Mark 14:18-25. Supper and Rite," JournTheol-
                SAfric 4:38-43.   (N 18-882)

1210   1971   K. Hein, "Judas Iscariot: Key to the Last-Supper Narra-
                tives?" NTS 17:227-232.   (N 15-879)

1211   1965   S. Dockx, "Le récit du repas pascal. Marc 14,17-26," Bib
                46:445-453.   (N 10-928)
                  [Republished in Dockx, O.P., Chronologies Néotestamen-
                taires et Vie de l'Église primitive: Recherches ex-
                égétiques (Gembloux: Duculot, 1976), pp. 199-206.]

14:21-25

See 1594.

14:21

1212   1956   J. Christensen, "Le fils de l'homme s'en van, ainsi qu'il
                est écrit de lui," ST 10:28-39.   (N 2-535)

14:22-25

1213   1977   Joachim JEREMIAS. The Eucharistic Words of Jesus. Tr.
                by Norman Perrin from the German 3rd ed. with the auth-
                or's revision to July 1964. London: SCM Press, 1976 and
                Philadelphia: Fortress, 1977. 278 pp.

1214   H. Merklein, "Erwägungen zur Überlieferungsgeschichte der

neutestamentlichen Abendmahlstraditionen," BZ 21:88-101,
235-244.   (N 22-108, 109)

1215   R. Pesch, "The Last Supper and Jesus' Understanding of His
             death," Biblebhashyam 3:58-75.   (N 21-755)

1216   Adrian SCHENKER. Das Abendmahl Jesu als Brennpunkt des
             Alten Testaments. Begegnung zwischen den beiden Testa-
             menten--eine bibeltheologische Studie. Biblische Bei-
             träge 13. Fribourg: Schweizerisches Katholisches Bibel-
             werk. 158 pp.

1217   1974   J. A. Grassi, "The Eucharist in the Gospel of Mark," AER
             168:595-608.   (N 19-961)

1218   1973   D. Flusser, "The Last Supper and the Essenes," Immanuel 2:
             23-27.   (N 18-124)

1219   E. J. Kilmartin, "The Eucharistic Prayer: Content and Func-
             tion of Some Early Eucharistic Prayers," in The Word in
             the World: Essays in honor of Frederick L. Moriarty, S.J.
             (ed. by Richard J. Clifford and Goerge W. MacRae; Cam-
             bridge, MA: Weston College Press), pp. 117-134.

1220   1972   J. Jeremias, "'This is My Body..,'" ExpTim 83:196-203.
                                                          (N 17-148)

1221   K. Kertelge, "Die soteriologischen Aussagen in der ur-
             christlichen Abendmahlsüberlieferung und ihre Beziehung
             zum geschichtlichen Jesus," TTZ 81:193-202. (N 17-544)

1222   1971   E. Nardoni, "Por una communidad libre. La última cena se-
             gún Mc 14,22-25 y el éxodo," RevistB 33:27-42.(N 16-185)

1223   1970   N. A. Beck, "The Last Supper as an Efficacious Symbolic
             Act," JBL 89:192-198.   (N 15-173)

1224   1963   W. E. Lynch, "The Eucharist: A Covenant Meal," TBT 1:319-
             323.
             [Republished in Contemporary New Testament Studies (ed.
             by Sister M. Rosalie Ryan, C.S.J.; Collegeville, MN:
             Liturgical Press, 1965), pp. 173-177.

1225   1962   J. A. Emerton, "To haima mou tēs diathēkēs: The Evidence of
             the Syriac Versions," JTS 13:111-117.

1226   1961   B. M. Ahern, "Gathering the Fragments: The Lord's Supper,"
             Worship 35:424-429.   (N 6-141)

1227   1959   J.-B. du Roy, "Le dernier repas de Jésus," BVC 26:44-52.
                                                          (N 4-92)

1228 1957 N. Turner, "The Style of St. Mark's Eucharistic Words,"
            JTS 8:108-111.   (N 2-295)

1229 1955 J. A. Emerton, "The Aramaic Underlying to haima mou tēs di-
            athēkēs," JTS 6:238-240.

14:22

1230 1977 A. R. Winnett, "The Breaking of the Bread: Does it Symbol-
            ize the Passion?" ExpTim 88:181-182.   (N 21-754)

14:24

1231 1974 N. Hook, "The Dominical Cup Saying," Theology 77:624-630.
                                                         (N 19-976)

1232 1972 W. Pigulla, "Das für viele vergossene Blut," MTZ 23:72-82.
                                                         (N 17-149)

1233 1964 J. A. Emerton, "Mark XIV. 24 and the Targum to the Psalter,"
            JTS 15:58-59.   (N 9-173)

14:25

1234 1973 D. Palmer, "Defining a Vow of Abstinence," Colloquium 5:
            38-41.   (N 18-125)

1235   J. A. Ziesler, "The Vow of Abstinence Again," Colloquium
            6:49-50.   (N 18-883)

1236 1972 J. A. Ziesler, "The Vow of Abstinence. A Note on Mark 14:
            25 and Parallels," Colloquium 5:12-14.   (N 17-953)

14:26-72

1237 1977 N. Walter, "Die Verleugnung des Petrus," in Theologische
            Versuche VIII (ed. by Joachim Rogge and Gottfried Schille;
            Berlin: Evangelische Verlagsanstalt), pp. 45-61.

1238 1971 M. Wilcox, "The Denial-Sequence in Mark xiv. 26-31, 66-72,"
            NTS 17:426-436.   (N 16-186)

1239 1966 E. Linnemann, "Die Verleugnung des Petrus," ZTK 63:1-32.
                                                         (N 11-726)
14:27

1240 1975 R. P. Schroeder, "The 'Worthless' Shepherd. A Study of
            Mark 14:27," CurTM 2:342-344.   (N 20-463)

1241 1967 M. Orge, "'Percutiam pastorem et dispergentur oves' (Mc 14,
            27; Mt 26,31). De momento scandali in genesi fidei

christianae," <u>Claretianum</u> 7:271-291.

14:28

1242   1974   R. H. Stein, "A Short Note on Mark xiv. 28 and xvi. 7,"
                <u>NTS</u> 20:445-452.   (N 19-565)

14:30

1243   1979   D. Brady, "The Alarm to Peter in Mark's Gospel," <u>JSNT</u> 4:
                42-57.   (N 24-119)

1244   J. W. Wenham, "How Many Cock-Crowings? The Problem of Har-
                monistic Text-Variants," <u>NTS</u> 25:523-525.   (N 24-442)

1245   1968   H. Kosmala, "The Time of the Cock-Crow, II," <u>ASTI</u> 6:132-
                134.
                [Republished in Kosmala, <u>Studies, Essays and Reviews</u>,
                <u>Vol. 2: New Testament</u> (Leiden: E. J. Brill, 1978), pp.
                79-81.]

1246   1963   H. Kosmala, "The Time of the Cock-Crow," <u>ASTI</u> 2:118-120.
                [Republished in Kosmala, <u>Studies, Essays and Reviews</u>,
                <u>Vol. 2: New Testament</u> (Leiden: E. J. Brill, 1978), pp.
                76-78.]

14:32 - 15:47

See 171a.

14:32-42

1247   1977   A. FEUILLET. <u>L'Agonie de Gethsémani: enquête exegetique et</u>
                <u>théologique suivi d'une étude du "Mystere de Jésus" de</u>
                <u>Pascal</u>. Paris: Éditions Gabalda. 345 pp.

1248   1976   A. Feuillet, "Il significato fondamentale dell'agonia del
                Getsémani," in <u>La sapienza della croce oggi, I: Atti del</u>
                <u>Congresso internazionale: Roma, 13-18 ottobre, 1975</u> (Tor-
                ino-Leumann: Elle Di Ci), pp. 69-85.

1249   W. H. Kelber, "The Hour of the Son of Man and the Tempta-
                tion of the Disciples (Mk 14:32-42)," in <u>The Passion in</u>
                <u>Mark: Studies on Mark 14 - 16</u> (ed. by Werner H. Kelber;
                Philadelphia: Fortress), pp. 41-60.

1250   G. Szarek, "A Critique of Kelber's 'The Hour of the Son of
                Man and the Temptation of the Disciples: Mark 14:32-42',"
                in <u>Society of Biblical Literature 1976 Seminar Papers</u>
                (ed. by George MacRae; Missoula, MT: Scholars Press), pp.
                111-118.

1251   1973   W. Mohn, "Gethsemane (Mk 14:32-42)," ZNW 64:194-208.
                                                              (N 19-116)

1252   1972   M. GALIZZI. Gesù nel Getsemani (Mc 14:32-42; Mt 26:36-46;
              Lc 22:39-46). Biblioteca di Scienze Religiose. Zürich/
              Rome: PAS-Verlag. xvi-317 pp.   (E 54-3141)

1253   W. H. Kelber, "Mark 14:32-42: Gethsemane. Passion Christ-
              ology and Discipleship Failure," ZNW 63:166-187.
                                                              (N 17-954)

1254   1970   R. S. Barbour, "Gethsemane in the Tradition of the Pass-
              ion," NTS 16:231-251.   (N 15-174)

1255   1966   T. Lescow, "Jesus in Gethsemane," EvT 26:141-159.
                                                              (N 11-247)

1256   1963s T. Boman, "Der Gebetskampf Jesu," NTS 10:261-273.

1257   1962   J. Héring, "Zwei exegetische Probleme in der Perikope von
              Jesus in Gethsemane (Markus 14:32-42; Matthaeus 26:36-46;
              Lukas 22:40-46)," in Neotestamentica et Patristica: eine
              freundesgabe, herrn professor dr. Oscar Cullmann zu sein-
              em 60. Geburtstag überricht (NovT Supplement 6; Leiden:
              E. J. Brill), pp. 64-69.

14:35-51

1258   1960   J. Bligh, "Christ's Death Cry (Mk 14,35-51)," HeyJ 1:142-
              146.

14:35-36

1259   1959   D. Daube, "A Prayer Pattern in Judaism," in Studia Evangel-
              ica 1: Papers Presented to the International Congress on
              "the Four Gospels in 1957" held at Christ Church, Oxford,
              1957 (Texte und Untersuchungen zur Geschichte der alt-
              christlichen Literatur 73; ed. by K. Aland et al.; Ber-
              lin: Akademie Verlag), pp. 539-545.

14:36

1260   1976   M. L. Amerio, "Il nesso abba ho patēr in Clemente Alessan-
              drino," Augustinianum 16:291-316.

1261   1970   W. C. van Unnik, "'Alles ist dir möglich' (Mk 14,36)," in
              Verborum veritas. Festschrift für Gustav Stählin zum 70.
              Geburtstag (ed. by Otto Böcher and Klaus Haacker; Wupper-
              tal: Theologischer Verlag Rolf Brockhaus), pp. 27-36.

1262   1961   W. Marchel, "Abba, Pater! Oratio Christi et christianor-
              um," VD 39:240-247.   (N 7-153)

__14:38__

1263   1964   F. Wulf, "'Der Geist ist willig, das Fleisch schwach' (Mk
              14,38)," GeistLeb 37:241-243.   (N 9-560)

__14:41__

1264   1955   G. H. Boobyer, "APECHEI in Mark xiv. 41," NTS 2:44-48.
                                            (N Experimental Issue - 32)
__14:43-52__

1265   1972   G. Schneider, "Die Verhaftung Jesu. Traditionsgeschichte
              von Mk 14:43-52," ZNW 63:188-209.   (N 17-955)

__14:51-52__

1266   1979   H. Fleddermann, "The Flight of a Naked Young Man (Mark 14:
              51-52)," CBQ 41:412-418.   (N 24-443)

1267   F. Neirynck, "La Fuite du Jeune Homme en Mc 14,51-52," ETL
              55:43-66.   (N 23-856)

1268   1973   R. Scroggs and K. I. Groff, "Baptism in Mark: Dying and
              Rising With Christ," JBL 92:531-548.   (N 18-498)

1269   1971   A. Vanhoye, "La fuite du jeune homme nu (Mc 14,51-52),"
              Bib 52:401-406.   (N 16-558)

__14:53 - 15:47__

1270   1978   Olivette GENEST. Le Christ de la passion: Perspective
              structurale: Analyse de Marc 14,53 - 15,47, des paral-
              lèles bibliques et extra-bibliques. Recherches 21 Théo-
              logie. Tournai/Montreal: Desclée/Bellarmin. 220 pp.

__14:53 - 15:41__

1271   1977   Haim COHN. The Trial and Death of Jesus. New York: KTAV.
              xxiv-419 pp.
              [First published New York: Harper & Row, 1971.]

__14:53-72__

See also 188.

1272   1970   G. Schneider, "Jesus vor dem Synedrium," BibLeb 11:1-15.
                                                             (N 15-175)

1273   1963   P. Winter, "The Marcan Account of Jesus' Trial by the San-
              hedrin," JTS 14:94-102.

14:53-67

1274   1976   P. Lamarche, "Procès et outrages (14,53-67)," in Lamarche,
                Révélation de Dieu chez Marc (Le Point Théologique 20;
                Paris: Beauchesne), pp. 105-118.
                [Previously published as "Le déclaration de Jésus de-
                vant le Sanhédrin," in Christ Vivant 1966: 147-163.]

14:53-65

1275   1977   M. Herranz Marco, "El proceso ante el Sanhedrin y el Minis-
                terio Público de Jesús," EstBíb 36:35-56.

1276   1976   J. R. Donahue, "Temple, Trial, and Royal Christology (Mark
                14:53-65)," in The Passion in Mark: Studies on Mark 14 -
                16 (ed. by Werner H. Kelber; Philadelphia: Fortress), pp.
                61-79.

1277   M. Herranz Marco, "El proceso ante el Sanhedrin y el Minis-
                terio Público de Jesús," EstBib 34:83-111; 35:49-78, 187-
                222.

1278   1973   John R. DONAHUE. Are You the Christ? The Trial Narrative
                in the Gospel of Mark. Society of Biblical Literature
                Dissertation Series 10. Missoula, MT: Society of Bibli-
                cal Literature. xi-269 pp.   (E 55-2904)

1279   1962   P. Winter, "Markus 14:53b. 55-64 ein Gebilde des Evangel-
                isten," ZNW 53:260-263.   (N 7-797)

14:53-54, 66-72

1280   1976   K. E. Dewey, "Peter's Curse and Cursed Peter (Mark 14:53-
                54, 66-72)," in The Passion in Mark: Studies on Mark 14 -
                16 (ed. by Werner H. Kelber; Philadelphia: Fortress), pp.
                96-114.

1281   J. Ernst, "Noch einmal: Die Verleugnung Jesu durch Petrus
                (Mk 14,54.66-72)," Catholica 30:207-226.   (N 21-401)
                [Republished in Petrus und Papst: Evangelium, Einheit
                der Kirche, Papstdienst. Beiträge und Notizen (ed.
                by Albert Brandenburg and Hans Jörg Urban; Münster:
                Aschendorff, 1977), pp. 43-62.]

1282   1974   R. Pesch, "Die Verleugnung des Petrus: Eine Studie zu Mk
                14,54.66-72 (und Mk 14,26-31)," in Neues Testament und
                Kirche: Für Rudolf Schnackenburg (ed. by Joachim Gnilka;
                Freiburg/Basel/Vienna: Herder), pp. 42-62.

1283   1956   G. W. Buchanan, "Mark xiv. 54," ExpTim 68:27. (N 1-187)

<u>14:55-65</u>

1284   1977   Donald JUEL. <u>Messiah and Temple. The Trial of Jesus in</u>
              <u>the Gospel of Mark</u>. Society of Biblical Literature Dis-
              sertation Series 31. Missoula, MT: Scholars Press. 223
              pp.   (E 58s-4961)

1285   1975   D. Juel, "The Function of the Trial of Jesus in Mark's Gos-
              pel," in <u>Society of Biblical Literature 1975 Seminar Pa-</u>
              <u>pers II</u> (ed. by George MacRae; Missoula, MT: Scholars
              Press), pp. 83-104.

1286   1974   S. Légasse, "Jésus devant le Sanhédrin. Recherche sur les
              traditions évangéliques," <u>RTL</u> 5:170-197.   (N 19-117)

1287   1970   G. Schneider, "Gab es eine vorsynoptische Szene 'Jesus vor
              dem Synedrium'?" <u>NovT</u> 12:22-39.   (N 14-874)

1288   1958   T. A. Burkill, "The Trial of Jesus," <u>VC</u> 12:1-18.(N 3-85)

<u>14:55-64</u>

See 1313.

<u>14:58</u>

1289   1978   G. Biguzzi, "Mc. 14,58: un tempio <u>acheiropoiētos</u>," <u>RivistB</u>
              26:225-240.   (N 23-476)

1290   1976   G. Theissen, "Die Tempelweissagung Jesu. Prophetie im
              Spannungsfeld von Stadt und Land," <u>TZ</u> 32:144-158.
                                                            (N 21-402)
<u>14:61-62</u>

See also 1164.

1291   1976   N. Perrin, "The High Priest's Question and Jesus' Answer
              (Mark 14:61-62)," in <u>The Passion in Mark: Studies on Mark</u>
              <u>14 - 16</u> (ed. by Werner H. Kelber; Philadelphia: Fortress),
              pp. 80-95.

<u>14:61</u>

1292   1961   E. Lövestam, "Die Frage des Hohenpriesters (Mark. 14,61
              par. Matth. 26,63," <u>SEÅ</u> 26:93-107.   (N 7-798)

<u>14:62</u>

See also 1480, 1531.

1293   1977   R. Kempthorne, "The Marcan Text of Jesus' Answer to the high Priest (Mark xiv 62)," NovT 19:198-208.(N 22-416)

1294 1968 F. H. Borsch, "Mark xiv. 62 and I Enoch lxii. 5," NTS 14: 565-567. (N 13-206)

1295 1966 N. Perrin, "Mark XIV. 62: The End Product of a Christian Pesher Tradition?" NTS 12:150-155. (N 10-929)
[Republished in Perrin, A Modern Pilgrimage in New Testament Christology (Philadelphia: Fortress), pp. 10-22.]

1296 1964 A. M. Goldberg, "Sitzend zur Rechten der Kraft. Zur Gottesbezeichnung Gebura in der frühen rabbinischen Literatur," BZ 8:284-293. (N 9-561)

1297 1961 O. Linton, "The Trial of Jesus and the Interpretation of Psalm cx," NTS 7:258-262. (N 6-142)

1298 1960 T. F. Glasson, "The Reply to Caiphas (Mark xiv. 62)," NTS 7:88-93. (N 5-411)

1299 1958 H. K. McArthur, "Mark xiv. 62," NTS 4:156-158.(N 2-536)

1300 1956 J. A. T. Robinson, "The Second Coming--Mark xiv. 62," ExpTim 67:336-340. (N 1-188)

1301 1955 E. J. Tinsley, "The Sign of the Son of Man (Mk 14,62)," SJT 8:297-306.

14:65

1302 1973 W. C. van Unnik, "Jesu Verhöhnung vor dem Synedrium," in van Unnik, Sparsa collecta: The Collected Essays of W. C. van Unnik. Part One: Evangelia--Paulina--Acta (NovT Supplement 29; Leiden: E. J. Brill), pp. 3-5.
[Originally published in ZNW 29 (1930):310s.]

1303 1962 P. Benoit, "Les outrages à Jésus Prophète (Mc 14,65 par)," in Neotestamentica et Patristica: eine freundesgabe, herrn professor dr. Oscar Cullmann zu seinem 60. Geburtstag überricht (NovT Supplement 6; Leiden: E. J. Brill), pp. 92-110.

1304 1960 R. H. Gundry, "LMTLYN: 1 Q Isaiah a 50, 6 and Mark 14,65," RevQ 2:559-567. (N 6-143)

14:66-72

See also 1237 - 1239, 1280 - 1282.

1305 1978 D. Gewalt, "Die Verleugnung des Petrus," LingBib 43:113-144. (N 23-477)

1306   1973   G. W. H. Lampe, "St. Peter's Denial," <u>BJRL</u> 55:346-368.
                                                                  (N 18-126)

1307   1961   G. Klein, "Die Verleugnung des Petrus. Eine traditionsge-
               schichtliche Untersuchung," <u>ZTK</u> 58:285-328. (N 7-154)

<u>14:68</u>

See also 1237, 1245, 1246.

1308   1956   W. J. P. Boyd, "Peter's Denials--Mark xiv. 68, Luke xxii.
               57," <u>ExpTim</u> 67:341.   (N 1-189)

<u>14:72</u>

See also 1245, 1246.

1309   1972   G. M. Lee, "Mark 14,72: <u>epibalon eklaien</u>," <u>Bib</u> 53:411-412.
                                                                  (N 17-956)

1310   1958   J. N. Birdsall, "<u>To rhēma hōs eipen autō ho Iēsous</u>: Mk xiv.
               72," <u>NovT</u> 2:272-275.   (N 4-93)

<u>Chs. 15 - 16</u>

1311   1978   Daniel PATTE and Aline PATTE. <u>Structural Exegesis: From
               Theory to Practice: Exegesis of Mark 15 and 16: Hermeneut-
               ical Implications</u>. Philadelphia: Fortress. x - 134 pp.

<u>15:2-5</u>

1312   1978   R. L. Overstreet, "Roman Law and the Trial of Christ," <u>BS</u>
               135:323-332.

1313   1961   G. Braumann, "Markus 15,2-5 und Markus 14,55-64," <u>ZNW</u> 52:
               273-278.   (N 6-792)

<u>15:2</u>

1314   1960   J. Irmscher, "<u>Su legeis</u> (Mk 15,2; Mt 27,1; Lc 23,3)," <u>Stud-
               ii Clasice</u> 2:151-158.

<u>15:8</u>

1315   1978   G. M. Lee, "Mark xv 8," <u>NovT</u> 20:74.   (N 23-121)

<u>15:14</u>

1316   1975s J. M. Ford, "'Crucify him, crucify him' and the Temple
               Scroll," <u>ExpTim</u> 87:275-278.

15:20b-41

1317   1976   T. J. Weeden, Sr., "The Cross as Power in Weakness (Mark
                15:20b-41)," in The Passion in Mark: Studies on Mark 14 -
                16 (ed. by Werner H. Kelber; Philadelphia: Fortress), pp.
                115-134.

15:21-41

1318   1974   J. H. Reumann, "Psalm 22 at the Cross. Lament and Thanks-
                giving for Jesus Christ," Int 28:39-58.   (N 18-884)

15:21(22)-39

1319   1978   M. de Burgos Nuñez, "La communion de Dios con el crucifica-
                do. Cristología de Marcos 15,22-39," EstBíb 37:243-266.
                                                            (N 25-103)

1320   1976   F. Vouga and M. Faessler, "Mc 15,21-39: La mort de Jésus,"
                Bulletin du Centre Protestant d'Études 28:25-28, 28-30.

15:21

1321   1975   G. M. Lee, "Mark xv 21, 'The Father of Alexander and Ruf-
                us,'" NovT 17:303.   (N 20-805)

15:25

See also 141.

1322   1966   A. Mahoney, "A New Look at 'The Third Hour' of Mk 15,25,"
                CBQ 28:292-299.   (N 11-727)

15:26

1323   1968   G. M. Lee, "The Inscription on the Cross," PEQ 100:144.
                                                            (N 13-891)

15:29-34

1324   1971   J. A. Dvořáček, "Vom Leiden Gottes. Markus 15,29-34,"
                CommViat 14:231-252.   (N 16-890)

15:33-39

1325   1978   R. A. Culpepper, "The Passion and Resurrection in Mark,"
                RevExp 75:583-600.   (N 23-446)

1326   M. Josuttis, "Die permanente Passion. Predigt über Markus
                15,33-39," EvT 38:160-163.

<u>15:34</u>

1327   1978   X. Léon-Dufour, "Le dernier cri de Jésus," <u>Études</u> 348-366-
                682.   (N 23-122)

1328   R. Rubinkiewicz, "Mk 15,34 i Hbr 1,8-9 w świetle tradycji
                targumicznej," <u>RoczTeolKan</u> 25:59-67.   (N 24-444)

1329   1973   G. Braumann, "Wozu? (Mark 15,34)," <u>Theokratia</u> 2:155-165.

1330   1970   F. W. Danker, "The Demonic Secret in Mark: A Reexamination
                of the Cry of Dereliction (15:34)," <u>ZNW</u> 61:48-69.
                                                                (N 15-531)

1331   1959   J. Gnilka, "'Mein Gott, mein Gott, warum hast du mich ver-
                lassen?' (Mk 15,34 Par.)," <u>BZ</u> 3:294-297.   (N 4-405)

<u>15:35-36</u>

See 1454.

<u>15:38</u>

1332   1974   P. Lamarche, "La mort du Christ et le voile du temple selon
                Marc," <u>NRT</u> 96:583-599.   (N 19-118)
                [Republished in Lamarche, <u>Révélation de Dieu chez Marc</u>
                (Le Point Théologique 20; Paris: Beauchesne, 1976),
                pp. 119-144.]

<u>15:39</u>

See also 1526.

1333   1978   K. Stock, "Das Bekenntnis des Centurio. Mk 15, 39 im Rahm-
                en des Markusevangeliums," <u>ZKT</u> 100:289-301. (N 23-123)

1334   1973   P. B. Harner, "Qualitative Anarthrous Predicate Nouns: Mark
                15:39 and John 1:1," <u>JBL</u> 92:75-87.   (N 17-957)

1335   1970   H. A. Guy, "Son of God in Mk 15:39," <u>ExpTim</u> 81:151.
                                                                (N 14-875)

1336   1969   R. G. Bratcher, "Mark xv. 39: the Son of God," <u>ExpTim</u> 80:
                286.   (N 14-172)

1337   T. F. Glasson, "Mark xv. 39: the Son of God," <u>ExpTim</u> 80:
                286.   (N 14-171)

1338   1968   P. H. Bligh, "A Note on Huios Theou in Mark 15:39," <u>ExpTim</u>
                80:51-53.   (N 13-591)

1339   1967   J. R. Michaels, "The Centurion's Confession and the Spear

Thrust," CBQ 29:102-109.   (N 11-1053)

1340   1956   R. G. Bratcher, "A Note on huios theou (Mark xv. 39)," Exp-
                Tim 68:27-28.   (N 1-190)

15:40 - 16:8

1341   1958   É. Dhanis, "L'ensevelissement de Jésus et la visite au tom-
                beau dans l'évangile de saint Marc (Mc., XV, 40-XVI,8),"
                Greg 39:367-410.   (N 3-362)

15:42 - 16:8

1342   1974   R. Pesch, "Der Schluss der vormarkinischen Passionsge-
                schichte und des Markusevangeliums: Mk 15,42 - 16:8," in
                L'évangile selon Marc: Tradition et rédaction (ed. by M.
                Sabbe; Bibliotheca ephemeridum theologicarum lovaniensium
                34; Gembloux/Louvain: Duculot/Louvain University), pp.
                365-409.

15:40

See 140, 573.

15:47

See 573.

Ch. 16

1343   1978   J. Cantinat, "Saint Marc et la résurrection de Jésus," in
                Réflexions sur la résurrection de Jésus (d'après saint
                Paul et saint Marc) (Paris: Gabalda), pp. 79-106.

1344   1977   A. Benito, "Marcos 16. Redacción y Hermenéutica," Salman-
                ticensis 24:279-305.   (N 22-783)

1345   H. Lubsczyk, "Kyrios Jesus: Beobachtungen und Gedanken zum
                Schluss des Markusevangeliums," in Die Kirche des An-
                fangs: Festschrift für Heinz Schürmann zum 65. Geburtstag
                (ed. by Rudolf Schnackenburg, Josef Ernst and Joachim
                Wanke; Erfurter theologische Studien 38; Leipzig: St.
                Benno, 1977, and Freiburg/Basel: Herder, 1978), pp. 133-
                174.

1346   1972   J. W. E. Dunn, "The Text of Mark 16 in the English Bible,"
                ExpTim 83:311-312.   (N 17-150)

1347   B. Metzger, "The Ending of the Gospel According to Mark in
                the Ethiopic Manuscripts," in Understanding the Sacred
                Text: Essays in Honor of Morton S. Enslin on the Hebrew
                Bible and Christian Beginnings (ed. by John Reumann;

Valley Forge, PA: Judson), pp. 165-180.

1348   W. Schmithals, "Der Markusschluss, die Verklärungsge-
               schichte und die Aussendung der Zwölf," ZTK 69:379-411.
                                                                (N 17-958)

1349   1971   H. W. Bartsch, "Der Schluss der Markus-Evangeliums. Ein
               überlieferungsgeschichtliches Problem," TZ 27:241-254.
                                                                (N 16-559)

1350   1969   K. Aland, "Bemerkungen zum Schluss des Markusevangeliums,"
               in Neotestamentica et Semitica: Studies in honour of
               Matthew Black (ed. by E. Earle Ellis and Max Wilcox;
               Edinburgh: T & T Clark), pp. 157-180.

1351   1965   N. Q. Hamilton, "Resurrection Tradition and the Composition
               of Mark," JBL 84:415-421.   (N 10-525)

1352   1964   D. J. Bowman, "The Resurrection in Mark," TBT 1:709-713.
                                                                (N 8-968)
               [Republished in Contemporary New Testament Studies (ed.
               by Sister M. Rosalie Ryan, C.S.J.; Collegeville, MN:
               Liturgical Press, 1965), pp. 161-165.]

1353   1959   G. Hebert, "The Resurrection-Narratives in St. Mark's Gos-
               pel," AusBR 7:58-65.

16:1-8

1354   1980   A. Lindemann, "Die Osterbotschaft des Markus. Zur theolo-
               gischen Interpretation von Mark 16,1-8," NTS 26:298-317.
                                                                (N 25-104)

1355   F. Neirynck, "Marc 16,1-8. Tradition et rédaction," ETL
               56:56-88.   (N 25-105)

1356   H. Paulsen, "Mk xvi 1-8," NovT 22:138-175.   (N 24-812)

1357   1979   F.-J. Niemann, "Die Erzählung vom leeren Grab bei Markus,"
               ZKT 101:188-199.   (N 24-120)

1358   1978   M. D. Goulder, "Mark xvi.1-8 and Parallels," NTS 24:235-
               240.   (N 22-417)

1359   H.-W. Kuhn, "Predigt über Markus 16,1-8," EvT 38:155-160.

1360   G. O'Mahoney, "The Empty Tomb," Clergy Review 63:207-210.

1361   1977   G. Mangatt, "At the Tomb of Jesus," Biblebhashyam 3:91-
               96.   (N 22-110)

1362 1976   J. E. Alsup, "John Dominic Crossan, 'Empty Tomb and Absent
             Lord'—A Response," in Society of Biblical Literature
             1976 Seminar Papers (ed. by George MacRae; Missoula, MT:
             Scholars Press), pp. 263-267.

1363   J. D. Crossan, "Empty Tomb and Absent Lord (Mark 16:1-8),"
             in The Passion in Mark: Studies on Mark 14 - 16 (ed. by
             Werner H. Kelber; Philadelphia: Fortress), pp. 135-152.

1364   M. D. Goulder, "The Empty Tomb," Theology 79:206-214.
                                                        (N 21-104)

1365   T. R. Longstaff, "Empty Tomb and Absent Lord: Mark's Inter-
             pretation of the Tradition," in Society of Biblical Lit-
             erature 1976 Seminar Papers (ed. by George MacRae; Mis-
             soula, MT: Scholars Press), pp. 269-277.

1366 1975   F. C. Synge, "Mark 16.1-8," JournTheolSAfric 11:71-73.
                                                        (N 20-464)

1367 1974   K. Aland, "Der Schluss des Markusevangeliums," in L'évan-
             gile selon Marc: Tradition et rédaction (ed. by M. Sabbe;
             Bibliotheca ephemeridum theologicarum lovaniensium 34;
             Gembloux/Louvain: Duculot/Louvain University), pp. 435-
             470.
               [Republished in Aland, Neutestamentliche Entwürfe (The-
               ologische Bücherei Neues Testament 63; Munich: Chr.
               Kaiser, 1979), pp. 246-283.]

1368   A. Ammassari, "Il racconto degli avvenimenti della mattina
             di Pasqua secondo Marco 16, 1-8," BeO 16:49-64.(N 19-566)

1369   H.-W. Bartsch, "Der ursprüngliche Schluss der Leidensge-
             schichte: Überlieferungsgeschichtliche Studien zum Mark-
             us-Schluss," in L'évangile selon Marc: Tradition et ré-
             daction (ed. by M. Sabbe; Bibliotheca ephemeridum theolo-
             gicarum lovaniensium 34; Gembloux/Louvain: Duculot/Lou-
             vain University), pp. 411-433.

1370 1973   T. Horvath, "The Early Markan Tradition on the Resurrection
             (Mk 16,1-8)," RUO 43:445-448.   (N 18-499)

1371   J. Radermakers, "Prêcher le Ressuscité," LumVit 28:67-80.

1372 1972   E. Güttgemanns, "Linguistische Analyse von Mk 16,1-8,"
             LingBib 11-12:13-53.   (N 17-151)

1373   R. H. Smith, "New and Old in Mark 16:1-8," CTM 43:518-527.
                                                        (N 17-545)

1374   1971   R. P. Meye, "Mark's Special Easter Emphasis," <u>ChristToday</u>
              15:584-586.   (N 15-880)

1375   H. Schlier, "Die Osterbotschaft aus dem Grab (Markus 16,1-
              8)," <u>KathGed</u> 27:1-6.   (N 16-187)

1376   1970   J. Delorme, "Resurrección y tumba de Jesús. Mc 16,1-8 en
              la tradición evangélica," <u>SelecTeol</u> 9:119-130.
              ⌈Originally published in French in Lectio Divina 50;
              see below, 1379.⌉

1377   1969   I. Broer, "Zur heutigen Diskussion der Grabesgeschichte,"
              <u>BibLeb</u> 10:40-52.   (N 14-173)

1378   J. Delorme, "Les femmes au tombeau, Mc 16,1-8," <u>AsSeign</u> 2:
              58-67.

1379   "Résurrection et tombeau de Jésus: Mc 16,1-8
              dans la tradition évangélique," in <u>La Résurrection du</u>
              <u>Christ et l'exégèse modern</u> (ed. by E. de Surgy et al;
              Lectio Divina 50; Paris: Éditions du Cerf), pp. 105-151.

1380   R. P. Meye, "Mark 16:8--The Ending of Mark's Gospel," <u>BR</u>
              14:33-43.   (N 14-877)

1381   1968   Ludger SCHENKE. <u>Auferstehung und leeres Grab. Eine tra-</u>
              <u>ditionsgeschichtliche Untersuchung von Mk 16,1-8</u>. Stutt-
              garter Bibelstudien 33. Stuttgart: Katholisches Bibel-
              werk. 117 pp.   (E 50-2622)

1382   1967   D. Dietzfelbinger, "Mk 16:1-8," in <u>Kranzbacher Gespräch:</u>
              <u>der Lutherischen Bischofskonferenz zur Auseinandersetz-</u>
              <u>ung um die Bibel</u> (ed. by Hugo Schnell; Berlin/Hamburg:
              Lutherisches Verlagshaus), pp.9-22.

1383   1963   E. Galbiati, "È risorto, non è qui (Marco, 16,1-8)," <u>BeO</u>
              5:67-72.   (N 8-593)

1384   1962   G. Hebert, "The Resurrection-Narrative in St. Mark's Gos-
              pel," <u>SJT</u> 15:66-73.   (N 7-155)

1384a 1959   J. L. Cheek, "The Historicity of the Markan Resurrection
              Narrative," <u>JBR</u> 27:191-200.   (N 4-94)

1385   G. Hebert, "The Resurrection-Narrative in St. Mark's Gos-
              pel," <u>AusBR</u> 8:58-65.   (N 5-412)

<u>16:1</u>

See 140, 573.

16:2

1386 1978 F. Neirynck, "Anateilantos tou hēliou (Mc 16,2)," ETL 54:
70-103. (N 23-124)

1387 1957 F. Montagnini, "'...Valde mane una sabbatorum veniunt ad
monumentum...' (Mc 16,2). Contributo ad una pagina di
armonia evangelica," ScuolCatt 85:111-120.

16:4

See 302.

16:5

1388 1969 J. H. McIndoe, "The Young Man at the Tomb," ExpTim 80:125.
(N 13-892)

16:7-8

1389 1977 D. Catchpole, "The Fearful Silence of the Women at the
Tomb: A Study in Markan Theology," JournTheolSAfric 18:
3-10. (N 21-756)

16:7

See 1242.

16:8

1390 1980 N. R. Petersen, "When is the End not the End? Literary Reflections on the Ending of Mark's Narrative," Int 34:151-
166. (N 24-813)

1391 1972 P. W. van der Horst, "Can a Book End With GAR? A Note On
Mark xvi. 8," JTS 23:121-124. (N 17-152)

1392 1969 J. Luzarraga, "Retraducción semítica de phobeomai en Mc 16,
8," Bib 50:497-510. (N 14-876)

16:8-20

1393 1970 K. Aland, "Der wiedergefundene Markusschluss? Eine method-
ologische Bemerkung zur textkritischen Arbeit," ZTK 67:
3-13. (N 15-176)

1394 1969 E. Linnemann, "Der (wiedergefundene) Markusschluss," ZTK
66:255-287. (N 14-878)

16:9-20

1395 1978 Joseph HUG. La finale de l'évangile de Marc (Mc 16,9-20).
Études Bibliques. Paris: J. Gabalda. 266 pp.

1396   1976   R. H. FULLER. <u>Longer Mark: Forgery, Interpolation, or Old</u>
              <u>Tradition?</u> Protocol of the Colloquy of the Center for
              Hermeneutical Studies in Hellenistic and Modern Culture
              18. Berkeley, CA: Center for Hermeneutical Studies in
              Hellenistic and Modern Culture. Pp. 1-11; responses,
              pp. 12-71.   (E 58s-4987)

1397   1975   J. W. Burgon, "The Last Twelve Verses of the Gospel accord-
              to St. Mark (Condensed by D. O. Fuller)," in <u>Counterfeit</u>
              <u>or Genuine? Mark 16? John 8?</u> (ed. by D. O. Fuller; Grand
              Rapids: Grand Rapids International Publications), pp. 25-
              130.
                  [This appears to be a condensation of a book by John
                  William Burgon, with the same title, published in
                  Evansville by the Sovereign Grace Book Club, 1959,
                  416 pp. That, in turn, appears to be a reprint of an
                  1871 edition.]

1397a   S. Zwemer, "The Last Twelve Verses of the Gospel of Mark,"
              in <u>Counterfeit or Genuine? Mark 16? John 8?</u> (ed. by D.
              O. Fuller; Grand Rapids: Grand Rapids International Pub-
              lications), pp. 159-174.

1398   1974   William R. FARMER. <u>The Last Twelve Verses of Mark</u>. Socie-
              ty for New Testament Studies Monograph Series 25. Lon-
              don/New York: Cambridge University Press. xii-123 pp.

1399   1973   G. W. Trompf, "The Markusschluss in Recent Research," <u>AusBR</u>
              21:15-26.   (N 18-885)

1400   1972   G. W. Trompf, "The First Resurrection Appearance and the
              Ending of Mark's Gospel," <u>NTS</u> 18:308-330.   (N 17-153)

1401   1971   J. K. Elliott, "The Text and Language of the Endings to
              Mark's Gospel," <u>TZ</u> 27:255-262.   (N 16-560)

1402   1967   F. Wagenaars, "Structura litteraria et momentum theologicum
              pericopae Mc 16,9-20," <u>VD</u> 45:19-22.   (N 12-184)

1403   1958   M. VAN DER VALK. <u>Observations on Mark 16, 9-20 in Relation</u>
              <u>to St. Mark's Gospel</u>. Coimbra: Faculdade de Letras da
              Universidade de Coimbra. 44 pp.   (E 41-1571)

<u>16:14-15</u>

1404   1979   G. Schwarz, "Zum Freer-Logion—ein Nachtrag," <u>ZNW</u> 70:119.
                                                            (N 24-445)

1405   1972   K. Haacker, "Bemerkungen zum Freer-Logion," <u>ZNW</u> 63:125-
              129.   (N 17-959)

16:15-20

1406   1970   G. Becquet, "La mission universelle de l'Église par la foi
                et ses signes (Mc 16, 15-20)," EspVie 80:297-300.

1407   1969   P. Ternant, "La prédication universelle de l'Évangile du
                Seigneur, Mc 16, 15-20," AsSeign 2:38-48.

VII.   THEOLOGICAL MOTIFS

Mark's Theology: Overviews

See also 107, 227, 232, 272, 290, 337, 385, 583.

1408   1977   Heinrich BAARLINK. Anfängliches Evangelium. Ein Beitrag
                zur näheren Bestimmung der theologischen Motive im Mark-
                usevangelium. Kampen: J. H. Kok. vii-313 pp.
                                                            (E 58s-4787)

1409   Phillip VAN LINDEN. Knowing Christ Through Mark's Gospel.
                Herald Biblical Booklets. Chicago: Franciscan Herald
                Press. 91 pp.

1410   1976   I. F. CHURCH. A Study of the Marcan Gospel. New York:
                Vantage Press. vii-200 pp.   (E 58s-4796)

1411   C. Senft, "La théologie de l'Évangile selon Marc," Bulletin
                du Centre Protestant d'Etudes 28:5-15.   (N 21-390)

1412   1974   Dale MILLER. The Adult Son. A Study of the Gospel of Mark.
                Des Moines: Miller Books. v-163 pp.

1413   Gottfried SCHILLE. Offen für alle Menschen. Redaktionsge-
                schichtliche Beobachtungen zur Theologie des Markus-Evan-
                geliums. Arbeiten zur Theologie, Heft 55. Stuttgart:
                Calwer Verlag. 99 pp.   (E 55-2882)

1414   1973   A. Stöger, "Das Kerygma des Markusevangeliums," BLit 46:22-
                29.   (N 18-119)

1415   L. Swain, "Preaching from the Lectionary in 1973: The Gos-
                pel According to St. Mark," ClerRev 58:342-349.(N 18-120)

1416   1972   T. A. Burkill, "Theological Antinomies: Ben Sira and St.
                Mark," in Burkill, New Light on the Earliest Gospel: Sev-
                en Markan Studies (Ithaca, NY: Cornell University), pp.
                121-179.

1417   K.-G. Reploh, "Das unbekannte Evangelium. Das Markus-Evan-
             gelium in der Theologiegeschichte," BK 27:108-110.
                                                          (N 17-925)

1418   1971   P. Schoonenberg, "Notes of a Systematic Theologian," in
             Theology, Exegesis and Proclamation (ed. by Roland Mur-
             phy; Concilium 70; New York: Herder and Herder), pp. 90-
             97.

1419   1970   J.-L. CHORDAT, Jésus devant sa mort dans l'évangile de
             Marc. Lire la Bible 21. Paris: Éditions du Cerf.
             111 pp.   (E 52-2533)

1420   1969   J. Roloff, "Das Markusevangelium als Geschichtsdarstellung,"
             EvT 29:73-93.   (N 14-154)
                [Republished in Das Markus-Evangelium (ed. by Rudolf
                Pesch; Wege der Forschung 411; Darmstadt: Wissenschaft-
                liche Buchgesellschaft, 1979), pp. 283-310.]

1421   1968   Christopher Francis EVANS. The Beginning of the Gospel.
             Four Lectures on St. Mark's Gospel. London: SPCK.
             88 pp.   (E 49-2602)

1422   1967   Roy A. HARRISVILLE. The Miracle of Mark: A Study in the
             Gospel. Minneapolis: Augsburg Publishing House. 128
             pp.   (E 49-2611)

1423   Johannes SCHREIBER. Theologie des Vertrauens. Eine redak-
             tionsgeschichtliche Untersuchung des Markusevangeliums.
             Hamburg: Furche-Verlag. 272 pp.   (E 49-2649)

1424   1966   Johannes SCHREIBER. Theologische Erkenntnis und unter-
             richtlicher Vollzug: Dargestellt am Markusevangelium.
             Hamburg: Furche-Verlag. 196 pp.   (E 47-2460)

1425   1964   E. Schweizer, "Die theologische Leistung des Markus," EvT
             24:337-355.
                [Republished in Schweizer, Beiträge zur Theologie des
                Neuen Testaments; Neutestamentliche Aufsätze (1955 -
                1970 (Zürich: Zwingli Verlag, 1970), pp. 21-42.]

1426   1963   W. F. J. Ryan, "The Preaching within the Preaching," TBT
             1:457-464.
                [Republished in Contemporary New Testament Studies (ed.
                by Sister M. Rosalie Ryan, C.S.J.; Collegeville, Minn.:
                Liturgical Press, 1965), pp. 165-173.]

1427   1962   P. Fannon, "The Four Gospels. I. St. Mark's Message,"
             ClerRev 47:404-414.   (N 7-149)

1428   E. Schweizer, "Anmerkungen zur Theologie des Markus," in

Neotestamentica et Patristica: eine freundesgabe, herrn
professor dr. Oscar Cullmann zu seinem 60. Geburtstag
überricht (NovT Supplement 6; Leiden: E. J. Brill), pp.
35-46.

1429   D. M. Stanley, "Mark and Modern Apologetics," TBT 1:58-64.
        ᵣRepublished in Contemporary New Testament Studies (ed.
        by Sister M. Rosalie Ryan, C.S.J.; Collegeville, Minn.:
        Liturgical Press, 1965), pp. 178-183.ᵧ

1430 1957   N. K. Bakken, "Avenues of Thought in Mark's Gospel," LQ 9:
              222-233.

1431 1957   T. A. Burkill, "St. Mark's Philosophy of History," NTS 3:
              142-148.   (N 2-51)

Mark's Theology: John the Baptist

1432 1977   C. Wolff, "Zur Bedeutung Johannes des Täufers im Markus-
              evangelium," TLZ 102:857-865.   (N 22-773)

1433 1975   R. P. Rousseau, "John the Baptist: Jesus' Forerunner in
              Mark's Christology," TBT 77:316-322.

Christology / Jesus

See also 114, 264, 289, 561, 873, 902, 1276, 1433.

1434 1980   T. R. W. Longstaff, "Crisis and Christology: The Theology
              of the Gospel of Mark," Perkins Journal 33:28-40.
                                                        (N 25-85)

1435 1979   W. D. Carroll, "The Jesus of Mark's Gospel," TBT 103:2105-
              2112.   (N 24-104)

1436   R. C. Tannehill, "The Gospel of Mark as Narrative Christ-
        ology," Semeia 16:57-95.

1437 1978   J. L. Blevins, "The Christology of Mark," RevExp 75:505-
              517.   (N 23-443)

1438 1977   W. J. Bennett, Jr., "The Gospel of Mark and Traditions
              About Jesus," Encounter 38:1-11.   (N 21-734)

1439   D. Lührmann, "Biographie des Gerechten als Evangelium. Vor-
        stellungen zu einem Markus-Kommentar," Wort und Dienst
        14:25-50.   (N 24-801)

1440   E. Schweizer, "Towards a Christology of Mark?" in God's

Christ and His People: Studies in honor of Nils Alstrup Dahl (ed. by Jacob Jervell and Wayne A. Meeks; Oslo: Universitetsforlaget), pp. 29-42.

1441 1976 K. Stock, "Gesú è il Cristo, il Figlio di Dio, nel vangelo di Marco," RassTeol 17:242-253.   (N 21-391)

1442 1975 H. Langkammer, "Chrystologia ewangelii Marka," RoczTeolKan 22:49-63.   (N 21-389)

1443   U. Luz, "Das Jesusbild der vormarkinischen Tradition," in Jesus Christus in Historie und Theologie: neutestamentliche Festschrift für Hans Conzelmann zum 60. Geburtstag (ed. by Georg Strecker; Tübingen: Mohr), pp. 347-374.

1444   P. von der Osten-Saeken, "Streitgespräch und Parabel als Formen markinischer Christologie," in Jesus Christus in Historie und Theologie: neutestamentliche Festschrift für Hans Conzelmann zum 60. Geburtstag (ed. by Georg Strecker; Tübingen: Mohr), pp. 375-394.

1445 1974 J. Delgado, "El silencio, lenguaje revelador del misterio de Cristo en el Evangelio de Marcos. Un estudio exégetico-teologico," Ecclesiastica Xaveriana 24:133-211.

1446   E. R. Martinez, "The identity of Jesus in Mark," IntCathRev/ Communio 1:323-342.   (N 20-100)

1447 1973 J. Lambrecht, "The Christology of Mark," BTB 3:256-273.   (N 18-877)

1448   É. Trocmé, "Is there a Markan Christology?" in Christ and Spirit in the New Testament: In Honour of Charles Francis Digby Moule (ed. by Barnabas Lindars and Stephen S. Smalley; Cambridge/New York: Cambridge University Press), pp. 3-13.

1449 1972 F. J. Schierse, "Das Christusbild im Markusevangelium. Neuere Untersuchungen zur markinischen Christologie," BK 27: 114-116.   (N 17-927)

1450   Harald WEINACHT. Die Menschwerdung des Sohnes Gottes im Markusevangelium. Studien zur Christologie des Markusevangeliums. Hermeneutische Untersuchungen zur Theologie 13. Tübingen: Mohr-Siebeck. 197 pp.   (E 54-3213)

1451 1971 L. F. Rivera, " Escribió Marcos para nuestro tiempo?" RevistB 33:195-224.   (N 16-870)

1452   N. Perrin, "The Christology of Mark: A Study in Methodology," JR 51:173-187.   (N 16-168)

[Republished in Perrin, <u>A Modern Pilgrimage in New</u>
<u>Testament Christology</u> (Philadelphia: Fortress, 1974),
pp. 104-121, and in <u>Das Markus-Evangelium</u> (ed. by Rudolf Pesch; Wege der Forschung 411; Darmstadt: Wissenschaftliche Buchgesellschaft, 1979), pp. 356-376.
A slightly revised version appeared as "The Christology of Mark" in <u>L'évangile selon Marc: Tradition et</u>
<u>rédaction</u> (ed.by M. Sabbe; Bibliotheca ephemeridum
theologicarum lovaniensium 34; Gembloux/Louvain: Ducu-
lot/Louvain University, 1974), pp. 471-485.]

1453   1968   D. Zeller, "Jesus als Mittler des Glaubens nach dem Markusevangelium," <u>BibLeb</u> 9:278-286.   (N 13-877)

1453a   1967   F. POEPPIG. <u>Das Markus-Evangelium. Die Sprache des kos-</u>
<u>mischen Christus im Markus-Evangelium</u>. Freiburg: Verlag
Die Kommenden. 247 pp.   (E 50-2613)

1454   1966   P. M. K. Morris, "Elijah and Jesus in Mark's Gospel," <u>Triv-</u>
<u>ium</u> 1:121-133.

1455   1965   U. Luz, "Das Geheimnismotiv und die markinische Christologie," <u>ZNW</u> 56:9-30.   (N 10-526)
[Republished in <u>Das Markus-Evangelium</u> (ed. by Rudolf
Pesch; Wege der Forschung 411; Darmstadt: Wissenschaftliche Buchgesellschaft, 1979), pp. 211-237.]

1456   1964   P. Vielhauer, "Erwägungen zur Christologie des Markusevangeliums," in <u>Zeit und Geschichte. Dankesgabe an Rudolf</u>
<u>Bultmann zum 80. Geburtstag</u> (ed. by Erich Dinkler in col-
laboration with Hartwig Thyen; Tübingen: J.C.B. Mohr
[Paul Siebeck]), pp. 155-169.
[Republished in Vielhauer, <u>Aufsätze zum Neuen Testament</u>
Theologischer Bucherei 31; Munich: Chr. Kaiser Verlag,
1965), pp. 199-214.]

1457   1963   L. O. Bristol, "Jesus in the Gospel of Mark," <u>RelLife</u> 32:
429-437.   (N 8-144)

1458   É. Trocmé, "Jésus, prophète du déracinement et du ré-enra-
cinement d'après les ch. 1 à 13 de l'Évangile selon Marc,"
<u>Le Christianisme social</u> 71:62-70.

1459   1961   J. Schreiber, "Die Christologie des Markusevangeliums. Beobachtungen zur Theologie und Komposition des zweiten
Evangeliums," <u>ZTK</u> 58:154-183.   (N 6-785)

1460   1954   P. E. Davies, "Mark's Witness to Jesus," <u>JBL</u> 73:197-202.

Christology: Jesus as Teacher

See also 113, 244, 349, 464, 468, 476, 1449, 1497.

1461   1980   P. J. Achtemeier, "'He Taught Them Many Things': Reflec-
                tions on Marcan Christology," CBQ 42:465-481.

1462   R. T. France, "Mark and the Teaching of Jesus," in Gospel
                Perspectives: Studies of History and Tradition in the
                Four Gospels, Vol. 1 (ed.by R. T. France and David Wen-
                ham; Sheffield: JSOT), pp. 101-136.

1463   1977   M. E. Boring, "The Paucity of Sayings in Mark: A Hypothes-
                is," in Society of Biblical Literature 1977 Seminar Pa-
                pers (ed. by Paul J. Achtemeier; Missoula, MT: Scholars
                Press), pp. 371-377.

1464   A. F. Graudin, "Jesus as Teacher in Mark," Concordia Journ-
                al 3:32-35.   (N 21-387)

1465   1972   Klaus BERGER. Die Gesetzesauslegung Jesu: Ihr historischer
                Hintergrund im Judentum und im Alten Testament. Vol. I:
                Markus und Parallelen. Wissenschaftliche Monographien
                zum Alten und Neuen Testament 40. Neukirchen-Vluyn: Neu-
                kirchener Verlag. xi-631 pp.   (E 54-3124)

1466   M. Smith, "Forms, Motives, and Omissions in Mark's Account
                of the Teaching of Jesus," in Understanding the Sacred
                Text: Essays in Honor of Morton S. Enslin on the Hebrew
                Bible and Christian Beginnings (ed. by John Reumann; Val-
                ley Forge, PA: Judson Press), pp. 153-164.

Christology: Messiah

See 374, 1026, 1027, 1030, 1284.

Christology: Son of God

See also 69, 1450.

1467   1980   H.J. STEICHELE. Der leidende Sohn Gottes. Eine Untersuch-
                ung einiger alttestamentlicher Motive in der Christologie
                des Markusevangeliums. Zugleich ein Beitrag zur Erhell-
                ung des überlieferungsgeschichtlichen Zusammenhangs
                zwischen Altem und Neuem Testament. Biblische Untersuch-
                ungen 14. Münchener Universitäts-Schriften, Katholisch-
                Theologische Fakultät. Regensburg: F. Pustet. xii-348
                pp.

1468   1979   Carl R. KAZMIERSKI. Jesus, the Son of God: A Study of the Markan Tradition and its Redaction by the Evangelist. Forschung zur Bibel 33. Würzburg: Echter Verlag. xv–247 pp.

1469   J. D. Kingsbury, "The Spirit and the Son of God in Mark's Gospel," in Sin, Salvation, and the Spirit: Commemorating the Fiftieth Year of the Liturgical Press (ed. by Daniel Durken, O.S.B.; Collegeville, MN: Liturgical Press), pp.195–202.

1470   1974   A.-L. Descamps, "Pour une histoire du titre 'Fils de Dieu': Les antécédents par rapport à Marc," in L'évangile selon Marc: Tradition et rédaction (ed. by M. Sabbe: Bibliotheca ephemeridum theologicarum lovaniensium 34; Gembloux/Louvain: Duculot/Louvain University), pp. 529–571.

1471   1973   L. Swain, "The Divine Face of Man: Mark's Christology," ClerRev 58:696–708.   (N 18–484)

1472   John R. RICHARDS. Jesus, Son of God and Son of Man: A Markan Study. Pantyfedwen Trust Lectures 1972. Penarth, Southeast Wales: Church in Wales Publ. 147 pp.
                                            (E 58s–4849)

1473   1964   J. Alonso Díaz, "Jesús 'Hijo de Dios' en el Evangelio de Marcos," CB 21:131–136.   (N 9–552)

1474   L. S. Hay, "The Son-of-God Christology in Mark," JBR 32: 106–114.   (N 9–164)

1475   1963   John A. PHILLIPS. The Son of God. An Explanation of St. Mark's Gospel. Melbourne/New York: Thomas Nelson. ix–166 pp.
                                            (E 47–2452)

1476   1955   J. Allan, "The Gospel of the Son of God," Int 9:131–143.

Christology: Son of Man

See also 171, 874, 1450, 1472.

1477   1977   H. Sahlin, "Zum Verständnis der christologischen Anschauung des Markusevangeliums," ST 31:1–19.   (N 22–98)

1478   1974   J. Coppens, "Les logia du Fils de l'homme dans l'évangile de Marc," in L'évangile selon Marc: Tradition et rédaction (ed. by M. Sabbe; Bibliotheca ephemeridum theologicarum lovaniensium 34; Gembloux/Louvain: Duculot/Louvain University), pp. 487–528.

1479   1973   Joseph COPPENS. De Mensenzoon-Logia in het Markus-Evangel-
              ie. Mededelingen van de Koninklijke Academie voor Weten-
              schappen, Letteren en schone Kunsten van België, Klasse
              der Letteren, Jaargang XXXV, nr. 3. Brussels: Konink-
              lijke Academie. 55 pp.

1480   O. J. F. Seitz, "The Future Coming of the Son of Man: Three
              Midrashic Formulations in the Gospel of Mark," in Studia
              Evangelica 6: Papers Presented to the Fourth Internation-
              al Congress on New Testament Studies held at Oxford, 1969
              (ed. by Elizabeth A. Livingstone; Berlin: Akademie Ver-
              lag), pp. 478-494.

1481   1972   R. G. Rank, "Who is this man? The Son of Man According to
              Mark," TBT 63:959-965.   (N 17-525)

1482   1970   L. S. Hay, "The Son of Man in Mark 2:10 and 2:28," JBL 89:
              69-75.   (N 14-866)

1483   1968   N. Perrin, "The Creative Use of the Son of Man Traditions
              by Mark," USQR 23:357-365.   (N 13-186)
                [Republished in Perrin, A Modern Pilgrimage in New Tes-
                tament Christology (Philadelphia: Fortress, 1974), pp.
                84-93.]

1484   1967   Morna D. HOOKER. The Son of Man in Mark. A Study of the
              Background of the Term "Son of Man" and its Use in St.
              Mark's Gospel. London/Montreal: SPCK/McGill University
              Press. x-230 pp.   (E 48-2424)

1485   H. H. Straton, "The Son-of-Man and the Messianic Secret,"
              JRT 24:31-49.

1486   1963   S. Sandmel, "'Son of Man' in Mark," in In the Time of Har-
              vest (ed. by Daniel J. Silver; New York: Macmillan), pp.
              355-367.
                [Republished in Sandmel, Two Living Traditions: Essays
                on Religion and the Bible (Detroit, Mich.: Wayne State
                University, 1972), pp. 166-177.]

1487   1961   T. A. Burkill, "The Hidden Son of Man in St. Mark's Gospel,"
              ZNW 52:189-213.   (N 6-783)

Christology: Theios Anēr

1488   1974   W. L. Lane, "Theios anēr Christology and the Gospel of
              Mark," in New Dimensions in New Testament Study (ed. by
              Richard N. Longenecker and Merrill C. Tenney; Grand Rap-
              ids, MI: Zondervan), pp. 144-161.

1489 1972 O. Betz, "The Concept of the So-called 'Divine Man' in Mark's Christology," in Studies in New Testament and Early Christian Literature: Essays in Honor of Allen P. Wikgren (ed. by David Edward Aune; NovT Supplement 33; Leiden: E. J. Brill), pp. 229-240.

The Disciples / "The Twelve"

See also 238, 244, 862, 1441.

1490 1978 E. Best, "Mark's Use of the Twelve," ZNW 69:11-35.
(N 23-837)

1491 1977 E. Best, "The Role of the Disciples in Mark," NTS 23:377-401. (N 22-96)

1492 R. C. Tannehill, "The Disciples in Mark: The Function of a Narrative Role," JR 57:386-405. (N 22-407)

1493 1975 Klemens STOCK. Boten aus dem Mit-Ihm-Sein. Das Verhältnis zwischen Jesus und den Zwölf nach Markus. Analecta Biblica 70. Rome: Biblical Institute Press. xxvii-228 pp.
(E 57-3791)

1494 1974 J. Delorme, "L'évangile selon Marc," in Le ministère et les ministères selon le Nouveau Testament: Dossier exégétique et réflexion théologique (ed. by Jean Delorme; Parole de Dieu 10; Paris: Éditions du Seuil), pp. 155-181.

1495 Günther SCHMAHL. Die Zwölf im Markusevangelium: eine redaktionsgeschichtliche Untersuchung. Trierer Theologische Studien 30. Trier: Paulinus-Verlag. xiii-170 pp. (E 56-2985)

1496 1969 K. Kertelge, "Die Funktion der 'Zwölf' im Markusevangelium. Eine redaktionsgeschichtliche Auslegung, zugleich ein Beitrag zur Frage nach dem neutestamentlichen Amtsverständnis," TTZ 78:193-206. (N 14-495)

1497 1968 Robert P. MEYE. Jesus and the Twelve. Discipleship and Revelation in Mark's Gospel. Grand Rapids: Eerdmans. 257 pp. (E 51-2397)

1498 1957 J. Coutts, "The Authority of Jesus and of the Twelve in St. Mark's Gospel," JTS 8:111-118. (N 2-292)

The Disciples: Their Lack of Understanding

1499   1975   C. Focant, "L'incompréhension des disciples dans le deux-
              ième évangile. Tradition et rédaction," RB 82:161-185.
                                                        (N 20-449)

1500   1972   D. J. Hawkin, "The Incomprehension of the Disciples in the
              Marcan Redaction," JBL 91:491-500.   (N 17-524)

1501   1961   J. B. Tyson, "The Blindness of the Disciples in Mark," JBL
              80:261-268.   (N 6-464)

The Disciples: Peter

See also 840 - 849, 1237 - 1239, 1280 - 1282, 1305 - 1308.

1502   1980   J. Ernst, "Die Petrustradition im Markusevangelium--ein alt-
              es Problem neu angegangen," in Begegnung mit dem Wort:
              Festschrift für Heinrich Zimmerman (ed. by Josef Zmifewski
              and Ernst Nellessen; Bonner biblische Beiträge 53; Bonn:
              Peter Hanstein), pp. 35-65.

1503   1978   E. Best, "Peter in the Gospel According to Mark," CBQ 40:
              547-558.   (N 23-442)

1504   1974   B. Rigaux, "Pietro e il Vangelo di Marco," Miscellanea
              Franciscana 74:294-317.

1505   1972   J. S. Setzer, "A Fresh Look at Jesus' Eschatology and
              Christology in Mark's Petrine Stratum," LQ 24:240-253.
                                                        (N 17-134)

1506   1967   E. Ravarotto, "La 'casa' del Vangelo di Marco è la casa di
              Simone-Pietro?" Anton 42:399-419.   (N 12-886)

Discipleship

See also 174, 261, 262, 863 - 871, 874, 920, 1016, 1596.

1507   1980   M. F. Kirby, "Mark's Prerequisite for Being an Apostle,"
              TBT 18:77-81.   (N 24-800)

1508   P. S. Pudussery, "The Meaning of Discipleship in the Gospel
              of Mark," Jeevadhara 10:93-110.   (N 25-89)

1509   1979   J. A. Estrada Díaz, "Las relaciones Jesús-pueblo-discípulos
              en el evangelio de Marcos," EstEcl 54:151-170.
                                                        (N 24-105)

1510   1978   H. F. Peacock, "Discipleship in the Gospel of Mark," RevExp
                75:555-564.   (N 23-452)

1511   E. Schweizer, "The Portrayal of the Life of Faith in the
                the Gospel of Mark," Int 32:387-399.   (N 23-112)

1512   K. Stock, "Vangelo e discepolato in Marco," RassTeol 19:
                1-7.   (N 23-113)

1513   1976   J. DEWEY. Disciples of the Way: Mark on Discipleship.
                Cincinnati: Women's Division, Board of Global Ministries,
                United Methodist Church. vi-149 pp.   (E 58s-4799)

1514   1975   J. Donaldson, "'Called to Follow'. A Twofold Experience
                of Discipleship in Mark," BTB 5:67-77.   (N 19-960)

1515   B. V. Manno, "The Identity of Jesus and Christian Disciple-
                ship in the Gospel of Mark," Religious Education 70:619-
                628.

1516   1973   W. Au, "Discipleship in Mark," TBT 67:1249-1251.(N 18-482)

1517   G. Bruni, "La communità nell'evangelo di Marco," Servitium
                7:123-136.   (N 18-483)

1518   D. Catchpole, "Discipleship, the Law and Jesus of Nazar-
                eth," Crux 11:8-16.

1519   1971   C. M. Murphy, "Discipleship in Mark as Movement with
                Christ," TBT 53:305-308.   (N 15-866)

Ecclesiology

1520   1974   P. H. Reardon, "Kenotic Ecclesiology in Mark," TBT 70:1476-
                1482.   (N 18-865)

1521   1972   P. S. Minear, "Audience Criticism and Markan Ecclesiology,"
                in Neues Testament und Geschichte: Historisches Geschehen
                und Deutung im Neuen Testament: Oscar Cullmann zum 70.
                Geburtstag (ed. by Heinrich Baltensweiler and Bo Reicke;
                Zürich: Theologischer Verlag / Tübingen: Mohr), pp. 79-
                89.

1522   1970   B. E. Thiering, "'Breaking of Bread' and 'Harvest' in Mark's
                Gospel," NovT 12:1-12.   (N 14-865)

1523   1967   J. Delorme, "Aspects doctrinaux du second Évangile," ETL
                43:74-99.   (N 12-171)

1524 1966   G. Schille, "Der Beitrag des Evangelisten Markus zum kirch-
             enbildenden (ökumenischen) Gespräch seiner Tage," <u>KD</u> 12:
             135-153.   (N 11-238)

1525 1962   J. M. Casciaro Ramíres, "Iglesia y pueblo de Dios en el
             Evangelio de S. Marcos," in <u>Concepto de la Iglesia en el
             Nuevo Testamento (y) otros estudios</u> (Semana Bíblica Es-
             pañola XIX; Madrid: Consejo Superior de Investigaciones
             Científicas, Instituto Francisco Suárez), pp. 19-99.

Ecclesiology: Universal Mission

See also 151, 1154.

1526 1980   S. J. Anthonysamy, "The Gospel of Mark and the Universal
             Mission," <u>Biblebhashyam</u> 6:81-96.   (N 25-82)

Eschatology

See also 1121, 1123, 1129, 1131, 1133 - 1135, 1137 - 1151, 1157, 1540.

1527 1978   G. R. Beasley-Murray, "Eschatology in the Gospel of Mark,"
             <u>SWJournTheol</u> 21:37-53.   (N 23-439)

1528 1976   A. BONORA. <u>La speranza del cristiano nel Vangelo di Marco</u>.
             Cognoscere il Vangelo 8. Padua: Messaggero. 142 pp.
                                                           (E 58s-4792)

1529 1975   J. M. Nützel, "Hoffnung und Treue: Zur Eschatologie des
             Markusevangeliums," in <u>Gegenwart und kommendes Reich:
             Schülergabe Anton Vögtle zum 65. Geburtstag</u> (ed. by Peter
             Fiedler and Dieter Zeller; Stuttgarter biblische Mono-
             graphien; Stuttgart: Verlag Katholisches Bibelwerk), pp.
             79-90.

1530 1969   E. Schweizer, "Eschatology in Mark's Gospel," in <u>Neotesta-
             mentica et Semitica: Studies in honour of Matthew Black</u>
             (ed. by E. Earle Ellis and Max Wilcox; Edinburgh: T & T
             Clark), pp. 114-118.
               ₍Republished in German as "Eschatologie im Evangelium
               nach Markus," in Schweizer, <u>Beiträge zur Theologie des
               Neuen Testaments: Neutestamentliche Aufsätze (1955 -
               1970)</u> (Zürich: Zwingli Verlag, 1970), pp. 43-48.₎

Eschatology: Parousia

1531 1978   G. R. Beasley-Murray, "The Parousia in Mark," <u>RevExp</u> 75:
             565-581.   (N 23-440)

1532 1975 F. Hahn, "Die Rede von der Parusie des Menschensohnes
Markus 13," in Jesus und der Menschensohn: Für Anton
Vögtle (ed. by Rudolf Pesch and Rudolf Schnackenburg, in
collaboration with Odilo Kaiser; Freiburg/Basel/Vienna:
Herder), pp. 240-266.

1533 1973 P. O. G. White, "The Resurrection and the Second Coming of
Jesus in Mark," in Studia Evangelica 6: Papers Presented
to the Fourth International Congress on New Testament
Studies held at Oxford, 1969 (ed. by Elizabeth A. Livingstone; Berlin: Akademie Verlag), pp. 615-618.

1534 1968 G. Bornkamm, "Die Verzögerung der Parusie: Exegetische Bemerkungen zu zwei synoptischen Texten," in Bornkamm, Ge-
shichte und Glaube (Beiträge zur evangelischen Theologie 48; München: C. Kaiser), pp. 46-55.
  [Originally published in In Memoriam Ernst Lohmeyer
  (ed. by Werner Schmauch; Stuttgart: Evangelisches Ver-
  lagswerk, 1951), pp. 116-126.]

1535 1966 J. K. Howard, "Our Lord's Teaching Concerning His Parousia:
A Study in the Gospel of Mark," EvQ 38:52-58.(N 10-921)

Kingdom

See also 234, 373.

1536 1980 A. Pilgaard, "Gudsrigebegrebet i Markusevangeliet," DTT 43:
20-35.   (N 25-88)

1537 1978 E. Breech, "Kingdom of God and the Parables of Jesus,"
Semeia 12:15-40.

1538 1974 Werner H. KELBER. The Kingdom in Mark: A New Place and a
New Time. Philadelphia: Fortress. xii-173 pp.

1539 1972 Aloysius M. AMBROZIC. The Hidden Kingdom. A Redaction-
critical Study of the References to the Kingdom of God
in Mark's Gospel. Catholic Biblical Quarterly Monograph
Series 2. Washington: The Catholic Biblical Association
of America. xi-280 pp.   (E 54-3120)

1540 1972 W. H. Kelber, "The History of the Kingdom in Mark--Aspects
of Markan Eschatology," in Society of Biblical Literature
1972 Seminar Papers I (ed. by Lane C. McGaughy; Los Angeles: Society of Biblical Literature), pp. 63-95.

Miracles

See also 134, 583.

1541   1978   E. Best, "The Miracles in Mark," <u>RevExp</u> 75:539-554.
                                                      (N 23-441)

1542   1977s R. L. Sturch, "The Markan Miracles and the Other Synopt-
              ists," <u>ExpTim</u> 89:375-376.

1543   1977   E. Best, "Exorcism in the New Testament and Today," <u>Bib-</u>
              <u>Theol</u> 27:1-9.   (N 22-95)

1544   P. Lamarche, "Les miracles de Jésus selon Marc," in <u>Les</u>
              <u>miracles de Jésus selon le Nouveau Testament</u> (ed. by
              Xavier Léon-Dufour; Parole de Dieu; Paris: Éditions du
              Seuil), pp. 213-226.

1545   1976   R. PESCH and R. KRATZ. <u>So liest man synoptisch. Anleitung</u>
              <u>und Kommentar zum Studium der synoptischen Evangelien.</u>
              <u>II. Wundergeschichten, Teil I: Exorzismen--Heilungen--</u>
              <u>Totenerweckungen. III. Wundergeschichten, Teil II:</u>
              <u>Rettungswunder--Geschenkwunder--Normenwunder--Fernheil-</u>
              <u>ungen.</u> Frankfurt: Knecht. 101 pp.; 99 pp.

1546   J. ROQUETA. <u>Lo sistema del miracle dins l'Evangeli segon</u>
              <u>S. Marc.</u> Fulhets Occitans de Reflexion Crestiana (del)
              Centre Teologic Interdiocesan 1. Montpelhièr [Mont-
              pellier]. 40 pp.   (E 58s-4852)

1547   1975   P. J. Achtemeier, "Miracles and the Historical Jesus: A
              Study of Mark 9:14-29," <u>CBQ</u> 37:471-491.   (N 20-802)

1548   Dietrich-Alex KOCH. <u>Die Bedeutung der Wundererzählungen</u>
              <u>für die Christologie des Markus-Evangeliums.</u> Beiheft
              zur <u>ZNW</u> 42. Berlin/New York: de Gruyter. xii-217 pp.
                                                              (E 56-2959)

1549   1974   Ludger SCHENKE. <u>Die Wundererzählungen des Markusevangel-</u>
              <u>iums.</u> Stuttgarter Biblische Beiträge 5. Stuttgart:
              Katholisches Bibelwerk. x-430 pp.

1550   1973   H. K. Nielsen, "Et bidrag til vurderingen af traditionen
              om Jesu helbredelsesvirksomhed," <u>DTT</u> 36:269-300.
                                                              (N 18-864)

1551   1972s T. Snoy, "Les miracles dans l'évangile de Marc. Examen de
              quelques études récentes," <u>RTL</u> 3 (1972):449-466; 4
              (1973):58-101.   (N 17-928)

1552   1970   Karl KERTELGE. <u>Die Wunder Jesu im Markusevangelium. Eine</u>

redaktionsgeschichtliche Untersuchung. Studien zum Alt-
en und Neuen Testament 23. München: Kösel-Verlag. 232
pp.   (E 51-2384)

1553   D. Merli, "Lo scopo dei miracoli nell'Evangelo di Marco,"
            BeO 12:184-198.

1554   D. M. Slusser, "The Healing Narratives in Mark," Christ-
            Cent 87:597-599.   (N 15-158)

1555   1968 H. C. Kee, "The Terminology of Mark's Exorcism Stories,"
            NTS 14:232-246.   (N 12-883)

1556   F. J. Matera, "Interpreting Mark--Some recent theories of
            Redaction Criticism," LouvStud 2:113-131.   (N 13-184)

1557   1966 Kenzo TAGAWA. Miracles et Évangile. La pensée personnel-
            le de l'évangéliste Marc. Études d'histoire et de philo-
            sophie religieuses 62. Paris: Presses universitaires de
            France. 213 pp.   (E 49-2657)

1558   1965 M. E. Glasswell, "The Use of Miracles in the Markan Gos-
            pel," in Miracles: Cambridge Studies in their Philosophy
            and History (ed. by C. F. D. Moule; London: A. R. Mowbray
            & Co.), pp. 149-162.

1559   1959 T. A. Burkill, "The Notion of Miracle with Special Refer-
            ence to St. Mark's Gospel," ZNW 50:33-48.   (N 4-85)

Sacraments: Eucharist

See also 755, 1213 - 1229.

1560   1978 A. Edanad, "Institution of the Eucharist according to the
            Synoptic Gospels," Biblebhashyam 4:322-332. (N 23-855)

Sacraments: Baptism

1561   1976 D. J. Murray, "Mark's Theology of Baptism," Dimension 8:
            92-97.   (N 21-92)

1562   1977 S. Légasse, "Le Baptême de Jésus et le Baptême chrétien,"
            SBFLA 27:51-68.   (N 22-774)

1563   1973 R. Scroggs and K. I. Groff, "Baptism in Mark: Dying and
            Rising with Christ," JBL 92:531-548.   (N 18-498)

("Messianic") Secrecy Motif

See also 125, 281, 293, 374, 612, 1455, 1485, 1487.

1564   1980   B. G. Powley, "Vincent Taylor and the Messianic Secret in
              Mark's Gospel," in Studia Biblica 1978: II. Papers on
              the Gospels. Sixth International Congress on Biblical
              Studies,Oxford, 3-7 April 1978 (ed. by E. A. Livingstone;
              JSNT Supplement Series 2; Sheffield: JSOT), pp. 243-246.

1565   1977   J. J. Kilgallen, "The Messianic Secret and Mark's Purpose,"
              BTB 7:60-65.   (N 21-738)

1566   F. J. Steinmetz, "Das Rätsel der Schweige-Gebote im Markus-
              Evangelium," GeistLeb 50:92-102.   (N 21-741)

1567   1976   Heikki RÄISÄNEN. Das "Messiasgeheimnis" im Markusevangel-
              ium. Ein redaktionskritischer Versuch. Schriften der
              Finnischen Exegetischen Gesellschaft 28. Helsinki: Finn-
              ish Exegetical Society. 192 pp.   (E 58s-4847)

1568   1975   C. F. D. Moule, "On Defining the Messianic Secret in Mark,"
              in Jesus und Paulus: Festschrift für Werner Georg Kümmel
              zum 70. Geburtstag (ed. by E. Earle Ellis and Erich
              Grässer; Göttingen: Vandenhoeck & Ruprecht), pp. 239-252.

1569   1973   W. C. Robinson, Jr., "The Quest for Wrede's Secret Messi-
              ah," Int 27:10-30.   (N 17-926)

1570   1971   W. WREDE. The Messianic Secret. Tr. (from the German:
              1901) by J. C. G. Greig. The Library of Theological
              Translations. Greenwood, S.C.: Attic and London: J.
              Clark (1972). xxi-292 pp.

1571   1970   J. D. G. Dunn, "The Messianic Secret in Mark," TynBull 21:
              92-117.   (N 15-513)

1572   1969   D. E. Aune, "The Problem of the Messianic Secret," NovT
              11:1-31.   (N 14-151)

1573   R. N. Longenecker, "The Messianic Secret in the Light of
              Recent Discoveries," EvQ 41:207-215.

1574   B. G. Powley, "The Purpose of the Messianic Secret: A Brief
              Survey," ExpTim 80:308-310.   (N 14-153)

1575   1968   C. Maurer, "Das Messiasgeheimnis des Markusevangeliums,"
              NTS 14:515-526.   (N 13-185)

1576   G. MINETTE DE TILLESSE. Le secret messianique dans l'évan-
              gile de Marc. Lectio Divina 47. Paris: Éditions du

Cerf. 576 pp.   (E 50-2605)

1577 1967 F. W. Danker, "Postscript to the Markan Secrecy Motif,"
            CTM 38:24-27.   (N 11-1043)

1578   L. S. Hay, "Mark's Use of the Messianic Secret," JAAR 35:
            16-27.   (N 11-1044)

1579   R. P. Meye, "Messianic Secret and Messianic Didache in
            Mark's Gospel," in Oikonomia: Heilsgeschichte als Thema
            der Theologie. O. Cullmann zum 65. Geburtstag gewidmet
            (ed. by Felix Christ; Hamburg-Bergstedt: Reich), pp. 57-
            68.

1580 1966 F. W. Danker, "Mark 1:45 and the Secrecy Motif," CTM 37:
            492-499.   (N 11-721)

1581 1965 E. Dhanis, "The Messianic Secret," TD 13:127-128.
            [Translated from an article in Latin in Doctor Communis
            (Vatican City) 15 (1962):22-36.]

1582   E. Schweizer, "Zur Frage des Messiasgeheimnisses bei Mark-
            us," ZNW 56:1-8.   (N 10-527)
            [Republished in Schweizer, Beiträge zur Theologie des
            Neuen Testaments: Neutestamentliche Aufsätze (1955 -
            1970) (Zürich: Zwingli Verlag, 1970), pp. 11-20.]

1583 1964 G. Strecker, "Zur Messiasgeheimnistheorie im Markusevangel-
            ium," in Studia Evangelica 3: Papers Presented to the
            Second International Congress on New Testament Studies
            held at Christ Church, Oxford, 1961 (Texte und Untersuch-
            ungen zur Geschichte der altchristlichen Literatur 88;
            Berlin: Akademie Verlag), pp. 86-104.
            [Republished in Das Markus-Evangelium (ed. by Rudolf
            Pesch; Wege der Forschung 411; Darmstadt: Wissen-
            schaftliche Buchgesellschaft, 1979), pp. 190-210.]

1584 1960 G. H. Boobyer, "The Secrecy Motif in St. Mark's Gospel,"
            NTS 6:225-235.   (N 5-87)

1585 1954s J. W. Leitch, "The Injunctions of Silence in Mark's Gos-
            pel," ExpTim 66:178-182.

Soteriology

See also 1003 - 1013, 1221, 1593.

1586 1976 F. G. Lang, "Sola Gratia im Markusevangelium: Die Soterio-
            logie des Markus nach 9,14-29 und 10,17-31," in Recht-
            fertigung: Festschrift für Ernst Käsemann zum 70. Ge-

burtstag (ed. by Johannes Friedrich, Wolfgang Pöhlmann
and Peter Stuhlmacher; Tübingen/Göttingen: J. C. B. Mohr
[Paul Siebeck]/Vandenhoeck & Ruprecht), pp. 321-337.

1587 1969 A. Strobel, "Die Deutung des Todes Jesu im ältesten Evangelium," in Das Kreuz Jesu: theologische Überlegungen.
Beiträge von Georg [i.e. August] Strobel (ed. by P. Rie-
ger; Forum 12; Göttingen: Vandenhoeck & Ruprecht), pp.
32-64.

1588 1965 Ernest BEST. The Temptation and the Passion. The Markan
Soteriology. Society for New Testament Studies Monograph
Series 2. Cambridge/New York: Cambridge University
Press. xiv-222 pp.

Theology of the Cross

See also 225, 1131, 1528, 1596.

1589 1977 M. de Burgos Núñez, "El Evangelio de San Marcos como 'Theologia Crucis.' La teología de la Cruz como instancia
crítica de la cristología y la eclesiología según el E-
vangelio de San Marcos," Communio 10:207-455.(N 22-770)

1590 1976 W. Harrington, "The Gospel of Mark: A Theologia Crucis,"
DocLife 26:24-33.   (N 20-787)

1591 1975 W. R. Bouman, "'Reflections on Mark from a Confessional
Theologian,'" CurTM 2:326-331.   (N 20-448)

1592 1974 M. Vellanickal, "Suffering in the Life and Teaching of
Jesus," Jeevadhara 4:144-161.   (N 19-558)

1593 1962 J. Alonso Díaz, "Historicidad del Evangelio de Marcos en
la presentación de la muerte de Jesús como meurte reden-
tora," EstBíb 21:23-36.   (N 8-143)

Theology of the Cross: Passion Predictions

See also 262, 855 - 859, 917, 918, 993.

1594 1979 D. Lorenzen, "Jesu lidelsesudsagn i Markusevangeliet," DTT
42:217-254.   (N 25-86)

1595 1976 A. Pérez Gordo, "Gli annunci della passione," in La Sapienza della Croce oggi. Atti del Congresso internazion-
ale: Roma, 13-18 ottobre 1975. Vol. 1: La sapienza della Croce nella rivelazione e nell'ecumenismo (Torino
Leumann: Elle Di Ci), pp. 106-125.

1596 1972 C. J. Reedy, "Mk 8:31 - 11:10 and the Gospel Ending. A
           Redaction Study," CBQ 34:188-197.   (N 16-884)

1597 1967s A. Feuillet, "Les trois grandes prophéties de la Passion
           et de la Résurrection des évangiles synoptiques," Rev-
           Thom 67 (1967):533-560; 68 (1968):41-74.   (N 13-195)

1598 1964 G. Strecker, "Die Leidens- und Auferstehungsvoraussagen im
           Markusevangelium (Mk 8,31; 9,31; 10,32-34)," ZTK 64:16-
           39.   (N 12-181)
           [Translated and republished as "The Passion- and Resur-
           rection Predictions in Mark's Gospel (Mark 8:31; 9:31;
           10:32-34)," Int 22:421-442.]

1599 1954s V. Taylor, "The Origin of the Marcan Passion Sayings," NTS
           1:159-167.
           [Republished in Taylor, New Testament Essays (London:
           Epworth, 1970), pp. 60-71.]

Bracht, W.: 229.
Brady, D.: 1243.
Brandon, S. G. F.: 250, 255.
Bratcher, R. G.: 126, 1336, 1340.
Braumann, G.: 531, 1000, 1313,
   1329.
Braun, H.: 516, 546.
Breech, E.: 1537.
Bregine, D. F.: 251.
Bretscher, P. G.: 427.
Breymayer, R.: 1093.
Brière, J.: 449, 467, 918.
Bristol, O. L.: 1457.
Broer, I.: 1377.
Brooks, J. A.: 331.
Brower, K.: 875.
Brown, J. P.: 177, 311.
Brown, S.: 651.
Bruce, F. F.: 316.
Bruni, G.: 1517.
Buchanan, G. W.: 1038, 1060, 1283.
Budesheim, T. L.: 181.
Bultmann, R.: 628.
Burgers, W.: 563.
Burgon, J. W.: 1397.
Burkill, T. A.: 185, 235, 293, 374,
   526, 560, 583, 643, 716, 743,
   801, 803, 804, 805, 945, 1193,
   1288, 1416, 1431, 1487, 1559.
Buse, I.: 149.
Busslinger, H.: 911.
Buth, R.: 565.
Butterworth, R.: 282.

Cabanis, A.: 503.
Caird, G. B.: 735.
Calloud, J.: 350, 496, 697.
Calmet, A.: 925.
Cantinat, J.: 1343.
Carlston, C.: 795.
Carrington, P.: 17, 258.
Carroll, W. D.: 1435.
Carton, G.: 1102.
Casalegno, A.: 673.
Casciaro Ramires, J. M.: 1525.
Castellino, G. R.: 594.
Castro Tello, C.: 270.
Catchpole, D. R.: 941, 1389, 1518.
Cave, C. H.: 484, 713.
Celada, B.: 968, 980.
Ceroke, C. P.: 96, 507.

Cheek, J. L.: 1384a.
Chilton, B. D.: 876.
Chordat, J.-L.: 1419.
Christensen, J.: 1023, 1212.
Church, I. F.: 1410.
Clark, D. J.: 119.
Clark, K. S. L.: 38.
Clark, K. W.: 1002.
Clévenot, M.: 354.
Cohn, H.: 1271.
Cohn-Sherbok, D. M.: 541.
Cole, R. A.: 39.
Collins, R. F.: 431.
Colpe, C.: 506, 586.
Combet-Galland, C.: 741, 1122.
Comblin, J.: 816.
Combrink, H. J. B.: 1009.
Comiskey, J. P.: 435.
Congar, Y.: 575.
Conzelmann, H.: 1147.
Cook, M. J.: 179.
Cope, L.: 567.
Coppens, J.: 1478, 1479.
Corsani, B.: 343.
Cortés, E.: 1049, 1050.
Coune, M.: 890.
Cousar, C. B.: 1131.
Cousin, H.: 1043.
Coutts, J.: 640, 1498.
Cowling, C. C.: 141.
Craghan, J. F.: 710.
Crane, T. E.: 357.
Cranfield, C. E. B.: 16, 420.
Cremer, F. G.: 529, 530.
Crosby, J.: 457.
Crossan, J. D.: 226, 573, 1035,
   1036, 1080, 1363.
Crotty, R.: 30.
Cullmann, O.: 402, 564, 934.
Culpepper, R. A.: 1057, 1325.
Cummings, J. T.: 720.

Dahl, N. A.: 256.
Dambrine, L.: 718.
Daniel, C.: 825.
Danieli, G.: 569.
Danker, F. W.: 817, 1156, 1196,
   1330, 1577, 1580.
Daube, D.: 1259.
Dautzenberg, G.: 107, 376, 377.
Davies, P. E.: 1460.

Fleddermann, H.: 920, 1266.
Fletcher, D. R.: 868.
Flückiger, F.: 1132.
Flusser, D.: 536, 1218.
Focant, C.: 1499.
Ford, J. M.: 1067, 1316.
Fortna, R. T.: 188.
Fowler, R. M.: 752.
France, R. T.: 1462.
Frankemölle, H.: 851.
Freyne, S.: 77.
Friedrich, G.: 760.
Fuchs, A.: 579, 887.
Fuchs, E.: 448.
Fuller, R. H.: 1396.
Funk, R. W.: 674.
Fürst, H.: 989.
Fusco, V.: 596.
Füssel, K.: 353.

Gaboury, A.: 146.
Gaide, G.: 477, 524.
Gain, D. B.: 300.
Galbiati, E.: 1383.
Galizzi, M.: 74, 1252.
Galot, J.: 975.
Gamba, G.: 501, 513, 537.
García Burillo, J.: 988, 990.
Garofalo, S.: 928.
Gärtner, B. E.: 42.
Geischer, H.-J.: 627.
Genest, O.: 1270.
Gennarini, S.: 892.
Geoltrain, P.: 556.
George, A.: 631, 995.
Gerber, W.: 898.
Gero, S.: 423.
Gewalt, D.: 1305.
Giesen, H.: 1048.
Gils, F.: 553.
Glasson, T. F.: 310, 1149, 1298, 1337.
Glasswell, M. E.: 367, 392, 1558.
Glusman, E. F.: 189.
Gnilka, J.: 1, 4, 498, 737, 1331.
Goldberg, A. M.: 1296.
González Faus, J. I.: 436.
Goppelt, L.: 1097, 1099.
Goulder, M. D.: 1358, 1364.
Graham, A. A. K.: 198.
Graham, H. H.: 373.

Grässer, E.: 727.
Grassi, J. A.: 769, 1217.
Graudin, A. F.: 1464.
Grayston, K. 1128.
Greenlee, J. H.: 301.
Greeven, H.: 877.
Griesbach, J. J.: 204.
Griffiths, J. G.: 867.
Grob, R.: 56.
Groff, K. I.: 1268, 1563.
Groupe d'Entrevernes: 747a.
Grundmann, W.: 5.
Guillemette, P.: 464, 473.
Gundry, R. H.: 1304.
Güttgemanns, E.: 1090, 1372.
Gutzke, M. G.: 32.
Guy, H. A.: 51, 130, 1335.

Haacker, K.: 652, 1405.
Haefner, A. E.: 187.
Haenchen, E.: 52, 368, 843.
Hahn, F.: 534, 616, 1532.
Hamann, H. P.: 212.
Hamilton, N. Q.: 1351.
Hamilton, W.: 80.
Hargreaves, J.: 78.
Harner, P. B.: 1334.
Harnisch, W.: 973.
Harrington, W.: 20, 98, 272, 1590.
Harrisville, R. A.: 1422.
Harsch, H.: 698.
Hartman, L.: 413, 1137.
Haufe, G.: 649.
Hawkin, D. J.: 268, 1500.
Hay, L. S.: 1474, 1482, 1578.
Hebert, G.: 1353, 1384, 1385.
Hegermann, H.: 595.
Hein, K.: 1210.
Heising, A.: 763.
Hemelsoet, B.: 937.
Hendriks, W.: 156.
Hendriksen, W.: 9.
Hengel, M.: 787, 1082.
Hennig, K.: 63.
Héring, J.: 1257.
Hermann, I.: 54, 57, 1138.
Herránz Marco, M.: 388, 486, 497, 872, 1275, 1277.
Hertzsch, K.-P.: 675.
Hiebert, D. E.: 35.
Hiers, R. H.: 761, 1056, 1062.

688, 711, 1177, 1274, 1332, 1544.
Lambrecht, J.: 176, 568, 572, 574, 600, 603, 611, 712, 780, 1135, 1136, 1141, 1447.
Lampe, G. W. H.: 1306.
Lampe, P.: 638.
Landier, J.: 19.
Lane, W. L.: 36, 333, 334, 1488.
Lang, F. G.: 269, 811, 1586.
Langevin, P.-E.: 335, 339.
Langkammer, H.: 378, 1129, 1442.
Langkammer, O. H.: 6.
Lanz, D.: 1124.
Lapointe, R.: 1130.
Laufen, R.: 200.
Laws, S.: 1126.
Leder, H.-G.: 442.
Lee, E. K.: 194.
Lee, G. M.: 520, 734, 833, 981, 1118, 1309, 1315, 1321, 1323.
Leenhardt, F. J.: 702.
Légasse, S.: 964, 965, 969, 983, 997, 1286, 1562.
Legault, A.: 418.
Legrand, L.: 733.
Leitch, J. W.: 548, 1585.
Lelior, L.: 810.
Lemcio, E. E.: 115.
Léon-Dufour, X.: 1327.
Lescow, T.: 1255.
Lewis, J. P.: 957.
Lewis, P. B.: 153.
Lindars, B.: 873.
Lindemann, A.: 1354.
Lindsey, R. L.: 215.
Linmans, A. J. M.: 686.
Linnemann, E.: 1188, 1239, 1394.
Linton, O.: 309, 821, 1297.
Livio, J. B.: 438, 460.
Lohfink, N.: 1108, 1109.
Lohmeyer, E.: 11, 12.
Lohse, E.: 86, 1037.
Longenecker, R. N.: 1573.
Longstaff, T. R. W.: 207, 1365, 1434.
López-Doriga, E.: 721.
Lorenzen, D.: 1594.
Losada, D. A.: 599, 736, 774.
Loslie, L. A.: 1042.
Louw, J.: 715.

Lövestam, E.: 588, 589, 938, 939, 1115, 1167, 1173, 1292.
Lubsczyk, H.: 1345.
Ludlum, J. H.: 218.
Lührmann, D.: 1439.
Luz, U.: 1443, 1455.
Luzarraga, J.: 1392.
Lynch, W. E.: 1224.

MacLaurin, E. C. B.: 459.
Maggioni, B.: 33.
Mahoney, A.: 1322.
Maisch, I.: 500.
Malbon, E. S.: 265.
Mally, E. J.: 53.
Malone, D.: 982.
Mánek, J.: 824.
Mangatt, G.: 232, 1361.
Manno, B. V.: 1515.
Manson, W.: 642.
Marchel, W.: 1262.
Marconcini, B.: 394.
Mariadasan, V.: 1026.
Mariani, B.: 237.
Marshall, I. H.: 79, 426.
Martin, J.: 991.
Martin, R. P.: 233, 242, 336.
Martindale, C. C.: 85.
Martinez, E. R.: 1446.
Martini, C. M.: 847.
Marxsen, W.: 243, 645.
Masson, C.: 245, 885.
Matera, F. J.: 1556.
Maura, C.: 1575.
Mauser, U. W.: 384.
Mayer, B.: 725.
Maynard, A. H.: 191.
Mays, J. L.: 841.
McArthur, H. K.: 676, 729, 1299.
McCaughey, J. D.: 241.
McCombie, F.: 823.
McCormick, M.: 299.
McCurley, F. R.: 906.
McDonald, J. I. H.: 921, 959.
McEleney, N. J.: 782.
McHardy, W. D.: 784.
McIndoe, J. H.: 1388.
McInnis, R.: 993.
Mead, R. T.: 502.
Meagher, J. C.: 348, 360.
Mees, M.: 966.

About the Author

Hugh M. Humphrey is an Assistant Professor of
Religious Studies at Fairfield University,
Fairfield, Connecticut. He received his doc-
toral degree from Fordham University in 1977
in New Testament Studies and is an active mem-
ber of the Catholic Biblical Association and
of the Society for Biblical Literature.